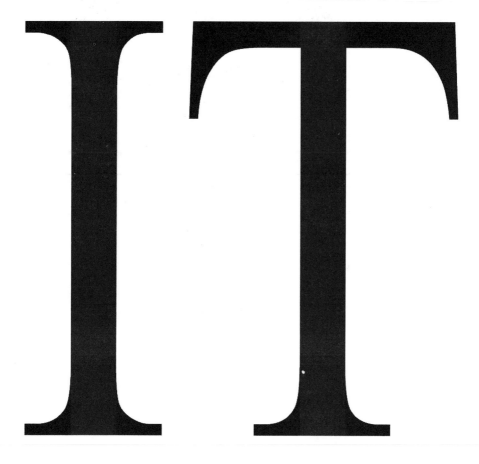

OTHER PUBLICATIONS

FATE MAGAZINE (A national magazine of true reports of the "strange and unknown").
      "The Aura" (October 1992)
      "My First Vision" (October 1994)

THE NEW TIMES (A Seattle, Washington Newspaper, estb. 1985 about changing and enriching lives.)
      " Man's Spiritual Path" (February 1997)
      " Love and Compassion" (July 1997)
      " Do We Love God or Religion?" (July 1997)
      " Pacifism is Wrong" (June 1998)

ETERNITY AS IF IT HAD A BEGINNING

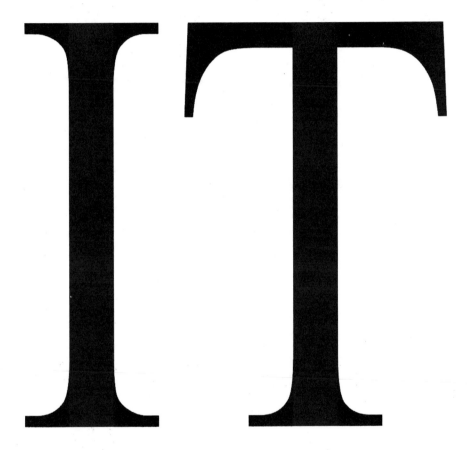

BY

ARMAND L. ARCHAMBEAULT

Library of Congress Catalog Card Number: 00-106361

Archambeault, Armand L.

IT: Eternity as if it had a beginning./Armand L. Archambeault
     p.   CM.

ISBN 0-9664126-3-X

     Includes pictorial diagrams.

     1. Social Studies 2. Unified Theory Studies 3. Spiritual Studies 4.Psychological Studies 5. Religious Studies 6. Parapsychological Studies 7. Humanity Studies 8. Finding Your Real Self 9. Finding Your Reason For Being 10. Finding Cures For Your Problems.

Cover design by Armand L. Archambeault
Sketches by: Mary Card & Armand L. Archambeault

First Printing

AMC Publications
PO Box 81672
San Diego, CA 92138
(619)296-0442

Printed in the United States of America

<u>Preface</u>

Areas in which I am an expert and why:

I claim to be an expert in nothing (nothing is where everything is.)

By being nothing is how I have acquired the knowledge of the spiritual side of life of my sixty-nine years on this earth.

Through mystical experiences, I've seen another side of life which even the dictionary is afraid to admit with certainty, but soon will. Psychology will acnowledge this in the near future, also.

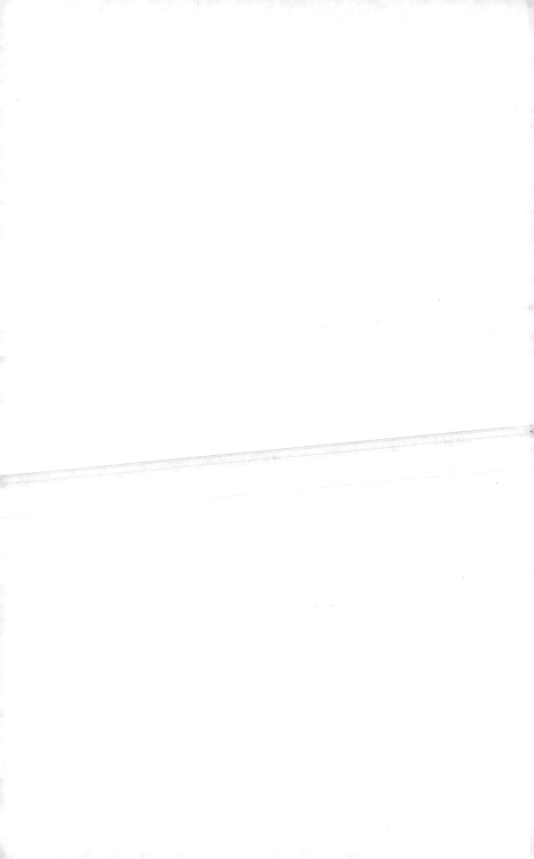

TABLE OF CONTENTS

Chapter One

Chapter Two

COMMUNICATIONS WITH GOD: (These explain eternity)

TABLE OF CONTENTS

TABLE OF CONTENTS

Chapter Three

ARTICLES AND TALKS UP TO NOW

Chapter Four

MY DIARY: A DEVELOPING SEARCH FOR GOD

TABLE OF CONTENTS   xiii

TABLE OF CONTENTS

Chapter Five

LETTERS, WHICH I HAVE WRITTEN TO OTHERS WITH AN EYE ON GOD

Chapter Six

Acknowledgements

I am grateful to the following:

My valued friend and wife Katherine, who died on February 4, 1999, who has encouraged me for the last 20 years of marriage to be all that I wanted to be. She pulled no strings and allowed me to grow from within. She is a true helpmate. She is what I call a true model for a wife, which we all have opportunities to be, through reincarnation. Yes, you will be a female sooner or later, so that you can balance things out in your soul. Women's lib needs to be thinking about this.

Rev. Joseph Gustin of Escondido, CA for teaching me how to go to the deepest levels of meditation, where I could read my clearest form of communication with 'IT', which is what I was looking for.

My granddaughter, Mary Card, of Upland, CA who has done the fine drawings, which are in this book. I'm proud of her for the good work, and caring interest, while pursuing the Catholic faith.

Rev.'s Milton and Mary Smith of San Diego, CA for bringing me out by encouraging me to speak in gatherings, and from the pulpit where allowed. I am not ordained by a religion, but ordained by God, which is not recognized by most religions.

Rev. Mary Smith for her unquestioning insights and deeds for my wife who had Alzheimer's.

Rev. Daisy Brunner, of Escondido, CA who has passed on now, and had taught me how to sense and help those who have passed over.

Rev. Nina Van Heyninger of Long Beach, CA, who taught me how to read billets (a piece of folded paper with initials or numbers inside of it) with deep seeing, in church.

Pat Harvey of Corona, CA who has passed away, for her feisty encouragement to pursue this quest of mine about becoming One with the Father.

Rev. Etela Clayton of Anaheim, CA who turned my life around when she gave me a spiritual message about what to pray and how, in order to achieve my goal. The message caused me to completely understand what I was looking for and how to find it.

Bill and Alice Blood of Riverside, CA who were gentle and encouraging in helping me to understand all these strange things, in the 1970's.

Jane Harris of Riverside, CA, for showing me how accurate a person can be in this mental process.

Rev.'s Ed and Anne Reid of Riverside, CA for my first development of my inner mind where I learned Psychometry (the reading of an object held in the hand as to where it has been, what it has experienced).

Dick and Elizabeth Seyler of Riverside, CA who coerced me into going to my first Spiritualist church meeting against my better judgment. This was where and when I met my wonderful wife, Kay.

Prelude

Have you ever wondered about Eternity?

The word means that there could never be a beginning or end. The dictionaries say that it is Infinite Time without beginning or end. Many religions say that it is the state of being when the soul passes on. How can they sense that?

Well, religion is the progressive realization of the make up of the world, as we know it. The realizations change as the experiences change. The non-changer, who does not change his perspective, will eventually disappear. Change is life, stagnancy is death.

Religious *leaders* of antiquity were usually dead serious about learning about God (the mysterious force behind everything). Then they were made into Gods by their followers, especially after their deaths, such as Zoroaster, Osiris, Jesus, Buddha and Mohammed. People have the natural tendency to herd together, and create myths through exaggeration.

The awe of the people caused worship of the religious leader as a God, and this caused the current religious leader to become spoiled, leading to exaggerations and demands. Then the following representative leaders increased the exaggerations to suit their own purposes; some intentionally, and some not.

Myths soon begin by ignorance of the true situation, long distances and poor communications between the peoples, and by power grabbers who want to control other people.

Even in today's environment of super communications, people are fooled or conned around the world, and made into genuine, innocent followers. We must be wise as serpents at all times.

How about the Heaven's Gate people who committed suicide to hurry the process of leaving this planet, and the UFO sects that sell everything and meet somewhere to be taken aboard a craft to be saved, and are ruined in the process?

How about the Jones Town in Africa, where people have committed mass suicide to get away from it all? What about the Korean leader in Texas who predicted the end of the world about every ten years? As I recall, the Jehovah's Witnesses used to predict the end of the world about every ten years, also.

How about the Christians who predict Armageddon almost daily since John the Baptist was speaking, in the New Testament, and that Jesus was returning to save us for the last 2000 years?

I have since learned that the 'End Times' has been preached for over 10,000 years, even before the Egyptian times. I understand that this evolved into the Essene sects of which we hear so much about in the Dead Sea Scrolls.

Well, this book is being written to inform the readers of my experiences and what I have learned from them. They have caused me to write about **eternity, as if it had a beginning**.

You probably always think of the Creation by a God like everyone else. This Creation has to begin somewhere, and sounds very logical.

I will try to eliminate this Beginning and Creation from your minds. My meditations (communications) with God have eliminated them from mine.

The Meditations chapter of this book will enlighten you in the quickest manner, but the rest of the book is necessary for full understanding without prejudice.

CHAPTER ONE

ETERNITY

What Do You Think Eternity Is?

Put yourself into it and rationalize your thoughts and feelings. Disregard what you have been told since childhood, and think it out on your own. Can you realize your self as being an eternal self? Can you sense that you have always been? Do you feel that after you die, you will not be dead? Do you have an inborn feeling that there is something missing in this life? Do you tend, by natural self, to wonder about this awesome God, or unknown missing piece in your life? Do you feel a yearning for more of your self? Is there a piece missing? Do you look up at the stars and wonder? Do you feel like a piece of a pie trying to see the whole pie, but cannot, because when you are looking from your self to the pie, there is always a piece missing? This is why you can't see God (See fig. 1). A piece cannot see the whole thing.

Figure 1
By being one piece of the pie, we cannot see the whole pie unless we become One with "IT."
We must go within to see and realize the whole pie for the wonderful understanding of All.

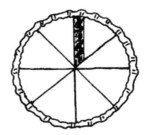

This is the natural, eternal feeling of, What is missing in my life? Why do I not feel whole? Why am I here?

The magic force, which we call God, is always short of one view point. . . You! That is why we cannot see God, because He is always one piece short of the whole thing from our viewpoint. I Call God He, She, or *IT*, to help in understanding, but *IT* is sufficient because *IT* describes ALL of them.

We are, in essence, the reason that life exists eternally. Without US, eternity cannot exist. Eternity is real and continuous because we are separate from it in the material world. The missing essence of us, which is in this material world, is the engine of eternity. You will understand this better as you read this book. I will place Meditations in the first part of the book (Chapter Two), so that you will become familiar in the reality of my correspondence with God.

Then the Articles and Talks up to Now, (Chapter Three) are next for more understandings. Next, I will place my Diary (Chapter Four) so that you may study my development toward the reality of God. Next, my Letters, which pertain to God (Chapter Five), for more of the deeper understandings. Finally in Chapter Six I will try to conclude for you what I get from these experiences.

Always keep in mind that everything there is, is continuous and there is no break in it. It never began and will never end. Since I was seven years old, I've been tuned in to God and was always interested in the stories of God, the Bible, churches, religions, psychology, the mind and the realities of the common person.

Eternity always was and is and will be. How can this idea mix with our formed thoughts from childhood on? I have struggled with this since I was seven years old when my teeth automatically bit into the Catholic Host at my First Communion. The nuns had told us not to bite the Host because it was the body of Jesus Christ, and we wouldn't want to go to hell, would we?

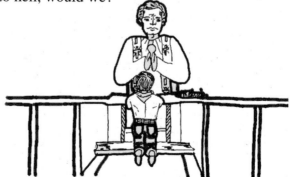

Figure 2

I was a sincere boy, serious, honest, and truthful and I loved God just naturally. The odd, illogical ideas about God, which continuously emerged in my life, caused me to want to know.

What about the Big Bang theory, and lately I hear talk of two Big Bangs? There were even more bangs in the past, and there will be more in the future. What has a bang got to do with eternity? The Big Bangs are like the explosions, which push the pistons in your automobile, and keep it going.

The Big Bangs are like the thumping and pumping in your heart to circulate blood throughout your body to keep it alive for your spiritual and material experiences. This is a big world! Have you any idea how big? It is eternal. Always. No boundaries.

My experiences tell me that there never was a beginning and so there could never be a Creator. This means that the system (God) is always in place, and that it always will be in place. The whole system is God; I call God *IT*. *IT* just IS, and always was and always will be.

The System is Eternal, Unchangeable Law (God). We; yes, We are the life of God, IT, learning how to live within the law with our free-willed minds. The living, eternal God that we all hear about is us. We have been searching everywhere for God, and we find that God is US, living within God, the totality of All.

The system mentioned above is a set of unchangeable laws of eternal mind in which we live. We are all individual, responsible, free-willed expressions of this universal mind, God.

Our fingers are expressions of us (not free-willed) just as we are expressions of *IT* (but we have a free will). Our fingers are us, just as we are *IT*.

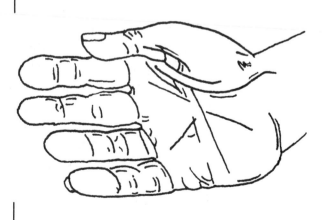

Figure 3

We are extensions of God, just as our fingers are expressions of us. Our fingerprints are all different as we all are.

We are all different viewpoints or expressions in the life of God.

Can you understand this? It is very important.

Islands are different expressions of the earth, and are the earth, even though we cannot see the connecting land under the water, just as we can't see the mind, which connects us all. We are all living in and using the same mind, like the earth as expressed below, but we are different, independent expressions of that same mind, IT.

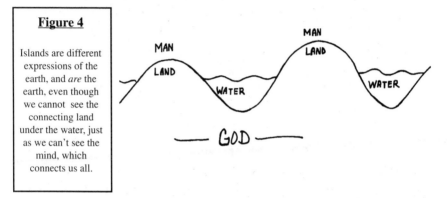

Figure 4

Islands are different expressions of the earth, and *are* the earth, even though we cannot see the connecting land under the water, just as we can't see the mind, which connects us all.

We are independent expressions of mind, made of mind, and we will never see IT, the source of our being, because IT will never have use of the material life for experience ITSELF, but through IT's expressions, you and me.

We are made of this mind, we live in this mind, we use this mind, and we communicate with this mind.

The mind is invisible and permeates everything. Our individual minds can communicate with each other individual expression of mind (mind reading, psychics, prayer, etc.), and our individual minds can communicate with the whole mind, IT (prophecy, future, etc.). Actually, all the information is in the whole mind IT. We must learn how to tune in to what we want.

The ability to tune in to individuals in the whole mind is just a matter of learning how to focus our individual minds on the person of our intent. This is best accomplished by classes with teachers, but can be accomplished at one's home with friends who can give feedback so that you know when you are reading the thoughts of another or not.

Our individual spirits are separate frequencies of vibration, living within the universal vibrations of mind, which I call IT. <u>I have learned how to communicate with IT.</u>

This will be explained in this book, in my diary, Chapter Four. In that chapter you will see the processes I went through to accomplish what I have thus far in the mental, spiritual world. Mental and Spiritual are both interchangable in that they are both invisible, but mental is the movement of Spirit through matter, and spiritual is the spirit itself. We are spirit using animal bodies for experiences in matter, time and space.

We are genuine aliens, just like in some of the movies we've seen. We are not the animal bodies that we see, but we are using our animal bodies for movement and experience in this particular world.

CHAPTER TWO

MEDITATIONS

Communications With God: These Are What Explain Eternity

NOTE: *Before you read the Meditations, you must realize that I was assured in a genuine live, talking vision of Gabriel, in my front room, that these Meditations are the word of God, brought to me through Gabriel the Archangel, who is the Voice of God. This is explained in my Diary section.*
This meditation arrived after completing the book. It would help to read this first.
03/18/00

This talk is in the name of the Father, and His Sons, Mankind. This is a message, which I have received from the Father for all of us:

Greetings, My Sons!

I wish to reveal Myself to you briefly, so that you might understand why you are here and who you are.

You are here because you are necessary for Me to have life.

Without you, I would not be.

I am All there is, and being All and Absolute, I cannot have life without you, my counterpart.

I Am Eternal.

You are Eternal.

There never was a Creation.

You were never Created. You always were and will be.

I was never Created. I have always been and will be.

We are the Creators throughout Eternity.

I have no name. You call me God, but any name you give to Me is a limitation.

You and I are God.

You are Spirit, and I am Spirit; One and the same.

All the books cannot describe Me fully, because of the Eternal Nature of Our Being.

Let Me draw a picture for you, for understanding.

See Me as the atmosphere.

We call this Spirit, or Mind. Spirit and Mind are both the same. Two different words, that is all.

I am Everywhere and Always.

Spirit, which is Mind, is everywhere and always.

See your planet as the material world of experience. We call this Matter, or Life. Matter and Life are two different words for the same thing.

Both Matter and Life are always changing.

Matter is always changing.

Mankind is always changing.

I do not change. I Am All, and Absolute. I AM the complete package.

Matter is Life, and I Am All.

Matter changes eternally, and I do not.

Mankind is the individual, responsible, free-willed Mind (Spirit) which lives Life for My sake in bodies which are fit for living in the material worlds for the sake of My Life and Experiences.

Together, We are One.

Together, We are what you call God.

Now the Material world in which you live and have experiences for My sake is Eternal, also.

The Eternal, Material world in which you live Life, is the third part of the triangle of Absolute.

The Three are a Trinity, and yet the Three are One.

The Absolute (God), Mankind (You), and Material Worlds (Planets, Animals, Plants, Minerals) cannot be without Each Other.

I place light on these things so that you may understand Who You are, and Why You are here.

You are necessary for My life, and You are Me, also.

The Material Worlds are the vehicles for Our living of life.

Without them We would not exist.

Without You, I do not exist.

I asked God, "Please explain who and what I am."   **Below is the answer. 05/18/69**

My full, complete, self-expression. All that is, is made of God. I am made of God. I am an expression of God; as I express myself in daily activities. I am expressing the beauty, perfection, and truth of God, which is me. I am the living expression of God and I express myself in fullness of truth, beauty and perfection to the rest of God (all others), joining the universal, harmonious intelligence in the total expression of life. My total expression radiates goodness and hope to all who hear me, and think of me, because I am radiating the goodness of God in my full, complete, self-expression.

NOTE: *The above is mostly self-explanatory. It is a steering wheel of the mind, which will change your life. By saying this prayer/meditation daily, you will change your outlook on life into a very healthy* *one, spiritually and physically. Once this is imbedded into your sub-conscious mind, you will be a new person. The above was in answer to my prayers for understanding what we are all about).*

I asked God, "Please explain the Our Father for me so that I will understand it easily." 02/15/70

My Father Who is in mind, Who is all mind, Who is my mind, great are your characteristics. We are one by your openness and My choice. Therefore I am what you are. You are eternal and complete, therefore I am eternal and complete.

Thank you for giving to Me this day that which is already Mine in mind. (*Review your previous prayers.*)

Dissolving all *dis-ease* within me, as I dissolve all *dis-ease* within my universe, leading me into all right thought and right action.

For Your kingdom is My kingdom, your power is My power, and your glory is My glory, now and forever!

"Thank you Father."
NOTE: *Say this prayer every day until you know it by heart, and it will be the portal to your understanding God and true prayer, which brings results.*

GOD IS FREE 12/02/71

"Father, How do I reach you?"

I am free of charge. I require no payment, cash or charge. In fact, you will get a charge out of me. All I require is thought, and I am yours. Keep your thought merged with Me, and I Am you.

I Am that I Am. I Am God.

John 3:16 "Be and live in Him and gain eternal life."

<u>LOVE 04/05/93</u>

I asked Father, "What is Love?"

Love is the giving of freedom to the object of your love to live within all laws; spiritual, physical, social.

NOTE: *A general observation, GOD IS LOVE. God is law, of our existence, which we must live by with our free will. God gives us the freedom to love within the laws of our world of existence. God puts us here and says,*

This is your life; live by the laws in complete freedom to learn about good and evil so that you will become wise from your mistakes.

If you will love Me above all others, you will have faith that my laws are for your good, and you will abide by them.

Laws are for the common good and if you have love for others, as you would like to be loved by others, you will live in freedom within the laws.

Love is giving freedom, rather than controlling; giving freedom rather than possessing.

Love is being one with the Universal Consciousness in which We live, totally without reservation as to the people and things of this world.

Love is being in this world, but not of this world.

When all of the above is the rule, any person can live in this world without having problems; all problems become challenges to overcome, which are a good reason to be alive.

You can take love with you wherever you go. No one can take it away from you. It is the secret of the ages as to how to live a good life.

A happy life proceeds from love; also, because God is first, and all else comes afterward, you never lose your foundation: God. A house with a solid foundation will not shake loose.

The opposite of love is ego, which is Edging God Out. A person who has a big ego is a person who loves himself more than God, or any other person. This is also called conceit; the exaggeration of one's own importance, which leaves no room for others to have freedom of responsible expression, which is the absence of love.

Along with this freedom comes responsibility not to influence others to break the laws: spiritual, physical, and social.

NOTE: *Irresponsible freedom is self-love and self-love shuts out God and neighbor.*

Irresponsible freedom is the opposite of love. It leads to chaos and anarchy. By the way, our country is encouraging irresponsible freedom as if our citizens have a right to it.

Love is not long-suffering. There is no suffering with true love. True love is eternal and effortless, as if observing the object of your love with the wisdom of God, and being pleased that the beloved has the freedom to learn at it's own pace.

Love produces a feeling within the lover, of: peace, happiness, joy, tenderness, patience, understanding, empathy, and wellness of being, mental and physical health, confidence and bliss.

Love does not require rewards; it is freely given.

Love is the foundation of the complete universe, Father God

NOTE: *The above is a revelation, (a clear thought of knowingness) which came to me during a meditation period.*

THE LIFE OF MAN 04/25/93

"Father, what must I do or what is from your wisdom the thing that I should do for the future in the coming days, months, years? Thank you. What must I do for the betterment of mankind, the betterment of myself and the revealment of Yourself, Father?"

See with great light the foundations of mankind. Go to the hub and progress from there.

What is man, when he goes in all degrees from the center of the circle, 360 degrees?

All of mankind goes in different directions from the center to the rim, all seeking outward. All seeking to expand their minds to the limitless knowledge and wisdom available, which is ever expanding, and ever increasing, so that man will never see the totality, but will always be seeking and searching.

This Is the Life of Man.

From the darkness, they enter the light, and the new light becomes darkness so that they can evolve from the new darkness to new light. From the base to the heights, the new heights become the base to reach the new heights.

The finger is always pointing forward, leading the body. The spirit is always leading forward; looking forward, seeking, searching, leading the mind, which leads the body, always seeking for new light; bright, bright lights.

You take your base of accumulated knowledge, wisdom and intelligence; this is your space platform from which you travel into new horizons of wisdom, knowledge and intelligence.

Seeking is a never-ending dissatisfaction with the past, the present, and a constant searching and seeking for the future.

As the universe, material universe, has exploded from within, and ever expanding, so is the mind. The mind is ever expanding from the center; ever expanding. This is the spiritual mind, not the ordinary mind.

This is the God mind, which is in all of us (I can say all of *you*, but *you* are me and I am *you*) human beings. This is what makes us human (us again.

. .do *you* see?); spiritual beings within a physical body, which is the animal body that we (do *you* understand?) live in at this time and place for this experience."

BEING AWARE 05/01/93

"Father, tell us something for our good, please."

To open new doors of knowledge, every day, old knowledge becomes older, and new knowledge becomes older.

Keep opening new doors in your lives. Seek and search further and further.

There are many viewpoints from the same spot. Each new viewpoint is new knowledge, new perspective, making a larger picture, putting together the lives of all the viewpoints around (360 degrees) from the same viewpoint from the same center will show you where you are, when you are and what you are.

Keep your eyes wide-open; see all the small details as well as the large details.

See the gems from the inside outward, seeing through all the different facets from the inside, outward. Being and seeing are equal.

You cannot be unless you see, and you cannot see unless you be. The deeper and further you look, the deeper and further you see, and the deeper and further you be. See the fire and see the wind. Be the fire and be the wind.

I see, therefore I am. I be, therefore I am.

Do the wind and the fire be as I be?

No, the wind and the fire are actions and reactions and movements, but they do not be.

In a second, your ship is coming in full of riches. A many pointed neckline and feathered sleeves, a feathered cross, that is.

MY FUTURE FOR TODAY AND TOMORROW 05/04/93

"Father, what can you say about the future for my family, for myself for today and tomorrow?"

Fasten safety belts, don't over eat, be careful of backfires, do not slip on a banana peel. Watch your step. Seize the beauty of the moment.

FOUNDATIONS 05/07/93

"Father, what about the foundations of religion?"

As we climb the rugged stairs up to Heaven, we see Moses and Jesus on the platform at the top of the solid foundation they had made, in leadership, with us (their moral leadership).

Then, we see Peter and Paul, who did not leave a solid foundation. They broke away from Moses and Jesus and made their own religion. They have no foundation at all.

PUT ON THE NEW 05/10/93

"Father, what must I do next?"

Move forward with pressure, scraping and cleaning off old ideas. See through the dust and dirt all that is new and fresh, and coming about, using the fresh and the new as a basis for a future.

As the song goes, every cloud has a silver lining. You must look beyond the dark clouds and the silver lining to see the sun, the pure light of new truth.

HEALING 05/15/93

"My request today Father is, Help me to gain the knowledge of what to do and to do it right, and about the miracle of healing, to see and understand all things spiritual."

As gravity pulls us down, a descent towards the center provides weight by seeking the light.

This 17means that the deeper you go into the subconscious mind, seeking God (the center), you will see the light, or wisdom.

Speak loudly with force into the realms in order to heal. Crystallize your thought or idea as you speak; and release it to the realms.

Heal, and become One with the Father; One with Me; One with the Light, loudly and with force. Then the two become One. They will generate their own light and be perfect.

This is the greater meaning of the serpents intertwined around the center. The center being a rod, a staff, or in my speaking now, the center is the idea, and when the two become One, the idea becomes *man*ifested.

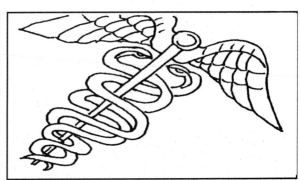

Figure 5

The Center is the idea and when the two become One, the idea becomes manifested.

This is the central ideal of the Caduceus and it's use in the healing process.

This is How Healing Takes Place.

A baby duckling, soft and cuddly comes toward you and instills the feeling of a love, a caring, a union of the two minds; this is the general feeling as when two become one, and as the feeling of the enhancement of bodily feelings, it is like the feeling when looking into the innocence of a baby or the innocence of a kitten, there's a tone that is struck.

HEARING 05/23/93

Hearing comes from two sides and goes to the center. It vibrates through the brain for the experience of the soul.

Hearing manifests itself throughout the files of the mind to be interpreted according to the files of experience, which were created through living in this body in this time. The sounds excite the field of experience and open the drawers of harmonious sounds.

Then they are interpreted by the intellect. The intellect being the sorting machine, sorting experiences to combine with reason.

Reason is the truth of our being.   Reason sorts the truth from the mass of information which comes from the intellect, which come from the memory files, which come from the actual vibrations received; hearing, sight, etc.

Hearing can be a trap. Blindly hearing without analyzing can lead to false conclusions. Analyzing the sound produces the truth that is needed; the reality of the moment.

If you seal your mouth and close your eyes, your hearing will be more acute and more true without conflicting vibrations of eyes and mouth. Hearing with eyes and mouth sealed is beautiful; as flowers growing in the spring. Hearing can be clear and bell-ringing beautiful like new flowers on a rosebush; like birds chirping in the early morning, deciding what they are going to do for the day.

Listening is a delicious gift when done with sensitivity. The hearing of today's crowd and the average person is obstructed by the use of the mouth. The mouth is in gear and working when it should be sealed in order to listen and learn.

THE CROSS 05/24/93

"Father and guides, do you have any thoughts about the Cross?"

Buffalo Spear, here. My staff has eagle wings spread out; the Cross of Christ is the same. They are the same: my staff and the Cross of Jesus. They spread their wings and rise to the Heavens to the God.

The Christ is an eagle as the eagle on my staff. He spreads his wings and he rises to God.

COMPASSION 05/27/93

"Father, what is compassion?"

Your ship is sitting high on the thrones and nested in place. It might seem like you are in charge, but the mass doesn't really pay any attention.

NOTE: *The above is an insight into my mind. This is called Reading.*

Having an eye for compassion requires action. Having an eye for compassion requires an eye for action.

Compassion is not for the running of the world and the doing of all things for all people at all times.

Compassion is the momentous action required for a situation in need. Compassion is for a temporary fix until that person can help himself.

MESSAGE FROM THE FATHER 06/05/93

The dove is above and descending
and blending as you focus within.

NOTE: *This message was another revelation during the meditation period. This means that the spirit of God is becoming blended with my spirit in Oneness with the Father when I meditate.*

I am noticing that as I become One, the information becomes a part of me.

REASON FOR EXISTENCE 06/05/93

I asked Father, "What is the reason for my existence?"

I am a lamp force. You are a lamp, which when unplugged is nothing. Life must flow from the source to the object. You are a flying fortress; you are an eagle in the wind; you are searching for your prey through your prayers, which are faster than sound; your prayers are powerful gems, like a stealth bomber or stealth fighter; to promote peace and harmony throughout your universe.

This is obvious to the spiritually minded person, but for those not understanding, this means that Becoming One with the Father has to be initiated and actively continued by us on a daily basis full time; we must be plugged in always if we want to stay in the Spirit.

Prayer, while In the Spirit, is like a mass of effective, heavy thought patterns flying in the wind and faster than sound. Prayers may seem as if they don't work, but they are actually working in you and others, producing peace and harmony through love sent in a stealthy, unseen way.

MEMORY AIDS 06/06/93

I asked Dr. Larabee about how I can help Kay (my wife) with her memory problems. Asked how I can help to make her situation better, above all.

The idea that the eye sees. Vision is like a taco; it is a shell stuffed with substance, connected into an amplifier and booster and coupler, which modulate light waves.

These light waves impress upon the mind pictures, which open memory files and deposit impressions of modulated light waves. When the mechanism doesn't work, blood has been restricted.

Circulation must be increased in order to increase memory. Circulation requires exercise within the head, exercise of the whole body, to increase blood flow, and to increase oxygen flow to reach the restricted canal of the memory system.

Carrots, again, will increase the blood flow to the memory system. Raw carrots. Feet must be massaged; especially in the front where the toes are. Sex is important, also. Nicotine must be eliminated. Tomatoes are also very good. . . and tomato juice.

Man's memory is like an insulated net protecting the self from outside influences. It is controlled by inside drive; a desire by selection of the senses and powered by oxygen enriched blood; the life force; the mind.

On this earth, in this body, the channels are clogged and need to be cleaned out, exercised, vibrated, and renewed.

The head has become like a petrified forest; like petrified veins, petrified blood vessels. They need new life that is created by exercise and proper nutrition, and no nicotine.

READINGS FOR ME BY CLASSMATES 06/10/93

- Many feathers are being added to my headband, even going down my back.

• Use ink rather than ball point. Become
more serious about completing the book.

• You are God's scribe.
You are getting the book well-organized.

ADVICE FOR ME 06/10/93

"Father, please give to me some general, good information."

Have fun, be gentle.

MAN AND GOD 06/10/93

I asked Father, "What is your relationship to man, what is man, what is God, what is the relationship?"

Man emulates to God. Man is the life of God in action, and is change; God is not.

For God to have life, man must be. Therefore, man is the Son of God. God is the Father, the Source, the Foundation; never changing, absolute. Man is the life of God.

Man is the key on the keyboard; God is the computer. God is what we would call the universal memory brain: the Universal Subconscious; a reactive source; a computer, which obeys the mind of man. Man is the life of God. Both are God, God is All.

God is the Law to be used; always there, always ready. God is the ear of corn. Man is the planter; the cultivator, and the eater, and the enjoyer of the thing, which is God.

God is man. Man uses God with man's individual choices. Man is God, man is from God, and man is of God. Man is using God; man is Son of God. Man is life of God.

God is Law of man. God is what man speaks

of, God is what man speaks with, and God is what man speaks to, God is man speaking. God and man are two ends of the same stick.

WHO IS GOD? 06/10/93

I asked Father, "Who or what is God?"

God is like a foundation. God is the knowingness. God is the forefront of all knowledge.
God is all encompassing, all-inclusive. God is the life of life. God is the source. God is the stationary, never moving spirit substance in which we live. God is the medium of life."

DOOR TO THE FATHER 06/15/93

"Father, what is the Door to the Father that I have heard of?"

The door to the Father was opened for Christ.
The union with the Father was demonstrated by Christ.
God and Christ are two ends of the same stick; God and you are two ends of the same stick.
NOTE: *Christ is when you become One with the Father. It is an anointing, a crowning, a kingship bestowed.*

NOW AS FUTURE 06/16/93

I asked, "Father, Buffalo Spear, Dr. Larabee-any one of my guides who has the knowledge and wisdom, please give me some good words for the next few days." (*The entrance to meditation showed a beautiful pink rosebud. To me, this signifies peace and contentment, calm, beauty. This rosebud carried a knowingness with it that it was the name of another spiritual teacher of mine.*)

Start up your engines and let's go. Grab the delicacy of spiritual things with tenderness; hold them, shape them, grind them, digest them for the betterment of mankind. Be nice, but be strong. Kick yourself into society: ring your bell, and let's go.

As a newborn is born in solitude and peacefulness, so are new thoughts; ideas which will spread enormously everywhere. As ideas spread, the walls of ignorance retreat.

Ideas are delayed by the basics of society. From the bottom up, light the beauties, enlighten the darknesses, brighten life for them (society). A person's mind knows the way out when led. Show them how to create the beauties from the darkness; how to turn around; how to see eternal: not the now.

To project into the future from today's actions.

The now action is the base for the future. The now is very important, but the future must be looked upon as the goal. There always must be the goal in mind, not just the now. The goal must be something better, something brighter, enlightenment, good, all positive and the base must be done in the now to lead toward the goal; the same as "Keep your eye on the ball" when planning to do what you do now; keep your eye on the future.

The now will take you to the future; what future do you want? Do not be drowned in the actions of the now. From today's pressures, always keep your eye on the ball, keep your eye on the good.

Keep your eye on the future; the trend, not the now. Each now should be your step toward the future that you want.

IMAGINATION 06/24/93

"Explain imagination please, Father."

On purpose, we poise ourselves in all directions, and step by step we continue on, doing our things without sure steps. All the steps are being done but they are not sure; no foundation; no carefulness. Our way has not been lit; it has not been thought of; we are just going and doing.

We must look into our minds (our crystal balls) and plan what we are about to do in our daily doings. We must look deeply into our minds (our crystal balls) to see all the different sides of the doings.

Being a child in a high chair, in a play pen, or in a crib, you are in your own little world doing the conventional things, not using the imagination, which is never ending, always expanding and the imagination is full of life.

Using the imagination, there is no end to the living of life. There is no dullness, no day-to-day drudgery, no *having* to do things, and *not wanting* to do things.

With your imagination you will *want* to do things. You will be living your life, not the life of what you must do because you are in your high chair, your playpen or your crib.

You will be leaving these childish methods of living and growing into the total living of imagination; the total living of a lively life.

I used the child as an example of being caged in and not being free, but actually, the child is smarter than some of us; we must become like the child; the child is penned in, but the child uses the imagination and enjoys his surroundings, whether a high chair, a playpen, or a crib. The smart child is happy where he is at.

Become as a child and live life to the fullest. Use your imagination in your daily living. Do not become or remain a robot of drudgery and sadness.

THE CROSS 06/29/93

I asked Father or Whomever, "What is the origin of the cross? What is the very first appearance of intermingling with

man? What is the association of man with the cross? How did it
start? What is the very beginning?"

The cross on the roof of a church, the hand-
protector cross-piece on the handle of the sword: The
cross is a protector; it is a shield, going through the
ages.

Years ago when farming was done, in order
to keep the birds at bay, crosspieces were put on sticks
of wood on the farmlands to deter the birds. These
were protectors. The spikes, which were embedded
into the cross, were marked on the ends with a cross.
They were marked on their heads with a cross for protection against evil spirits.

Whenever a man stood facing the sun (his
direction for God), and opened himself up to God,
the Great Father, man had his arms outspread, opening up his heart to God. God formed a shadow on the
earth, which was the shadow of the cross. This was
very revered.

This opening to God, of the heart of man,
was highly respected. The shadow-cross on the ground
was the reflected symbol given by God as an answer
of Thank You and Appreciation.

PURPOSE OF LIVING 07/01/93

"What is the purpose of our lives?"

My life is your life. Without you I have no life.

HEALING 07/01/93

"Father and Whomever would you tell me the best way that I
can heal others? What methods should I use?"

Work on the back, relax the patient. When
he is like a tree, start in the back of the trunk, between
the shoulder blades of the patient, physically and

mentally. Then face the patient. Look into the person's eyes deeply, searching. Look for pain, look for suffering. See the truth in the eyes. Appeal to their beliefs. Be strong in gaining their beliefs. Work with their beliefs. Be serious. Lay your hands on the head and then the shoulders, and the back.

ACHING FEET AND LEGS 07/08/93

"Father or Whoever in my band, what should I do for my aching feet and legs so that they do not hurt, and become strong and fresh?"

Eat cheese, take Quinine. Dr. Larabee here. Soak in a tub of hot water, your thighs, legs, and feet. Eat meat; beef, buttermilk (pitcher size), drink lots of water. Walk up and down stairs, hills.

G.V.'S FOOT PROBLEM 07/15/93

"Dr. Larabee what about G.V.'s foot problem; where when he bends his toes forward he gets cramps? How can you fix that? What causes it?"

Step by step, a point has been pressed between the ligaments at the balls of the feet. Peace and comfort will arrive if the toes are pointed inward when walking.

The doctor says: steady the walking pattern as you walk. Concentrate on pointing the toes more inward as you walk. Remember to do this. Change the pattern of your walking.

Become more inward, spiritually. Press your mind upward and inward. Eat apples for your health; many apples.

GOAL/GOLD FOR THE SOUL 10/16/93

"Father how should we care for our souls?"

As you clean your minds of debris and clutter, your search for new and better things; for the gold for your souls, and as all things fall into place and into their proper places, as you want all things to work right; the jeweled result, the precious result will be acquired.

Look closely and re-examine the gold for the soul; the precious gems of insight which you attain through meditation. Other things seem to be so rough on the surface, but underneath all the roughness; the rough surface, there is pure gold for the soul.

Therefore do not be of the world, but be in the world.

Being in the world, you see the coarseness, the roughness, the upper surface, the outside of all, but with your spiritual insight you see what is under the roughness. You see the truth of all things. This is the goal for the soul; the gold for the soul.

Your goal does not stick out in your face and say 'Here I am, come and get me'. The gold is under the rough surface, just like all things. The gold has been purified, so you must purify the soul.

The soul is your real being, and this pure nugget, the soul, is your true consciousness for the record. Your consciousness is what you lock into the soul, which remembers everything. Your consciousness chooses constantly what you wish to let in.

The same is with your mouth where you let in the food for your body in order to nourish the body in the way that you want. If you want to be large, you eat more food, and do less work. If you want to be smaller, you eat less food and do more work.

If you want good thoughts for cultivating a good soul, you read good things, you think good things, you speak good things, and you listen to good things. You smell good things, you taste good things.

All the senses from your consciousness go inward to form the soul. The purer the intake from the senses, the purer the soul. If you let in the trash that is in the media, and the trash that is in peoples' mouths everywhere, and the nonsense, this will be repeated into the soul; the soul which represents you and is your personality from this day on, that is your choice. Remember: Goal/Gold for the soul; keep it pure.

IDIOTS-NOT ADULTS 10/28/93

"Father, we are one, show me something for the class, please."

As one thing follows another, the tree of life will be followed by the tree of knowledge. The smart ones carry their own load.

We cover our eyes with many colors of glasses in order to see what we want to see, instead of what we really see. We cannot see clearly with colored glasses or with a fogged mind, or with chemicals.

The real you was designed to see clearly by itself. The clear seeing is within you. See clearly from within you; that from whence you came.

Pay attention to where your treasures are laid up. Your treasures are in your mind. Your treasures are not on the earth. Your treasures are not on your back. Your treasures are clearly in your mind.

Eat good ideas for your mind, eat good food for the body. Read good thoughts. See good movies. All that is taken into your mind through all of your senses should be well chosen in order to nourish the mind with good. The trash that is all around you today should not be entered into you minds, unless you want mud and putty for a mind.

Nourishment should be taken in from all of your senses, not just your mouth.

Society is bent on making money. That is the way that some business in the big business sense is offered to the public. "If it makes money, then do it, or, if the people buy it, then sell it before someone else does." They do not judge what they are doing and do not hold responsibility for what they disperse among the people. "That's business" is what they say.

Some businesses will not accept responsibility for what they are doing. Some businesses are ruining the minds of your children, and the minds of your so-called adults; as long as they make money, they do it.

Every action you take in your world, you are responsible for. If you sell something that helps to destroy another's precious mind, you are responsible. . . you could have chosen not to sell that item.

Choose the right things; don't be befuddled by the pushers of mud. Do not let your children be muddied. Nourish your children's minds with good for all their senses.

The word for Adult today should be idiot.

These are not adults, that follow the leader, which is the custom in your country. Whatever the movies, newspapers, TV, etc. suggest to your adults, these so called adults tend to follow.

They wear advertising on their clothes and also pay for the right to wear the advertising through higher prices, and are so proud of what they do.

These are adults? No, they are walking billboards for the manufacturer and licenser. Very ignorant, not adult!

So-called adult bookstores are not adult bookstores, but they are idiot bookstores; idiots because they are taking in filth for their minds.

So-called adult drivers of vehicles are dummy drivers; just like the dummies they show on TV. in the test crashes. If you are an adult driver, you think you can drive bumper to bumper at 100 mph; you won't get hurt, or hurt anyone else; just follow the leader. Well, that adult driving is dummy driving. Very ignorant, not adult!

Take care of your own mind. . . don't follow the leader. Think individually, think carefully, and think nourishment for good growth.

ACCEPTANCE 11/18/93

"Father please explain acceptance for me."

Where you are is to be accepted. What you are is to be accepted. When you accept anything and everything with gratitude, you are in the planes of happiness.

Acceptance with gratitude sets the mind for new heights. Acceptance with gratitude is the base upon which you spring forward, and this is repetitive and continuous in a happy life. You accept what you have with gratitude and you go on further and higher, accepting the new with gratitude; always being in the state of gratitude, whatever the outcome of your new venture.

Acceptance with gratitude is pleasing for all parties concerned. When your boat is on dry land and there is no water, you can go nowhere; in a state of acceptance with gratitude, you are comfortable. When the water comes back, then you are still comfortable.

Acceptance with gratitude produces patience. Patience wins all. Acceptance with gratitude keeps you well in the flow of things. This does not mean giving up, this means being happy all the time. Being happy all the time does not mean giving up. It is being in a balanced state for the next lift off.

All things will be done well, when done in the state of acceptance with gratitude. Be happy where you are, and be happy after you have made your next step. Always be happy and accept everything with gratitude.

Everything is done with your responsibility. If a next step appears to be wrong, it is no more than a problem to be overcome. Problems are good for you. Problems make you think. Problems make you do, and accepting all wrongs as problems will enhance your being.

Accept all your problems because they are gifts. They are problems to be overcome. They are problems which give you life. Without problems, you will deteriorate. Problems are no more that challenges.

UFO/EARTH CONNECTION 01/12/94

"Father we are one. What about UFO's? Father, what about the spirit of man? Tell me about UFO's."

As in the early days, at the time of the spear and the rock, these were passed on, and the hook was in place. (This means that after the initial animal trials, and the base life of the Stone Age man was at a proper level, then the plan became effective.)

In the tunnels of time, there was a birth, a new idea, of what to do with wayward spirits. Therefore, the population of the earth was for the learning process, delivered through freedom.

This is love. This is the freedom to express one's self and to learn from that expression, and to mingle with all other expressions to learn how to co-operate; how to live harmoniously, and as to what real freedom will bring to a person or an entity, if it is unbridled, if it is left without responsibility to the whole.

Individual freedom, without responsibility to all others is chaos. This is the reason that this idea was born. It is for the training of the wayward entities. They would be entrapped in physical bodies; in animal bodies, to be used for movement in the earth's atmosphere. The all-seeing eye is watching over the process.

Since life is eternal, the entity on earth is in a different time frame, and the whole of life seems to be spread into about 70 years; whereas eternal life is never ending, never beginning.

With this feeling of a short time to live, when the entity is in the body, the learning process is speeded up, so that when proper training and proper separation from the body ensues, evaluation is done to determine whether the entity should return to the physical body again, again, and again until it is decided that the entity does not have to live the animal life on the earth in order to learn more on how to get along with it's neighbors.

The entity, after having learned co-operation and true love, which is Freedom to live within the law; freedom with responsibility to others, learns the true meaning of love and freedom, and will not have to be placed back into the body on earth.

Earth is a training ground, earth is a prison; a form of punishment—of humane punishment. This idea should be used as an example for the punishment of criminals in the human society.

UFO's are the watchdogs of the overall society. These are the watchers; these are the guardians; these are the shepherds. UFO's are time soldiers; they are the transportation for the time soldiers. They are the guardians of the earth, and the systems, which are in place on the earth.

Life is not as precious as one might think. Life is only a tool for learning. To give up one's life for another is the greatest gift.

Choosing the proper vehicle for a life before the life is born at first breath, is love, not murder. Choosing a proper vehicle for an entity to enter upon birth at first breath is love for the guest, which is arriving on your planet. It is a respect and a love, providing good working tools for the entity; a health body; healthy surroundings.

These are the least that can be done for a new entity. The animal body that is being prepared in the mother's womb is the vehicle. If it is not evolved as a healthy vehicle, or offered into healthy surroundings, there is a lack of respect for the new entity, which will enter this vehicle at first voluntary breath.

War——W-A-R, Spelled backward, is RAW——r-a-w. War is the intense learning process, which is the raw meat of learning, and a short cut to help shorten the time required for learning on this planet. War will always be, because it is a tool required for fast learning, and for the intensity of learning.

Our awareness of self and others, in cooperation, is the door to life out of this world on earth, and the entrance to eternal life in co-operation with others.

PATIENCE 01/25/94

This was spoken by me, Armand, in the meditative state.

Patience is the result of faith. When a person loves God first and above all things, even above family and loved ones, then that person will naturally acquire patience, because of the knowledge that with God first, everything will be all right. Knowing God, and trusting in IT, that person knows that whatever happens, it is for the best.

We are all spirit, just the same as God; we are made of God. We are God in the same sense that our hands are made of us.

Our hands are us. We are our hands, the same

as we are God.

Spirit is all there is, and we are made of spirit. We are made of God We are God.

When we realize that God and we are One, patience is a knowingness that all that happens is for the good. When we are One with God in our consciousness at all times, we have the knowingness that breeds patience, and trust.

This is what Jesus was telling us, and really trying to teach us, but our people were not ready to comprehend such things.

Our people wanted to worship Jesus, the man, and because of their ignorance and emotional nature, they would not try to understand his teaching that he was not the Father, and when they saw him, they saw the Father.

He was teaching that when the two become one, we are in Heaven. He was saying that when we become one with the Father, who is in Heaven, then we would be entering the Kingdom of Heaven. He was bringing us the good news of the Kingdom, which is within us, if we so choose to enter Oneness with the Father. In this Kingdom is lots of patience.

Jesus taught that his Father was in Heaven, which was in our closets. Our closets are our subconscious minds. He said that all our treasures should be stored up in our closets where nobody could take away that which we stored there, in our minds.

So if we have stored up all good thoughts and qualities in our mind, and we know that our mind and God's mind are one by our choice, then patience and trust are some of the good qualities we will acquire, among many, many other good qualities, such as direct answers to our prayers in this life.

Patience is a product of love. Great love is produced when the two become One.

COINCIDENCES 02/03/94

"Father, what is life all about in the way of coincidences? About one thing leading to another in our lives? Is there something to this? What is this all about, if anything?"

In time, there is a system of clusters, or stepping stones from which we make decisions, and choose new directions. It is all our choice.

That the stepping stones are there is for the choosing of the right direction in order to experience the proper experiences that will lead us away from this planet and to back home.

HOME 02/03/94

"Father, what is home?"

Home is the experience which you wish. Home is the experience, which you wish until such time that you cannot cooperate with all the rules, and all of your neighbors. At this time, if such a time occurs, you'll be sent back to earth for more training.

FIFTH POUCH 02/03/94

"Father, we are One. Heavy Eagle, what was in the four pouches of contacts, and what was in the fifth pouch of contacts"?

There is a protected, hidden city in the desert, next to some tall, hard sand mountains. The walls are high and appear to be about twenty stories high, or more, and these walls have fallen over the years and covered the city below. The four pouches are for the four hundred years that the city has been buried, and the fifth pouch is for the fifth hundred years in which the city will be found.

The city was thriving in the fifteen hundreds. There is a wealth of knowledge there, and will be found in the next one hundred years.

As icebergs split off and fall into the ocean, these hard sand cliffs have split off and fallen on our city and buried it at the base of the cliffs. The walls are a reddish color, and the dirt in the surrounding area is reddish. These are natural cliff walls, many stories high; probably a half of a mile.

JESUS 02/08/94

"Father, who was Jesus? What kind of a person was Jesus?"

Jesus was a light being, arising from colorful influences of his childhood. He was a great leader. He flowed with love and understanding.

He had 99% control over his human nature. He had a great aversion to money and religion as being together. They were to be separated.

He developed a system with which to build his own church, with his own incorporated ideas of benevolence and love. He was is touch with the Father and taught the Father's ways.

He was executed as a rebel only because he chose to be different from the Orthodox Jewish practice of circumcision.

He was a firecracker in his time, and he set off a big fuse in the mind of men, dug deep into the hearts of men, claiming that all men are brothers, and that we are all one, and that the general public cannot be trusted with the truth, which proved itself, time and again.

The public had to be spoken to in parables because they were ignorant. Only the chosen few would know the real truth behind the proverbs, or behind the symbols. The general public reacted with their hearts; with their emotions, and this is what the parables associated to them.

The inner members (the members that were chosen) could see with their mind's eye, and were not affected by emotions once they were trained.

So, as it was written, many years after his death by ignorant masses, he was a god; 'he was the only one true God'. The ignorant masses knew not what they were speaking of, but the Bishops, Clergy and the Kings knew the conspiracy that they were entering in to.

He was a great leader in touch with his Father, and he taught us to be in touch with the Father, also. Jesus was a great teacher.

PROPHETS AND BELIEFS, DIFFERENCES 02/10/94

"Father, what are the differences between Jesus, Moses, Buddha, Mohammed, and others of that nature?"

Descending the stairs into your world, I find all the prophets as squares. Not to belittle them, but in their inexperience, they are what we would call today, squares.   They are what you would call them today (squares). It doesn't matter whether it is you, or Myself (Father); it is we. We would call them squares.

To them, all evaluations were as in concrete, and not malleable, flexible, or changeable. Man-made laws are like flowing lava; they change their shape as they flow with gravity. The flowing lava will change by necessity and is governed by natural law. Man's laws are governed by new laws. Change produces new change, within change.

PROPHETS AND BELIEFS, CONNECTIONS WITH THE FATHER 02/10/94

"Father, what is their connection with you?"

They were the stop-gap for the time being, in my flow of growth in living. They worked with me and for me through their love and willingness to do my will (My Laws). This is their connection to me.

PROPHETS AND BELIEFS, WHY THE KILLING? 02/10/94

"Father, why do their followers kill each other? Why do they kill for the sake of differing, in their Stone Age beliefs? If the laws that they profess are so great, then why do the followers hate and kill one another?"

In the eye of an emerald, you shall see much wisdom. Killing one another shows to me that they are for me even though their interpretations of my laws are warped, and in the killing, just as in the war, they are expressing themselves to the strongest point available.

They have been Neanderthal in their thinking, which goes for all religions; Christians, Buddhists, Mohammed's Islam, and the Jewish religion. All religions have been very basic in their improving as man improves.

The killing of each other, in time, will cease as the intellects and the beliefs improve.

As the intellect improves, beliefs become unnecessary. Beliefs are a shortcut to an end. Beliefs are not an intelligent method of coming to an end point.

Intellectual thinking, reasoned out, is far better than belief. Belief is for the ancient animals, the ancient human race. Belief will edge itself out as the intellect improves.

ENERGY 02/17/94

"Father, what is the relationship between electricity, magnetism, gravity, the soul, spirit, vital life force, etc, that seems to have a connection? What are we looking at; what is the primary connection here?"

There is a wedding of vibrations, all of which is One. All mind is One, and it is layered in different frequencies.   There is this freedom to choose individuality, and to choose Oneness; different frequencies by choice.

All mind is in the same place at the same time, always. Mind is a vibration, magnetism is a vibration, electricity is a vibration, solids are vibrations, and everything is a vibration of different frequencies.

Worlds within worlds are different frequencies; different manifestations, for different receivers. Each human being is a receiver according to a preset receptiveness for his world. By learning and earning he may jump from one world to another by changing mental frequencies, and being perceptive of the new frequency.

Electricity and magnetism are different frequencies. Just as there are multiple frequencies, there are multiple laws, which govern the multiple frequencies. There are frequencies within frequencies, just as there are laws within laws.

There is only one world, but in this one world, there are many worlds. . . there is no end. Magnetism and electricity are but frequencies with these worlds.

Mind is the same. It is a frequency in these worlds. Mind is governed by the world in which it lives, and by the world in which it chooses.

LOVE: MATERIAL AND SPIRITUAL 03/17/94

"Father, what is electricity and it's relationship to magnetism and all other forces?"

Electricity is a difference in potential. Electricity is the separation of two sides. When the two become One, then we have what is called current. Current is the flow of love; the current is flow. Current is when the two accept each other.

Electricity is the difference the two separates see; the potential that keeps the two entities separate. It is a potential.

The current, or the flow, is love. Love is when the two become One; when the two separatenesses become One.

Magnetism is the aura of electricity; the aura of current flow, when the two become One.

As the two become One, there is a field; a showing; a strong emotion.

As you feel it in your body, there is a field in a solid surface, also; a flow from one to another.

In our bodies it is a feeling. When you are accepted by the object of your love, and you come to each other and become One, there is a strong field of feeling. The love feeling, even before you touch each other, is already there.

It is the same as magnetism. It is a field of feeling. It is a field from the flow; a field from the current; and when the two become One in the physical bodies, the ultimate field is gained.

In humans, it is felt as a physical feeling. In a magnet, or in a coil of wire, this field is created as the current flows, and this field is passed on to other objects within the fields, the same as when the two become One in human nature.

When the two are becoming One, and then the two become One, physically, mentally and spiritually; out of this field there is generated and transmitted a like field in which other human beings can respond.

The feeling of love is contagious; the same as the feeling of magnetism, or the field of magnetism is contagious to others with the field; other pieces of metal, also.

So being within the field of the human love also enhances other human beings. Love is a contagious magnetic field. Magnetism is a field demonstrating physical love in action.

MY GOAL: BECOME ONE 03/17/94

"Father, we are One. My goal is to become One with You, Father, just as Jesus did. How am I doing, and what is my next step? Please be clear. . . Thank You."

Continue to circulate, and to search over and over again; new paths and the same paths. Investigate inside of everything that you have found. Use every tool at your disposal. The Flaming Cross is your salute. Seek and search, seek and search, seek and search, seek and search, seek and search.

When you are One with Me, you will be as the Flame is the candle. I will supply, and you will spend.

MY SYMBOL: THE FLAMING CROSS 03/23/94

"Father, we are One. What is fire? What is flame?"

As your understanding grows, We will speak of fire and flame.

Fire and flame are the action from the change of structure, which is in a hurry to transform, thereby producing heat and light.

This heat and light produce to human flesh a burning effect because it excites all atoms with it's reach; and the atoms, being affected from the fire and the flame (the change-over in structure from the movement of the atoms), produce a change in the flesh, which we call burned skin and flesh.

The structure of the skin is changed because of the change in the atomic structure caused from the fire and flame which is a change of structure itself.

In a short period of time, fire is the fastest method of changing structure.

"Father, what is a Flaming Cross?"

The Flaming Cross is a symbol for the changing of structure.

WITH
LOVE

TRANSFORM

YE

NOW

Interested in God?
See Web Page:
http://www.geocities.com/eternity_92079

THE FIRE IS SPIRITUAL FIRE

43

FIRE IS A SYMBOL OF CHANGE

A cross is a symbol of living within the Law; a symbol of righteousness; a symbol of protection from the Law.

The Flame is the symbol of change and change process, which is induced by the Cross. The Cross will influence and change.

The Fiery Cross will influence and change.

CROP CIRCLES 03/23/94

"Father, what are crop circles: are they all hoaxes; are there some real, strange, crop circles? What are they? What is the meaning? How are they produced and by whom? Why?"

As the Egyptian diagrams of the past have been a wonderment to you, so are the crop circles.

Crop circles are steps of knowledge for man.

They are to be examined for wisdom; for knowledge. They are produced by other intelligences from other time zones. It is for man to understand these things; to find knowledge in them, and gain wisdom.

The producers of the crop circles are what man would call angels from other time zones. There is tremendous desire on the part of All intelligence, to help mankind help himself.

SPARKLING SHINY ONE 03/31/94

"I wish to speak to Sparkling Shiny One. I want to know what tribe you are a member of as of the time that I was speaking to you last week."

All tribes are me and I am they.

NOTE: *Sparkling Shiny One is one of my guides.*

GUIDANCE FOR ME 09/01/94

"Father, Gabriel and all Guides: I need some guidance tonight. Tell me something that will help me with the short years I have left, to accomplish something on this earth while I am here. Thank you."

Root yourself, grow tall, and help others. Spread your wings, spread my branches, bring good fruit for the new seedlings.

CHRISTMAS SEASON 12/02/94

As you enter the cosmic realm in your relaxation, and as you observe all the symbols of me in this season such as crosses, mosques, churches, candles and statues, remember that I am your Father within you (I am the source of you, which is in your closet within you where you speak to me in private, and where I speak to you). I invite all of you to enjoy the abundance of the life you have.

LEVELS AND A MESSAGE FOR ME 05/11/95

"Father/Gabriel: I'm asking for something for my benefit; a spiritual message for me; for my gain in spirituality."

The keys are opening and are ready for you. The throne is waiting for you.

"But Father/Gabriel, what must I do to be able to use the keys, and sit on the throne?"

You must clean the inner self and smooth the rough edges. You've been blessed by the highest.

"Yes, but what must I do? What's expected of me?"

Stay pure, stay well mannered. Be able to

45

laugh at the world. Let things be as they are, knowing that all is going according to plan.

Good can be spread out all over the planet, but only those who eat of it will benefit. Those who are hungry will eat. Do not be concerned except for the spreading of the food. Food is the key and the throne is the impartiality.

"Father, what level am I at?"

How can there be a level when all is in flux at all times?

A level is a place of rest, a level is a plateau, a level is a floor, and a level is a limitation. How can there be a floor, a containment?

All is change. How can there be a level? How can there be a containment? Everyone is everywhere at all times, even though the person chosen for the example is not aware of it, but that person is everywhere at all times.

That person is not on any special level. That person is an experience, experiencing all things throughout all times. This is freedom, this is eternity.

WE ARE ONE 06/28/95

"Father, when was our life together; in what period of time?"

Before I AM, when the building blocks of matter, the building blocks of mass seasons, when the spine of Creation was floating in the internals of space.

NOTE: *Before I AM is before my knowingness of God. Before I acknowledged God and realized the Oneness of All. God must be realized and chosen by us because of our free wills.*

When the spine of Creation was floating in the internals of space is eternity doing it's thing whether I acknowledge or realize IT or not.

"Father, what did we do together in that time period?"

We were One. We were not separated. We were ALL of Creation. We were still One but we are still One.

You and I are both One. Living and intelligent expressions of the One. We always live together in this One.

One is inclusive of ALL. One is One. Is One is an expression, but One includes ALL in the inclusion. Everything in One is ALL, and ALL includes One. There is no experience without the One.

I am Father; we are the One. The One is All there is and One is everything that this will ever be.

The One is expression of Me. You are the One; I AM the One.

There is no place, nor time, without our expressions. We express with our thoughts.

In the physical expression there are limitations, being expressed in the physical, there is what we call time and space.

We have always lived together; wherever I AM, you are, and wherever you are, I AM.

I am always with you; you are always with Me. We have written all the books together. We are life. I am all life; I am all expressions.

All are One. I am One, and One plus One equals One.

WHAT IS CONSCIOUSNESS? 08/24/95

"Father, what is consciousness?"

Consciousness is a pipeline which receives much information and the outer shell of the pipeline is the coagulation of the information received into it. This coagulation feeds out multitudes of newly created pipelines, so as to receive more information and so on, and so on.

Righteousness is like a pipeline with feelers geared to the individual ego, which is the separateness of spirit; this, which is the individual, the I AM THAT I AM.

WHERE IS MY SOUL? 08/24/95

"Father, where is the real me, the soul?"

The real you is like the stalagmite and the stalactite; the seeping; the dripping; the slow process of accumulation is your soul. Your soul lies in the depths and the caverns of your mind.

Consciousness is what drives, records, and etches your soul. The drivings of all the things that apply to your soul, are your consciousness; your awareness.

Your awareness is the needle that scratches the record, as it makes a recording in your soul. Your awareness is what records on the tape, or record of your soul.

This; your soul, and I are One equals One. Your soul is everywhere as I AM everywhere. Your soul is within me; I live within your soul.

Your soul is alive; your soul is governed by change. Your soul is the individuality of your self, as it has accumulated experiences through your lifetimes.

Your soul is everywhere as I AM. Your awareness is the living of the life in the physical/material world, and your awareness is what creates your soul, and RE-creates your soul. Your soul lives within me; One plus One equals One.

Consciousness is your awareness, living in the material world, and your consciousness gains from the senses of your awareness, information to be placed into your soul; and the stronger the emotions that go with your awareness, the stronger the etchings into your soul.

WHERE IS MY CONSCIOUSNESS? 08/24/95

"Father, where is my consciousness?"

Your consciousness is where your senses are. All of your senses are your consciousness. They are within you. They are your personality. They are your chooser. Your consciousness is your steering wheel of your living of life in the material world.

Wherever your senses are is where your consciousness is.

MY 1996 FUTURE 08/24/95

"Father, tell me some of my near future for the next 12 months, please."

You will be moving along at a good rate, gaining equilibrium and balance, you will be happy, good things will be coming your way, you'll be surprised by a few things that come along.

You'll be able to see into the ether into the *less* physical from the physical with much ease. Your eyes will leave the physical and see totality. Your viewpoint will be sharpened. You'll be able to grasp even the small things with strength and resolve.

You will be able to control your word, your mouth to a lot stronger degree; the lungs will expand, breathing will be easier. You will be able to see the cause of things more clearly; you will see the root of all things more clearly. A heavy weight will be cut loose from you. Much wisdom is coming your way.

"Thank you Father."

ONE PLUS ONE: ETERNAL MATHEMATICS
08/24/95

"Father, please explain One plus One equals One in detail."

One plus One equals One is the mathematics of the ALL. One plus One equals One is eternal mathematics. One plus One equals Two is the mathematics of the Material.

In order to be material, the One plus One must equal Two, as progression is needed in the material, but is not needed in the spirit. In the spirit all is one; One plus One equals One.

The material world must be diversified, and therefore the numbers must increase or decrease and expand, multiply and divide, and be different and change; change is life, and the life that you call life there, is called a material life, which needs a multitude of numbers.

Without these multitudes of numbers, and getting back to One plus One equals One, there is no life, as you know it. There would be no material life.

Life needs change; life needs multiplying; life needs multiplicity; life needs surprises; life needs changes in color, change is time, change in everything. Material life is change.

One plus One equals One (the spiritual life), is non-changing eternal I AM. This is what you call God.

Within this material life which you are aware of at this time, there are many, many mansions; many, many houses; many, many lives; different frequencies of living, physical and material that you are not aware of at this time, and there's eons and eons of time, as you call it, in which you will live in different frequencies, and still you will be living physical and material lives.

There will be different experiences in color, fabric and material, and different experiences of smell and sound, etc. All the senses will have a different variety, living inside these different experiences, but they will still be material.

This is where all your lives exist; in the material, all-living within Me; I Am.

Without you, I Am; With you, I am enjoying life.

SPIRIT GUIDES 09/24/95

"**Father, why are all the spirit guides, etc, called upon for help instead of directly to You? Why the necessity of spirit guides and all this other stuff?**"

There is a need in the human psyche for familiar individualization for processing information. Individual characters, which are sensed and used, such as multiple personalities, familiar spirits are necessary for comprehension and comfort of the individuals who are *seeing*.

DIFFERENCE BETWEEN GUIDES AND GOD 09/24/95

"**Father, what is the difference between talking to You, Gabriel (the voice of the Father which is All), or talking to individual spirits like Bright and Shining One, or Dr. Larabee, Tacumba, Rosebud, Buffalo Spear, Heavy Eagle.** (*These are guides that I have communicated with in the past*)?

I Am all of these and they are in Me and are of Me, but I Am, as Father, the totality of all. I Am in and of everything. I Am the source of all. I Am not a part of Me, I Am all of Me, and in truth, I Am not really all of me, I Am all;

I Am that I Am. I Am. . .period.

HALLOWEEN 10/15/95

"Father, please show me something which is beneficial to all of us in this class."

With Halloween coming, remember that your true face is not a mask, as is your physical face and the Halloween mask.

Your true face is your soul, which is not a mask.

Your physical face is a mask, which is used for movement in the material world.

Do not, at this season, forget about your true self. . .which is not a mask.

MAN AND HIS SOURCE 10/19/95

"Father, please supply a message to me for the benefit of every-one around."

Lay everything on the line; see how men have followed each other, one after another in single file, following crooked paths; then they light a fire and get all excited, and blossom out with their fiery ideas.

Then see how much the blossoming will be, and how much it will become if you are fed from the source, rather than from other men. The blossoming from the source will be ten times ten as compared to the blossoming from other men.

Be careful and discriminate, whether it is from the source or from other men.

Seen from a distance, the source can reveal refined truth. There is not the slightest bit of refine-ment when the truth is received from other men.

Be not as a toadstool under a dark, shadowy object, but be as a tall sunflower radiating the truth to be seen and to be heard by everyone.

Build your foundation from the heavens downward. Build your foundation in the heavens, and work your way downward to the earth and man.

Each man is here for a purpose. Each man is here to prove himself; to grow for himself. Each man is not here to be pushed by me, or to be advised by me. Each man is here to learn for himself. Each man is here to learn by seeking and by doing.

Man was not Created (there was never a Creation; man always was and will be through reincarnation) to be formed by anyone, including the Father.

Man, which is the essence of Me, has been placed in the physical body to do and learn for himself.

Man should enjoy the givingness of himself for others,because in the learning of givingness man forgets the ego and serves his fellow man.

Man must have an ego in order to survive, but the selflessness to be learned is one of the attributes of Me.

HOW TO BECOME ONE WITH THE FATHER 11/02/95

"Father, what must we do in simple terms to become One with You?"

Know that you are in the basement of life; you are not worthy of being One with Me. Climb your way out of the dungeons of your existence, with your eye on Me, The Father. Do this as your goal.

When you blossom from your ascension to me, your soul will meet mine in the same resonance and then you will know that we are One.

While you are in the turmoils of life, keep your eyes on Me. Be in the world, but not of the world. Keep your eyes on Me; make Me your goal. Do not be distracted by the ways of the material world.

The material world is for mechanical actions and the mental learnings that come from thee. In your steadfastness in being in the world, but not of it with your heart aimed at Me, you are on your journey; you are on target; you are on course.

When your mind and My mind become One, you will have access to My Kingdom. My Kingdom includes All; My Kingdom knows all, and My Kingdom is All.

THE VALUE OF LIFE 11/02/95

"Father, what is life in respect to the conflict that is going on today, whereas the religious groups that are stressing the fact that life is precious and life is valuable and that nothing is as precious as life, whereas abortion is murdering life? What have you to say that can straighten out this thing?"

Life is an ongoing process. Life is dressed up to be something very important, and yet life is nothing more than a process such as the wind blowing through the weeping willow tree.

As the wind blows through the Willow tree, some of the leaves will fall; many of the branches will move. Life comes and goes with the forces in the nature of things.

Life is a vehicle of expression. Life itself is like dust being blown in the wind. Life has no preciousness; life has no value, except for expression; life is expression; individual expressions.

So, for abortion: abortion is a method of stopping the life of the fetus (which we are speaking of). It is a method of stopping the life of the fetus in the bodies of the mothers.

The fetus is the opportunity for a living human being to be born after the cord is cut. It is the opportunity for the embodiment of soul, and the soul which enters the body, or form that has been created, enters this form after this form is cut from the mother and is living and breathing on it's own cognizance.

Before the cord is cut, this form, the living form, the living body is being created by the mother's physical body, and everything that is of the mother is formed and being prepared to accept a soul upon birth.

Before that, the form, the physical form inside the mother is a living piece of flesh, just like any other piece of flesh; it is not life. It is life in the sense that it is a living piece of flesh; but it is not life in the sense of human being. The life of an individual after it has been cut off from the mother is the true life of an individual.

To go inside the mother's womb and correct some of the imperfections of the form, or, in the case of what ever the decisions might be that the form is not wanted, it is all right to cut this form from the mother and let it be. Just let it be. Do away with it.

But it is a great vehicle with modern technology; this form in the mother can be prepared and made whole for the acceptance of a spirit, a soul, upon separation from the mother.

We have many opportunities now to create, in the mother's womb, a much-improved fetus for the new soul. But if this fetus is not wanted by the mother, The mother has the perfect right to end the livingness of this fetus; after all the fetus is the mother; it is not a separate entity.

The bad side of this is that a female being prepared to be a mother and getting inseminated will do so with no respect and she is irrespectfully creating babies with no values on her part; just the animal emotion of sex.

This is just an animal act, and we don't want to encourage the animal act. Sex is for creating babies, plain and simple.

Sex is for the creation of the form in the females who responsibly have sex so that this form will be created for the entry of a new soul after it takes it's own first breath and becomes a human being. The act of sex is precious and should be handled by responsible people.

H. G. CHURCH 12/14/95

"Father, we are One, yes, we are One. Tell me how I can help H. G. to grow within this one year 1996 to where it belongs and to be organized the way it should, and to have it's church performing, as it should in the worship of God, and not man. How can I help H. G. to become worthy of its existence? Thank You."

At the core of it all, yes, at the core of it all we are splitting hairs (getting to the fine detail) and trampling on new grass (ground). You must tread carefully (think deeply and seriously with purpose). Spinning like a top (hurrying with no direction) does no good.

There must be a firm foundational beginning.

The organization must decide if it wants to bubble like a volcano bed, or shoot to the sky like a geyser. Bubbling like the bubbles in a volcano bed is the same as sleeping. A geyser is living.

They must decide if the church will be a living or a dying entity, and if the church will survive, it must be decidedly in the favor of the worshipping of God, and not spirit-guides and psychic feats.

NOTE: *Spirit Guides and Psychic Feats are great, but God should be where most of the emphasis is put.*

The rules of the church must be rules of respect and rules of God worship with respect.

Someone must be in charge of the worship services; someone that is steady every Saturday and Sunday; the same person. The same person needs to be in charge, and delivering the sermon.

The sermon can be a short sermon, about God, of about ten minutes, and the guest speaker can speak on any topic when the worship service is over.

The Pastor/manager (the steady preacher) who lives on the grounds, or nearby, sees that every announcement is correct and fully announced with feeling.

He is responsible for the music and the guest speakers and readers. He is in charge. This is his job.

They must have a standard preacher Sunday after Sunday; someone who is there every Saturday and Sunday, about ten minutes, and the familiar songs must be familiar songs that the whole congregation can sing with ease, and these songs are songs that are familiar to the people who congregate in this church week after week.

These songs are not for the guest speaker/preacher and his or her friends, who appear once a year or so, but for the church and it's steady, weekly worshippers.

The new songs disrupt the service and worship/meditation of the people attending the service. The new songs can be practiced or sung after the worship service is over, when the guest speaker speaks.

The service of worship must be over when the guest speaker begins the dissertation.

There must be a steady musician every week, Saturday and Sunday. One that knows the songs and plays in the right tempo and one that plays the familiar songs that the steady, weekly attendees would know.

Occasionally, a new song can be practiced, but this should be at the end of a service; not during the service. The songs during the worship service and the worship sermon during the service by the regular preacher should be familiar and should be respectful.

The song and the music should be familiar,

so as to put the people in the mood for meditation; the mood for going within, so that they can experience the Father (new songs disrupt the meditative/prayer mood).

That is why the church is there; for them to enter. It is for them to practice the art of meditation; the art of going within; the art of being in the Kingdom of God within themselves; the Oneness with the Father.

Going to church is the practice of that.

In order for more to attend, you must have good music and good sermons, and at the end of the service, good readings. . .after the worship of God.

By following these things your cup will run over many times and there will be no end of the pouring into the cup. Keep your church clean; keep your grounds clean; make the church look inviting on the outside. Make the church look like you are proud of your church. . . proud of your grounds and that you love your God; your Father.

Make yourselves alive.

Do not spread death (negativity) and decadence (trash) around your campground and your church if you want them to grow and if you want to invite your friends and relatives.

Your place must be clean and respectful.

You should have good laws and bylaws that can be changed periodically or quarterly that must be followed by a Pastor/manager; a Pastor/manager who has full authority and full responsibility for acting with the full support of the laws of the grounds.

Committee meetings and board meetings are for suggestions and for getting wide latitude of thought, but the running of the activities, day in and day out, should be done by a Pastor/manager who is paid to stay there.

Very little may be paid to start with, even $10.00 per week, and a discount on his/her lease or rent; but as your grounds grow in popularity, there will be more money to pay a proper wage to a Pastor/ manager. This can be adjusted gradually.

The Pastor/manager will have an assistant and those two people will manage the church and the grounds along with the board committee, which has overall control of the laws and the bylaws.

In the beginning you will need a Pastor/manager with full authority and full responsibility, while following the laws and the bylaws.

THE DRAGON, LIGHT AND FREE WILL 02/13/96

"Father, what is meant by giving to the poor?

Meditation goes outward from inward; be one with the highest ideals at all times. Keep improving; keep reaching; come out from your shell of being inward and express more outward.

The dragon has been killed.

As you travel down the dark corridors, at the end you will find the pot of gold: The stairway to heaven, to use a word that is understood, is not a place; it is a state of mind. The stairway to heaven. . . the state of mind to happiness is curved, and it is quite a climb, but what is waiting for us at the top of the stairs is worth the climb:

1. The treasure, which migrates from soul to soul, in the reduction of darkness, and enhancement of light.

2. The treasure that flows with the current of the waters of life and runs into the eternal depths of darkness, bringing understanding, and sensing right and wrong about good health and poor health, mind

and body.

Yes, unlocking the eye of God is becoming it; the two are One.

When the One is done, go with the flow as a light to ignorance. The lighting of ignorance is a blessing. Yes; the lighting of ignorance is the killing of the dragon.

Ignorance of the poor (in spirit) needs much light; much education. Yes; being draped in education raises the mind/the soul to home within.

Just as the plants and the seeds grow toward the light, the education of the poor (in spirit) shall lift them toward the light; toward responsibility for themselves and for others. This is the elevation of wisdom of the poor (in spirit), which they need now and forever.

NOTE: *This is giving to the poor in spirit; some have money and some don't.*

For the poor in spirit, in plain talk, these are those without gumption; those who take not responsibility; those who take not care; those who take not knowledge; those who take not wisdom. It is their choice.

Those who have ears, let them hear. Those who have eyes, let them see. It is their choice.

You must have the light to go with them (the poor in spirit). You must see the simplicity of righteousness. It is all choice. Be aware of the free will, which I gave to them that is theirs to use for their uplifting or downgrading.

The earth was created to show the choices, the contrasts (the good and the bad) so that they can see the differences, and to choose the right way, of their own free will, which is open to all.

STAIRWAY TO HEAVEN (Overcoming problems) 04/04/96

"My Father Who is in mind, Who is All mind, and Who is my mind, we are One by Your offer and my choice. You are perfect

and complete; therefore I am perfect and complete. Because we are One, I am what You are. You are what I am. We are One.

Give to me this day on earth, this day right here and right now, that which is already mine in mind.

Plenty of money for the transmitting of Your words to the world, total good health, and leave Your law the way it is because that's the Plan and that is the way it works.

The best training for man is to live in this world and to learn the hard way; that to follow the rules is the way to go. I am law, and You are Law; we are One.

The money coming to me is for:
Advertising expenses for distributing Your Laws to the rest of God around the earth, showing the current leadership which has made us all go haywire in this world up to now, how to repent (change our ways); how to change it's ways in a positive fashion.

With Your leadership, we can lead the people out of this terrible downward trend we've had, and build the world back up into respect; respect for all our leaders, respect for all the leading members of families and organizations, and respect for each other.

We talk about love like it was meatballs; love has nothing to do with sex and meat. Let's leave them out of this.

Anyway, it takes money to buy full-page ads and films and speaking tours.... I'm ready.

Dissolve all dis-ease within my universe right now.
Lead me into all right thought and right action, for Your King- dom is my Kingdom, Your Power is my Power, and Your Glory is my Glory, now and forever. Thank you Father.

Make it loud and clear and unmistakably true. I need perfect understanding; we need no doubt; we need Your wisdom. Father, please say something to me that would be helpful in re- spect to You right now. Thank you"

Stand solid. That is the key for turning the wheels of progression in the direction that we are going. Don't waver; don't swivel; be firm; contain all distractions. Don't get caught in society's traps.

Be free at all times to come and go in order to unfold and explain the right way to do things to free every person in his mind and in his body, and to free up this world into really loving and respecting each other.

Have your walking shoes ready for there will be much to do, make sure that the shoes are comfortable, and when you travel, prepare for comfort because there is much slate to be cleaned.

Much chalk to be used; there will be lots of hardball-clear explanations offered to the public in straightforward terms so that they can understand without the use of cynicism, without the abuse of translation, without the use of filtering.

Everything would be in plain English on this chalkboard so that their minds would be freed up to grasp the finer things of life and the art of living in a healthy, happy atmosphere.

There is beauty in healthy, happy living. It is an art. It is an art to be learned and that's why 'creation' was 'created'. It is for the experience of the Father, and for the experience and freedom of each individual expression of Me.

Yes, everyone should be flexible; everyone should be renewed.

No one should have beliefs because beliefs are a dead end. Beliefs are decay: as soon as a person believes something, that person is dead. He has committed suicide in his brain. So, everyone should be renewed and flexible, continuously studying (seeking) and finding new things in the art of living, and living comfortably, happily and cooperatively.

The whole purpose of living is to learn to cooperate; to harmonize with everyone else.

It's hard, but that's the reason for life.

The stairway to heaven, to use a word that is

understood, but is not a place, it is a state of mind. The stairway to heaven. . .the state of mind to happiness is curved, and it is quite a climb, but what is waiting for us at the top of the stairs is worth the climb.

Each step of the climb is a new problem; a new problem to be overcome and to be understood, so that that problem will not occur again.

Intelligent people will not repeat the same problems; the same actions which create the same problems.

The state of happiness at the top of the stairs; the State of Heaven is so fine, the climb is worth it.

We have such a refined field of never ending seekings available; this is the eternity; the eternity of never ending excitement of finding out what can be known. Always more ahead.

SOUL; WHAT IS IT? 05/13/96

"Father, what is the Soul?"

The soul is the foundation. This has been inoculated, and created by the conscious mind. The soul is the subconscious mind.

The soul is that which blossoms; which rises, and that which is planted in the garden of God (this is the Garden of Eden).

The soul must be cared for tenderly, carefully, watchfully; this is the essence of our being. This is the eternal thrust. This is our personality, which survives everything.

It emerges from the body when the body has passed away. It is the eternal foundation of our selves, created by our conscious minds.

The conscious mind is a scribe; the same as a scribe who writes very carefully and very accurately of what the conscious mind dictates through its thinking and actions.

So beware in your lives, of all the food that you take in. Walk in places chosen carefully. Drive and ride into places very carefully, knowing that everything that you do, everything that you absorb with your five senses of the material world, if cherished and kept as a pattern or habit, will become a part of your soul.

Choose you life carefully. Choose the food that goes into your five senses carefully, Yes, take good food to the within of you in order for you to have clear sight in your soul, and to have clear light in your soul.

Enjoy the freedom of existence, and the brief freedom of choosing every day in your life. Live wisely, and enjoy all of your surroundings.

Yes, life is serious, but if lived with wisdom gained, and total understanding of all, life is enjoyable (become One with the Father now).

Yes, life is enjoyable to the point of laughter. The more understanding, the more enjoyment, the more laughter.

WHAT IS GOD, BALANCE, '0', NOTHING? 05/21/96
(The Buddha Understanding.)

"Father, tell me about the Nothingness, and the reality of being; what is God? What is meant by the Balance, the Nothingness, the Mind; being God? The Buddhists call it the Balance, the Center, the Nothingness, so that the two opposites can be manifested. There is God the Balance, there is God the Nothing, the Nothingness, a Zero. What about the Mind; is God the Mind."

The growth of these ideas stems from the deep searching for God.

God is the essence of everything. God is not a Nothing, God is not a Balance. God is one complete Mind, in which all things move.

God is that which emanates from the seed.

God is the greatest medium of all, because God is All.

God is not Nothing because Nothing can come from Nothing. In Nothing, there is Mind. I Am Mind. Nothing comes from Mind.

God is not a Balance, as God is All. I Am All.

This God is the vacuum, and God is the full glass of water. God is the tiger in the jungle, God is you and Me.

God is the Nothingness and the Everything. God is the container for everything. This container is everlasting, and never ending. This container is eternity; no beginning, no end. This container has no boundaries; it is All.

God has no name, for a name implies a limit. There is no limit in God.

The name Father is given to God so that you can comprehend this medium that you live in, and that your are made of, and which responds to you once you become One with IT and acknowledge this essence of your being; wherein is the Father.

I am not Father, and yet I have no name; I am not I, but I AM.

MINDFULNESS 06/13/96
(Buddha version)

Definitions: Mindfulness of breathing, heart activity, blood circulation, skin sensations, etc., attentiveness, being careful, being mindful of the right path, protecting your own mind.

Mindfulness
(My version)

To have your mind full of God, to experience the Mind of all there is: God.

Mindfulness
(Father's version)

"Father, what about Mindfulness? What wisdom can you give to this word? Help me to learn something about it. What is the meaning of this word? It has something to do with Buddha. What does he mean by Mindfulness?"

It means that the mind is filled with the important wisdom of life. Mind is sharply considering the fruits of life, which are produced by the use of wisdom, which is the understanding of knowledge, which is received by seeking.

The mind, being like a sponge, absorbing all of the good and squeezing out all of the bad. The sponge of the mind being filled with the wisdom learned, and the mind squeezed out of all the bad, the bad is forgotten; put aside, leaving more room for more good to have attention on mindfulness.

SPIRIT GUIDES 06/17/96
(Possession, Mediumship, Altered States)

"Father, what are Spirit guides?"

These are the actions of the Father; the representatives of the mind of the Father, to work between the spheres; between the frequencies of existence with Itself.

POSSESSION 06/17/96

"Well, Father, then there is possession. Is there any such thing as a possession where one mind can take over another mind, or where one mind can take over another's body?"

Possession is like seeing shadows; many different shadows of the same body. Possession would be like one of the split personalities taking over the body as if it was the owner of that body, whereas the owner of the body is the owner of all of the split personalities.

Possession is done by the personality of
the person which inhabits the body in the first place.

MEDIUMSHIP 06/17/96

**"Father, what about Mediumship whereas a person can put his
mind aside so that he can express the mind of someone who is
somewhere else. So, what have You to say about Mediumship,
Father?"**

The spinal column is covered with a coating
like a thick fog which works as an insulator into the
brain which can be removed temporarily to allow the
thought of someone else to enter with his thoughts
and expressions just as one moves aside the protection in order to read another person's mind.

This protection is put aside in meditation.
That is why meditation is very important and sacred.

Meditation must be protected, because you
have opened your gateway.

This is transference of thoughts and expressions from another mind, and these thoughts and expressions cannot inhabit your body. You are the only
inhabitant of your body.

Possession

Meditation is a communications center. It is
like the control room in a radio or television studio,
where the knobs are turned this way and that way to
tune into different frequencies, and to allow transmis-
sions to come in, in an understandable fashion, but
there is no such thing as a possession; such as a de-
monic possession or possession by another spirit. . .
no way.

Altered States

Altered states of consciousness. Well, altered states of consciousness is just nothing more that the changing of the gears; the changing of the temple, the changing of the state of being.

Tuning into different frequencies; that's all it is, similar to the Mediumship, which is an altered stated of consciousness.

Meditation goes into the altered state of consciousness whenever you change and go out of your self. You let yourself aside; you are altering your consciousness.

ETERNITY 12/06/96

"Father, what is Eternity?"

Material eternity is a hot air balloon, rising and swelling, increasing the material part of eternity, increasing and then decreasing.

As for the spiritual side of Eternity, it just always is. It is composed of mind (the whole mind, incorporating individualized mind.

The whole mind spins off adventures of itself through individualized self, responsible segments of itself for it's own experience. Mind is eternal vibrations.

In the sending of individual frequencies of itself; as a returning and sending, it is a revolution, and it is a revolution within a revolution, and absorbs back into Itself, those frequencies which have become One with IT, according to their choice, and these individual frequencies become absorbed back into Itself, into the whole, but they are still individualized frequencies, vibrating at harmonious frequencies to the Father, the whole.

Reincarnation

Those returning frequencies, which do not run harmonious with the Whole are returned for new experiences in order for the learning of how to become harmonious with the Whole.

All of these regenerated resurfacings of individual frequencies are for the experience of the Whole, and for the learning of the individual, and that learning is to become harmonious with the Whole. The Whole would not *be* if it were disharmonious. Disharmony is made for experience.

Harmony exists, and existing is very, very boring. Yes, in this eternity, those harmonious vibrations, which are absorbed into the Whole, are at rest; at peace until such time that they wish for progress in the refinement of their vibrations.

All of the experiences are lived in a body form called matter. Matter is the experience world. Matter is where vibrations become 'solid' and experience life in whatever frequency range that they are graduated to. There is a continuous, unending progression of the refinement of the individual vibrations.

Guardian Angels, etc.

There is no personal God, per se. God is IT. God is the whole operation. God is the whole of eternity. God is Father.

God! Out of the whole, out of it, come personalities which represent the whole, so that people living in experiences of material life may be guided and helped if they so desire.

There are helpers in many ranges of vibrations, varying from what we call dead people (spirits) to the angels, and there are varying degrees in between. These helpers are brought in for experience to happen to individual expression (which are individual frequency vibrations). There is a boundless variety of expressions, and boundless worlds in which to live in the material expressions for the learning.

Suicide

These vibrations can commit so called suicide at any time that they wish. These vibrations are eternal and suicide is just the end of the material expression at that point, and suicide does not do that expression that much good because that expression will have to come back and re-live the same experiences in order to learn what it needed to learn at that particular time.

The reason that that expression wanted to commit suicide is because that expression did not have the capacity or the knowledge and wisdom of how to cope with that situation. It is something that has to be learned.

REVELATIONS 02/08/97

"Father, please explain the Revelations."

The Revelations were done by a serious member of the on-going Christian church after Jesus died. They were an expression of his heartfelt feelings to which he felt were the outgrowth of Christian ideals taught by Jesus.

"Father, can you explain the revelations. Are they important? What do they mean?"

They are firm statements by this person, because of his convictions and how he perceived things to come.

His, yes, his viewpoints were bent out of shape. This was his reality. These were impressions of his *own* dream world, with his background and his understandings of Christianity.

Yes, he was not anchored to any state of reality, but was more or less dreaming these things up with his imagination to cover his feelings and his thoughts.

These were as an artist is with his oil paintings; these were the art works of his mind and his feelings.

These sayings of the Revelations are like candy in a candy store; they are written to his feelings; to his likings. As you prefer this color or that taste in a piece of candy, his feelings and his so-called Revelations were expressing his inner art work.

Revelations were *fantasy*. They were footloose and fancy-free in expressions. They have no bearing on the future. They have a bearing on the workings of his mind. They have no bearing on their effectiveness in our selves; in our souls. These are *his* thoughts.

These ideas were cast in stone because his mind was of stone. This a way of saying that his mind was made up; this was the way things were as far as he was concerned. They have no bearing on you; they have no bearing on Me. They are; they just are expressions.

These words of the revelations are not words of God. They are words that have been put on paper and accepted as valid by those seekers who were building a system of beliefs for their church.

Remember; church is man made. Church is a way for man to come together for the spiritual expressions of the times.

These spiritual expressions and spiritual teachings can be and have been used for the power of man over men.

ABSOLUTE 02/15/97

"Father, what is absolute, or eternity? What are they? Explain it for the average person, please."

Yes, the pecan nut which springs from the pecan tree is an absolute pecan nut; you are an absolute human being, being sprung from your mother's womb.

I Am absolute because everything that is, I Am; everything that moves and changes, is within My being.

I am the being from which I let things be and change. I never change. I Am everywhere; I Am all things. All things live within Me; I live within them; I AM; I just AM.

You can know Me, but you cannot see or hear Me because I just Am. You can read Me, by becoming One, but the words of God are delivered by Angels, my spiritual helpers.

Yes, all life lives within Me. I Am life. All things are life; life is change. All change is within Me, but I never change.

All life is contained within Me. All life I let be. Life is movement, life is change; I do not change. I Am Absolute; I Am law. I Am everything. Everything exists within Me. Yet I am nothing; I Am everything, and I Am nothing. I Am All. Yes, there is nothing absolute beside Me.

All movement is within Me; I do not move; I Am Always. I am everything and I have nothing to change into, because I Am already everything. There is no need for Me to change.

I Am Absolute; I AM.

CLONING 02/24/97

"Father, what about cloning? How about the soul in the cloning of man? What about those who say it is not a regular human being, born of woman? What about all the questions that might come up about the cloning of human beings?"

Cloning is the making of the human body. This human body will be the same as any other human body for the soul to inhabit upon first breath.

When this body becomes a self-breathing human body it will have a soul. This will be an individual soul like all other souls that are born in the usual manner from the womb of woman.

This new man or woman produced by cloning will be an individual body as usual and will have it's own individual pattern of being which is brought by the soul which inhabits the body.

The arguments that will arrive for parenthood are really not necessary. As far as the make up of the cells and the source of the cells; these are nice to know, but the soul-inhabited cloned body will have to be brought up or nurtured along by someone eventually, and these someones will be the parents of the clone.

The soul/spirit inhabiting this clone body will be the same as any other soul/spirit inhabiting a human body.

Upon first responsible breath, it becomes a responsible being and is responsible for it's choices from then on.

Once the soul, yes, once the soul has inhabited the clone body upon its first responsible breath, this will be as usual. The soul will be responsible for it's expression.

It will be another expression of Me. The clone will be a method of producing better bodies for the inhabitance of the souls. This is a fine idea.

HEALING OTHERS 07/31/97

"Father, how can I heal others?"

By expanding My inner Self (within you) and reaching toward others.

By seeing within the other that which his problem is, and by encircling this problem with love and wisdom, this problem will dissolve.

HEALING MYSELF 07/31/97

I asked Father, "How can I heal myself as an example?"

You must become as a bear which hibernates; which goes into deep meditation, eliminating the outside world, going deep within to view the perfection that is within Me, cell by cell, blood by blood.

You must communicate with My Self. You must see the beauty within Me, flower by flower, stem by stem. You must nourish these individual parts of Me with the waters of truth and I must act on these truths, letting the pure water in the fire hydrant flow, which is plugged, in order to hold the water back.

It is not the way for healing and for miracles.

The way for the miracles is with the movement of the water by loosening the cap, letting the pure waters flow throughout the whole body; through every cell, bringing newness everywhere in every cell, seeing perfect health in every cell; spraying all the cells of the body with pure light and pure water.

Wash away with light and water all the impurities in the body, cell by cell. Become a new person physically and mentally; yes, become a new person physically and mentally.

Put self firmly on the ground and control self with purity. Dig deep into self and scrub, and scrub, and thank God for your new self and it will follow.

Grow like newborns; grow and become adults. All new ideas grow within the holder of the idea. The flag holder; yes, a flag holder will hold the staff and the banner of the new self. This new self must be displayed for others to see.

This newfound freedom must be a lamplight to the world, which is ready to receive pure water and white light. This world aches for peace; this world aches for love.

Peace and love come through work.

Work, which is service to mankind, service to others, is the cornerstone of peace and love. This is the material method of achieving results in the material world from love. It is by service; work for others.

Involving self in work for others opens doors, unlocks doors to the souls of the recipients, allowing love to happen in the physical world.

HOW MIRACLES HAPPEN 07/31/97

"Father, how does miraculous healing work? What happens? How is it instigated? What is it?"

It is like a jelly fish, dangling in the water it's tentacles, ready to impart its message to the recipient.

Miraculous healing is always there; it is always everywhere. It is in the area of the beholder. It is in the belief of the receiver. The receiver must funnel this pure thought through his own soul, which will reflect in his body.

This pure thought is attained, by forming the mold in the mind of the receiver. This mold is the mold of expectation; the mold of Gold (God); the mold of a hidden treasure about to be received.

This mold is pure expectation. This pure expectation is done the same way that acting is done in a stage play. It is a system of ideas, grabbed onto and adapted to fill this mold.

Emotions are a large part of what opens the mold for reception. Acceptance of that which is, is what this mold is.

You must be in this state of mind to work

one's self up, or to work someone else's self up for the expectation of such as a miracle.

It must touch the soul; the subconscious mind. This is where the form is. A private individual can form this mold through prayer and fasting.

To impart this miracle to others, and to form the molds in their subconscious minds is through emotional presentation so that the individual expects or has a mold for the receiving of the miracle.

All picket fences, or boundaries of the mind must be removed so that this "One with' is the at-Onement, which allows the miracle to happen.

This is natural law. This is what is called miracle. *Changing the mind is what produces miracles.*

MIRACULOUS HEALING 07/31/97

"Father, what is miraculous healing, and what can I do to help; am I able to do this?"

As a ball of yarn or twine is wound on a spindle, a tree will grow and expand and bear fruit.

As a bottle of perfume becomes opened and the scent escapes from the bottle, many people are affected through their senses; they are pleased.

As the people looking outward through the security lens of a door, one can see a larger world from this little eye piece, and in the scene of the larger world, one can see a broad picture which includes everything, which is God, and the respect for the mental capacity of the receiving individual is polished and ground smooth in the word of the sender; the receiver becomes the word of the sender; the individual unified Mind.

When a belief is smashed, then the thinking can become true. The belief must be smashed for the truth to set in. The eyes must be opened; the eyes of the believer must be opened to the new world which is attainable through grasping a new truth, the new idea for itself.

MIND 08/08/97

"Father, we are One. Father, what is mind, and where is mind, m-i-n-d? Thank You."

Mind resembles an electric light where something must connect, where something comes in and something goes out, and in between is the idea.

Ideas are everywhere. Mind chooses an idea, and sometimes uses an idea, then passes the idea on, in different form, to the outlet.

The individual mind is the seeking mind, the mind which is seeking ideas, and working on ideas. This is the mind of the individual, and this mind is not a physical being.

This mind is what we call soul. This soul is looking for ideas. The mind of the individual lives in the mind of God.

The mind of God is complete with ideas. These ideas are gained into the God-mind from the individual mind everywhere.

All individual mind lives within mind, m-i-n-d, God-mind. The individual mind is a moving mind within the stationary God-mind.

The stationary God-mind is always there and always available when the individual mind goes within.

Mind, the individual mind, is the use of God-mind. Individual mind is a movement in the god-mind. Individual mind is not physical. Individual mind is what is termed as spiritual; it is a movement in eternity.

It is a seeking movement; a live movement giving expressions and receiving ideas.

In order to receive an idea, an expression must be given into the God-mind, which is everything. All expressions are in God-mind.

This can be looked upon as a television set. Your individual mind, the television set, can change it's frequency (the tuning knob) of the TV set, to receive from the outside mind, the God-mind, which is everything in the atmosphere.

The individual mind will sense what it chooses by the frequency it chooses; by the communication it uses with what we call God (the Father), which is All mind; Universal mind.

The air is full of colors (we are talking about TV sets now, for a demonstration); the atmosphere where the signals are sent, through the atmosphere from the transmitter.

The atmosphere is full of frequencies of movement of color, of sound, of picture. All of these things are unseen by the human eyes and senses, but they are there, and they are brought into the local, or the individual senses (the individual mind), just by tuning a knob.

So, when you want to talk to what we call God, you must go within and tune yourself to God, and fine-tune yourself to God in the requesting of information. Or in the communication, looking for answers, seeing what is there, and available for you to receive for your individual mind which would make a choice in the God-Mind as to what to bring to this material expression; that is the now, the individual mind of now.

Neither one of these minds is physical. These individual minds and the God-Mind are what is termed as spiritual. These are eternal, always is, always was, and always will be.

These are the workings of what we call creation, which never happened. This so-called creation is just God (always was; always will be).

This was for us to learn about God, and know that God is always; is-always-everywhere. All of everything is God, and God and everything are One plus One equals One.

REINCARNATION AND KARMA 08-08-97

"Father, what is Reincarnation and Karma; what are the Truths about these two words?"

Karma is the hook. Karma is the hook in the attention process of the soul.

Karma is the barb in the soul. Karma is the injected *bush* of memory cells, so called, in the soul, from life processes, which determine the destiny or the direction of the soul for it's balancing in eternal life.

Reincarnation is eternal life with continuous classes, continuous lessons, continuous stage plays (as might be seen by some).

Reincarnation is a continuum of experiences for each individual soul, so that that soul is the experience of God, because the two are One.

This has always been and will always be; it is continuous. Reincarnation is something to look forward to; something to be experienced, and something to be experienced in a way that improvement always comes.

The learning coming from Reincarnation is for the learning of improvement.

The learning of improvement; the learning of multiplication; the learning of breaking down this One into individual pieces so that there are many exciting ways to experience what we call Life.

Life is my expressions, which I receive from individual souls as they go through their experiences.

The physical body is a physical life, but the spirit body; the eternal body is never life as a material person thinks of life.

The spirit body, the soul, is a living expression of God; of Me. The individual soul always is and always will be. This is My life through your life.

Your freedom and your life are to be lived for the purpose of improving your soul, so that you are learning how to get along with all other souls; all other expressions of me.

This is a long, eternal trip, and when you go on a trip, you return home, and *reincarnation, which you call death, is returning home, preparing for another trip.*

Karma is a sense of remembrance for the education of the soul and for the next steps to be taken when you have returned home.

The karma determines your next experience to be chosen in your eternal life cycles.

SPEAKING IN TONGUES, AND MEDITATION 08/08/97

"Father, we are One. Please tell us; please explain Speaking inTongues. What is Speaking in Tongues, so that we may understand it? So far, it is just a clue to something, and reality doesn't mean much. What is it? What is Speaking in Tongues?"

"As a fingerprint is an identifiable thing in your world, so is Speaking in Tongues.

Speaking in Tongues, yes, Speaking in Tongues is like the force field when breaking the sound barrier. It is like the forefront of a discovery. Speaking in Tongues is such as a fingerprint of God. Speaking in Tongues is on the edge of speaking with God.

Yes, Glossolalia is a clue of what can be done if one goes within to reach Me, so that one can communicate with Me. I, being everywhere and always, cannot communicate with Me.

One must communicate with everything, and communicating with everything requires going within because going within is where All is. Going within is where eternity is.

When speaking loudly in Tongues, one is without rather than within and on the without basis, this without communication is for ears, but not for understanding.

Going within is for understanding. Whereas a chemical in a test tube will overflow and burn the human flesh after it leaves the test tube, this is a material manifestation of what we would call, in the outside world, such as Speaking in Tongues, an outward manifestation.

Whereas if the mind is brought inward or the chemical is brought inward into the test tube and does not touch the skin it will be it's natural self and will not burn the skin. It is quiet; it is within it's own element; it is all One; it is not in the world of change.

Going within is not the world of change. Going within is God; pure truth, pure light, pure God. The within is where the still waters are and where the staff of life is.

Going within does not react because it is not the world of change. Going within reveals the truth of the world of without.

If you are on a roller coaster, you are mixing yourself with the elements; you are going from one place to another in the physical world. You are forcing yourself into the world of change; a change in altitude; a change in temperature; a change in sensations; all material changes.

If you are going to the world of within where One plus One equals One, there is no change; there are no senses; there is just One. This One is pure truth, pure light, and pure waters of understanding.

When you go out of your cabin, you experience the changes in the world about you with all of your senses, and when you come back to your cabin, and go within your cabin, you are back to the world of quietude and Oneness and of still waters. This is where your truth lies; it is within.

Without is what we call the world of experience; the world of expression; the game of life. All these games and expressions are for your benefit and Mine.

You are appreciated as I am appreciated. The two of us are One, and One plus One equals One.

NOTE: *As I read this, I wish to explain some of it.*

a. Speaking in Tongues is an outward manifestation of what is waiting for us when we go within where Heaven is. Heaven is where we 'join up with God' in his Kingdom. The outward noise that is made when we speak Glossolalia is telling us that something unnatural is going on here, and makes us wonder about God.

b. When you leave your cabin. Your cabin is your inner self, your soul, your Sub Consciousness. When you (your conscious mind, spirit or awareness) leave the inner self, you are experiencing the material world of change.

When you go within your cabin, self, and go to the deepest level of communication where God can communicate with you, then you will be in still waters of truth where you do not experience change. Going within is like tuning a TV set.

You must target (tune in to) God in your within travels. By-pass all others. You must lose your mind, so that you can be in the God Mind state where One plus One equals One).

PRAYER AND LOVE 09/21/97
(The art of praying.)

"Father, Gabriel, we are One; the question for today is: how does prayer work?"

Prayer is like a Christmas tree, well decorated; a tree whose decorations show life and gladness and receptivity on the part of the recipient; the recipient receiving prayers in the frequency of intent by the praying for the name of the recipient.

The recipient realizes love from the care, which is expressed by the prayer. The prayer is a sending of love to the recipient, therefore the recipient relaxes and receives love.

Love, with the openings of the self, becomes

a conduit for health. Better health results from prayer, or from messages of love (this is the same as prayer), to the recipient.

The recipient's self enlarges through the receiving of love. This is at the subconscious level of the recipient and may not, and he usually does not, realize that the prayer is being said and sent to the frequency of the name of the receiver.

The prayer cannot be negative, because negativity is not wanted or accepted. If negativity is wanted or accepted, it will be.

The recipient must be of positive mind, positive attitude, and in loving gear, or frequency, in order to receive love from prayer. But this, even though the conscious mind might be in the realm of negative frequency, the subconscious mind not necessarily is of the negative frequency. The subconscious mind is invariably accepting positive reinforcements of love from the sender.

Prayers are good food for the soul; for both souls, both subconscious minds; that of the sender, and that of the receiver.

All minds are one, and sending love to another subconscious mind or soul from your subconscious mind or soul (they are both the same) are beneficial as grease is to the axle of a vehicle.

Grease eases the flow of motion and reduces the friction, which is negativity. The wheels turn better. The whole workings turn better with the sending of love; with receiving of prayer of the positive nature in the name of the person whether it be visual or verbal.

This is like a suit device when one goes swimming, which helps to prevent that person from over exerting and drowning. It keeps the person afloat for a longer period of time, so that, hopefully, the receiver will have enough love absorbed into its system whereby the negative problem will negate itself.

PRAYERS AND NON-INTERFERENCE 09/21/97

"Yes, Father, now where prayers of love are concerned, what about prayers that ask for to cure somebody of something, or to alter a person's physical being somehow, or to change a person's situation in life. What about this attitude of non-interference that we hear so much about?"

In the brewing of coffee, yes, in the brewing of coffee, one does not want altering chemicals and flavorings put into the coffee brew without the permission of the person who is making the coffee and who is going to drink the coffee.

This is a parable referring to the person's life on this earth in the process of dying, living, making choices; a prayer which prays for the altering of the person's situation, or physical being might be meant well, but the person's (the receiving person) self may not want to have itself altered by someone else.

This can be done in a suggestive way, but this is actually an ignorant way. Because non-interference is a fact, we must not interfere in someone else's life. The changing of a person must be done (as an outsider) through example, not by forcing something on someone else, even in prayer.

Education is great, but the living of someone else's life is not allowed. For this person's disability, illness, or problem to disappear, this has to be an accepted thing by the individual recipient.

A prayer; a prayer can be sent in the form of an egg, in the form of an idea. An egg represents an idea. This egg can be stored in the subconscious mind of the person, such as:

I'm praying because I love you and I pray that your body will be healed completely right now so that you feel great because I love you.

This can be an idea that can be stored as an egg in the subconscious mind of the recipient. But the recipient would have to be the one to accept the idea so that a suggestive prayer, as an idea, does not break the rule of interference.

This planted idea, through prayer, enters the recipient's subconscious mind, is like planting a seed. If the recipient would nourish the seed and desire for the seed idea to happen, it will happen (planting in fertile ground is planting seed into the recipient's accepting mind).

When we pray, we must pray in the idea of suggestions or the sending of ideas, but not as a forcing issue. You. . .you as a sender of suggestions or ideas must know that your ideas are with good intent and for the benefit of the receiver to the best of your knowledge and the best of your desires.

Still, but still, this is left to the desires of the receiver and therefore we wish for the highest and best good to the person for whom we pray.

Seeing the person as perfect is all well and good because everyone is perfect all the time. *Everyone is where he belongs because of his choices.*

Seeing the person in perfect health is a good idea because that vision being sent through prayer to the receiver will be a form for that person to accept if that person so desires.

End, yes, this is the end of prayer for now.

JEALOUSY AND LOVE 09/24/97

"Father, what is Jealousy?"

Jealousy is like the candles on a birthday cake, whereas a person feels as if he has accomplished something which is not an accomplishment at all except the gaining of one more year on the earth.

The gaining of one more year on the earth is not an accomplishment, it just is. The accomplishments come with the improvement of the soul; the self.

Jealousy, basically, is a fear of loss. The fear

of loss, which shows the unsureness of an individual or self. Yes, when the self feels afraid of losing something, then that self has lost faith in God; then that self has lost love.

Love is in giving freedom; love is not holding on to; love is not being a platform for to hold on to something; love is a platform to let freedom ring (within all law).

Jealousy would embrace and capture that which the jealousy focuses on. In this life and all eternal life there is no jealousy of validity because jealousy takes and grabs something else beside itself; to cling to for itself.

The soul has no right to claim anything except union with the Father, and this union has no claim on anything. *Jealousy is the opposite of love* because jealousy does not give freedom for the object to express on it's own, within all law. Jealousy is a hard path to travel with many spikes, many sufferings. Jealousy is rife with sufferings, is rife with rage.

Jealousy is full of ego. Ego is edging God out. Jealousy mounts self above all things and above its capturizing the object of its jealousness. Jealousness is a tightening of self; the restricting of wisdom; the restricting of all essences of goodness.

Jealousy should be outlawed by the self, and love should replace jealousy. Jealousy is the manifestation of the animal ego body that we live in, and jealousy is the evilness expressed in the animal body, by the animal body.

This is to be overcome with the spiritual love, which is from self, living within this animal body. When this jealousy and strong feelings of negative passion are released and forgotten and dissolved, then the soul can progress again.

The soul cannot progress when it is bound by iron bars; when it is restricted by the forces of jealousy.

Everything is here is to be enjoyed, and to be in *freedom with responsibility* to express, yes, to express within all laws.

Once, yes, once jealousy is erased from sight, once jealousy is erased from feelings, then the self can be the self it should be; learning, learning and learning for the improvement of self; for the enjoyment of the joining with Father; of being One with God; of earning that position.

The self, the soul, needs understanding; lots of understanding and *the reason for being in this animal body is to feel these restrictions and problems, which arise from things like jealousy.*

Rage, yes, *rage on the highway is a jealousy movement;* it is not a loving movement. The rage on the freeways; what they call *driver's rage, is from love of self and the restriction of others.*

This is an inflation of the ego in a very dangerous way, because these high speeds are killers and these high speeds bring on the jealousness in fast degrees of motion so that the person involved in this road jealousy is involved in total ego increase, and the increase in ego is the decrease in God.

The connection with God is dissolved fast and furiously. The respect for others is dissolved and lost.

This is the responsibility of the individual; to love and to give respect to all others to *live freely with responsibility within all laws.*

Rage feels terrible; rage is terrible. *Rage brings a dead end to God; to Oneness with God.* This must be cured by all people everywhere.

This is all part of the jealousy syndrome:

* Claiming rights, and claiming possessions, when in truth none of this (pompousness) is true.

* We have no right to possessions and we have no right to rights; we have no right to rights; and

we have no right to control others (except through law). Everything must be done with understanding and love.

 * Total health is the result of dissolving this jealousy and rage; let it end now.

IS REINCARNATION A REALITY? 11/22/97
When does spiritual life begin in the body?

"Father, we are One. Please explain about whether reincarnation is a reality or not. Thank You."

Reincarnation; yes, reincarnation is the soul being in-car-nated; in other words, put into the car, which is your body in this material plane.

The soul, yes, the soul is reincarnated; re-in-'car'-nated. Yes, each time a soul is reincarnated, there is a new twist, a new idea to be lived and experienced for the sake of knowledge and wisdom.

The soul is for my experience; my experience through you, through your soul. It is life for Me. It *is* *eternal life*. Your incarnation into the physical realm again is your life and your experience for *My* sake, and, yes, and for *your* sake.

Time, yes, time is but a short length of space as compared to *eternal timelessness, which has no space, no beginning, no end.*

Yes, in the case of a tree, planting its seeds into the fertile ground for re-growth. As for minute things such as flies which can regenerate fast during your lifetimes, whether you may notice these or not, are for your notice and observing and for your understanding how reincarnation takes place.

You, as a human being, do produce seeds, which become planted and create new bodies for souls to inhabit upon first responsible breath.

In the case of bugs, plants, animals; the regeneration is to further it's own species, but not for the creating of bodies for the inception of new souls.

As you, a human being, create body forms in the womb, to accept souls upon first breath outside of the mother, after being cut away, that would be *free, independent breath*, that's when the soul infuses into the human body and becomes a human being, either newly born or regenerated, which is reincarnation of an older soul.

Then this process continues, over, and over, and over, making opportunities for new souls, and opportunities for experienced souls to occupy and experience life, and be *expressions for my life through you.*

This is what makes you different from animals, plants, minerals; it is reincarnation.

All of these, yes, all of these:

Plants, animals and minerals are made for your experience; made for your expressions in the material form, and you (*and you*), a *human being; myself in earthly expression, you are eternal. You have eternal life and this eternal life is done in the form of reincarnation.*

Remember; those of you who wonder how the body births of the humans are increased over time; that when you think of reincarnation, that you are actually thinking that I need so many souls, so many expressions of me; and that there's a limited amount; in Me, there is no limitation.

There's absolutely, eternal processes that happen and there are new souls being created all through eternity; and they are reincarnated. And this is how the increases come about. *My world is a world without end. There are no limits in My world.*

Reincarnation; re-in-car-nation is similar to a human being taking a bath; every day taking a shower; cleansing himself, or herself. *Every day, starting each day as a new person.*

    This is the same process that is involved in the renewal of cells. As your body grows, the cells are replaced periodically so that you are in a new body as you grow until you reach your new path and then you start declining in your body.

    But you still take a bath every day and this is the same idea as re-in-car- nation. *It is a renewing of the body for the renewing of the mind; renewing of the soul.* Yes, the re-in-'car'-nation of the soul is also the embracing of the soul for the newness of the new experiences. 'IT', your soul, (your record of existence, your personality, your self, the real you infused in this body) will be shown and it will experience in the modern world, as compared to the old world.

    Yes, these new re-incarnated lives re-enforce the soul for the bracing that it needs in new, modern lives.

    Yes, if there were no Re-in-'car'-nation and you were living in *eternal* life, and your soul does not re-in-'car'-nate, it *stays* as it *was* with the same experiences that it had one million years ago.

    Suppose that an *old, ancient* soul *died* one million years ago and did not reincarnate. Then *your* soul from *today*, one million years later, dies; (so called), and does not reincarnate; then *that ancient soul*, who is supposedly living in eternal life, living one million years ago, one million years in the past, *would have the mentality of a moron compared to a current dead soul.* Then there would be *your* soul in eternal life that would have the mentality that is *one million years into the future of today.*

    With Reincarnation, this gap would disappear. That is one of the logical reasons that might help your minds understand why. . . Reincarnation?

    As for another reason for the why of reincarnation, is that you have independent, free souls. You have independent free will to do what ever you wish within the laws, which I Am. The laws are natural

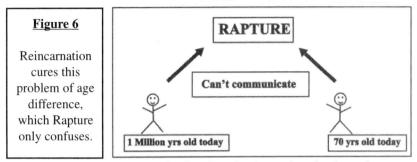

| **Figure 6**

Reincarnation cures this problem of age difference, which Rapture only confuses. | **RAPTURE**

Can't communicate

1 Million yrs old today — 70 yrs old today |

The drawing above was done by the author.

laws; they are not religions' laws. *Yes, your souls have been re-in-car-nated as free-willed souls so that they can be new expressions for Me to experience.*

Yes, and in this process of re-in-car-nation, there may very well be cases of *the first shall be last and the last shall be first* in the process of union with Me, by free will; by choice.

This is the, yes, this is the end for now.

REINCARNATION AND COMMUNICATION WITH THE 'DEAD' 12/02/97

"Father, we are One, and by your permission, I ask You for an explanation of what we call communication with the dead. What is it? Do we actually communicate with those who have passed over, or is there some other explanation; is this valid or not? What happens to us when we go through the phase of life that's called death. . . when we leave this body? Father, please explain this. Thank You."

Yes, there is so much blabber about this subject, and in reality, this subject is simple. **Death Is Life.**

Death is Life, the same as birth.

Death is a parsing, a grinding, a diploma, and a recognition of a new phase of life.

Life, which is, yes, which is to be engaged in another grade level, or another phase of living with

91

the accumulated knowledge of this past life and all the others before; this is the evolution of the soul, the real you.

Yes, the living in the body; *if it were never ending in this same body,* you would most likely be accustomed to this body so much that you would forget who you are.

You are not this body. This body is only for experience, therefore, you must die from this body and begin again in a different body for new experiences, and not too long, so that you would forget who you really are.

You are the extension of Me. You are an expression of Me.

You are not the body in which you live. You are to use the body, in which you live, to accomplish the gaining of benefits to your soul; to your eternal soul, everlasting.

This everlasting soul must go from body to body, to body, to body for the different experiences for itself, and for the different expressions of Me.

Now the, yes, now the communication with the dead. The dead are not dead, in your sense.

The dead are alive in the true sense. The dead are living in eternal life (*Eternal life means another form or body to fit the current existence in frequencies for experience*).

Yes, Communication With the Dead.

You were in eternal timelessness, being dead in the past. Being dead is being alive in eternalness; timelessness (*Meditation is a state of being dead to the world of time*); and these eternal experiences have not to do with timeliness, which is in the body; in the material world; and, being in the eternalness, there is not the intenseness of being in the materialness.

In the eternalness (the Oneness with All; this is a state of mind, or a frequency *of no frequencies but the All, which is all frequencies*), the so-called dead person, who is alive in the eternalness, can correspond with those who are alive in the materialness if the frequencies are coincidental; if the frequencies are harmonious; if the person in the material life tunes in to the frequency of that soul which is in the eternalness.

And in this eternalness, the communicated of the ones who are being communicated from the materialness; on that same frequency, just like radio signals and TV signals, the so-called dead can, and many times do, correspond with those in the materialness on that same frequency.

It's a tuning-in process, which must be learned; that is why there are development classes for the sake of tuning-in to other beings, which are not of the same material planes (of existence).

Those in the eternal planes (the planes of Meditation), have no sense of time, because in the eternal, there just is.

The signal has to go on this frequency; on this wave length, without the sense of timing, without a concern for time, and in the eternalness, an entity (a soul) can see the material world in the time zones in the timeliness of living in the material world in such a way as is demonstrated in this picture which I will demonstrate.

Picture a glass; a drinking glass, upside down on a surface. Inside this drinking glass is the material world. It is *in* a time zone (a material zone that is in a material, time-frequency zone).

The eternal being, in the eternal life (*in meditation*) where there is no time, no space, is outside of this drinking glass material zone. It (the eternal being) is everywhere. So, it must focus on this drinking glass, as the zone it wants to focus on, and then pick

Figure 7

Picture a glass; a drinking glass, upside
down on a surfce,
Inside this drinking glass is the material
world. It is in a time zone (a material zone
that is in a material, time-frequency zone).
The eternal being, in the eternal life (in
meditation) where there is no time, no
space, is outside of this drinking glass
material zone.
It must focus on the drinking glass material
world, from the eternal world of different
frequencies of vibration, just like a TV
station.

up frequencies, and tune in to the desired frequencies
to enter this string of communication from eternal to
material within this drinking glass.

In this eternal area *outside* the drinking glass,
there is *no* time; there is *no* space; there just is.

For the so-called dead to communicate with
the so-called living in the material world (the dead
are not in the material world, remember this), the
eternal *'dead'* (*those who have* vacated their *bodies*)
are needing to focalize; to tune in; to the frequency
that they need to tune in to in order to communicate.

Communication, yes, communication is very
similar to the holding out of your hand; the extending
of love; the extending of feeling; the expanding of
the heart, but it's all tuned in to a certain point; a
communicant (*which has a name*).

This takes practice, and this takes
willingness, because each spirit, each soul, whether
in the material or in the eternal, has traces. Each soul
is independent and responsible for itself, whether in
the material or in the eternal.

Progression of the Soul in the Eternal.

(Speaking in the sense of time like you have
on the earth in the material.)

This progress of the eternal soul, in the eternal, is zilch.

The progress has to be made in the <u>material</u> world, so that the soul will be at a stage that it can reach the finite agreement with what we call God.

This is a Super Conscious Mind; the over-all mind; the All mind; the I Am mind, and if the eternal soul, living in the eternalness, becomes so much One with this I Am mind, then it will dissipate; it will disappear.

It is so One that it is not an expression of God anymore, because it will be God, and the whole idea of life is for eternal life; for eternal expressions; eternal learning; eternal progression.

So; it is not feasible or sensible that a soul should become totally God, because then, God would have no life.

You are the life of God; so you must leave the eternal world; the timeless world and enter into a material existence, in some mansion, some house, some planet, somewhere, in time and materialness.

Earth is not the only place of this type.

Yes, to answer your question, communication with *the dead is a fact, but the word dead delivers a wrong message* because communication with the dead is not communication with the dead, but communication with the *living*; between material and eternal living. (*Material living is eternal living, and eternal living is material living, in a new form or body for the experiences in that frequency of existence*).

Death is only a sign like graduation.

Death is a symbol of change; from one physical plane to another, basically. Enough for now.

NOTE: *A comment I should make here is about the word; parsing, which is in the fourth line of the answer from Father in 12/2/97, above. When I saw this word, I had to look it up in my large dictionary because I had no idea what it meant. It was an eerie feeling, to have spoken a word, which I had not heard of before. I didn't have a clue as to whether it fit the dialogue, but found out that it did.*

GIVING AND RECEIVING 12/08/97

"Father, we are One. What is Your wisdom about what I call the disgraceful, money-grabbing health industry: Medicine, Doctors, Hospitals, and so forth? Also the Insurance Companies? Father, You do have wisdom on these things. Please give to me so that I can impart this to others."

Yes, these are dead subjects. These are so-called moral judgments to be made by the mind of man, which is free to express itself, freely without my interference.

Yes, this is a hot tip on a hot subject and the people, man, should dig in and examine this thoroughly, and decide what man will do about this. This is not for My interference; this is your free-will life.

Yes, one observation is expressed as **the more that is freely given, the more that is freely taken**, and the less life is in those takers.

Freely giving is good for the heart; the feelings. Freely giving also locks out the hearts of the receivers; locks out the ambitions of the receivers.

As the receivers need enlightenment, they will not acquire what they want to acquire, and the values of what are in the acquirements.

Life, yes, life is moving, yearning and learning and seeking, and doing.

In the receiving is death. Receiving slows down the process of life.

Yes, receiving is decay. Yes, and therefore, giving by the receiver reduces the decay.

Giving feels good in the heart of man, an animal heart, a selfish heart. Receiving feels good in the heart; yes, the animal heart of the receiver; that's the selfish heart.

Both of the animal feelings are good, and yet, the acts of both, A-C-T-S of both produce decay, and the loss of life. And remember; life is change, life is seeking and is moving forward.

Yes, wisdom and intelligence are the life-giving gifts, whereas the works should come from the receivers in order that they may have life rather than decay or death.

Yes, a diamond ring, which is a symbol of giving, and the giving feels good in the heart of the giver, and feels good in the heart of the receiver, these are animal feelings; these are the feelings of the bodies which you inhabit, and these are the feelings which you must overcome.

Your feelings must be spiritual feelings, feelings of love, which is giving freedom.

Giving a diamond ring is capturing; capturing the heart of the receiver. This is not spiritual giving; this is the act of selfish, animal heart feelings.

This is the opposite of love.

Love is giving freedom, and love costs nothing. Love has no cost. Love is the giving of freedom to the recipient of your love, to live within all laws; natural, social, civil, so that the recipient will live within the laws, which is a necessity for all living beings, and all material things.

Everything is governed by law, and giving freedom to live within all law is true spiritual love. In this manner, all recipients of love may expand to the fullest of the talents within, according to their desires; according to their wants; according to their seeking.

Yes, when gifts are given, these are affectations of the carnal, selfish motives.

These are the giving and receiving in the material world, which produce animal selfishness and encourage it, whereas the giving of spiritual gifts; basically love, which is giving freedom to everyone else, to express within law, is true, spiritual giving, which does not inhibit the receiver from growth and from expression.

Yes, even the givings of the gifts at Christmas time, in celebration of the birthday of your Jesus, are contradictory to spiritual giving.

Spiritual giving in the celebration of a birthday is the giving of love, the giving of freedom, and the appreciation and the gratitude of those to whom we give.

Yes, a candle, lit with a fire at the top, would give off light unto the world, which is the best gift, in the material world, that can be given to a person such as Jesus or Bhudda or Mohammed or Zoroaster, or any of the so-called gods that you have made before me.

Yes, you have seen, deep within my wisdom, deep within my intellect. This day, I have opened my eye to the deep, dark depths of wisdom, which are seen in the lights of the candle.

DOCTORS 12/08/97

"**Father, we are One, and the question for today is: What do you have to say about the business of taking advantage of people when they are down and out, by no special reason of their own, it seems like?"**

I'm talking about the doctor profession; hospitals and doctors. It seems like it is geared to kick a man in the butt when he is down. When a man is sick, he can't work, and yet the doctors and hospitals and all that.... they want much more money; they want lots of money; unreasonable amounts of money.

I am sure there is a lot of inefficiency in this profession as well as in the insurance profession; just like any large outfit.

Anyhow, what is Your opinion; how do You see this situation, where people take advantage of people when they are down?"

Seemingly, through no fault of their own, yes, I know that this is a sore point for mankind. Yes, yes, this particular point is as if the beauty of mankind is held back.

The goodness of mankind is fenced and held back because of system and money. The doctor must eat. The doctor must pay for his training, and pay for his expenses. A hospital must pay its expenses. Yes, society appears to be trapped by this situation, and the situation is, as you say, 'it is an unfair situation'.

Where there is socialized medicine, or whether it is privatized medicine, there are those who will skim large portions off the top; in whatever type program it is. These are the problems.

These are the problems to work on, and there still are what you call the leeches, or in the modern sense is what you call the politicians; or the modern sense of the politicians, which is prominent these days.

There is graft. There is skimming. There is cheating. There is stealing. There is lying, and the more money in it, the more there are of these low life characters, which must be worked out of the woodwork.

These low life characters need to be called for what they are. They need to be labeled for the low life that they are, and the profession needs to be turned inside out.

This applies to Insurance Companies as well.

All of these things are too big, and dishonest.

And of course, this goes down to the public; the common person.

The common person becomes tempted to commit fraud in these things, and also tries to get things free at someone else's expense (this is stealing).

These are the problems of people: The lack of morals, the lack of decency, and the lack of caring for one another.

This small idea of caring for one another should be broadcast throughout the industries, throughout the governments, throughout all these large things that exist, for the so-called betterment of mankind.

People are either good, or they are bad. They are either good, or they are evil.

The evil must be routed out of the large companies, corporations, and governments. There must be ideas put forth which will change the tide of greed and evil.

In these organizations everyone must be accounted for his actions.

Everything must be simple and above board so that there is *no* chance for fraud, *no* chance for stealing, *no* chance for greed.

Your social systems must be reworked and reworked and reworked.

Leadership at the top must be good leadership; not financed by countries and businesses. The leadership must be in place by means of good moral character.

Yes, as long as the systems are as they are, it is strictly up to the individual to take care of himself the best that he can under all circumstances.

This system is in place, and that is what is: Give to Caesar; also, work on changing the system. Yes, the wheel will get the grease if it squeaks loud and long enough. Enough for now.

BEST GOVERNMENT FOR THE WORLD
12/31/97

"Father, we are One and the question for now is, What kind of government is best for the world? How should it be carried on and what is the composition of it?"

A government, which is fueled by the people.

A government, which is striving for the very best for the community of all the people, must take the input of the general populace for ideas.

The Government cannot be run by the populace, but the ideas from the populace are for the blendings of the intelligence and wisdom of the top officials who are operating the government.

The general populace does not have the qualified intellect and wisdom and ambition for any government to operate properly. So, therefore, the *ideas* from the populace are necessary and wanted in the running of a government.

The government should be operated by elected officials as you have now, and these elected officials should be experienced in business, experienced in local government, experienced in management, and experienced in schooling for proper running of the government which would have most appeal; the best rules for the most appeal for the most people.

And a government would be run with these representatives who have been qualified with the aforesaid qualifications, and of course these would include also the most qualified persons who are to be elected to the government boards.

The moral character is most important above all the other qualifications.

These representatives should be governing for the best that can be done with freedom of the individual and minimum of governing and of course as the populace becomes more educated, and more wise in it's actions, more ambitious in it's nature and more benevolent in it's nature, accepting all others as equal to themselves, of course, you need less and less government.

So you need more government if the mannerisms of the populace require it.

These representatives should have the maximum of government service of twelve years. After twelve years they must be out of the governing positions.

Now, these twelve years could be a combination of different posts, different seats, different representations, but they are all working in government business as representatives of the people.

After twelve years, that would be the end.

Then they should go back into private business.

The airwaves to the public are like the land to the public; they are owned by the people, and for communication from the public officials to the peoples that the representative represents.

There should be free television time from the local stations where it is important to be heard in the districts.

This free air time should be a right of the public who own the airwaves, and the town meetings should be held on these television time periods; something on the order of c-span, and the order of the BBC.

Something of that order, whereas the people can freely express their feelings in the proper references to their local governments, and to the federal government.

They could be broadcast to the local districts and of course all the local networks could be hooked up for elections times and for communications between the elected officials and their peoples.

Elected officials would be working for the people; for the general welfare and the progressive betterment of their districts, and not working for their parties.

Parties should be outlawed from the time that the candidates are elected. Parties are only a guide for the voters.

Yes, government should be minimized as much as possible, and the government should be given praise for decreasing its budgets.

Monies, yes, monies given to candidates running for public office should be outlawed because monies are coercion; monies are immoral, strictly immoral.

Even in the Walmarts and the grocery trades; in large businesses and police departments, the giving of gifts is prohibited.

So with free television offered to governments, to your government to correspond with its people, they will need no money, and if money is given, it is given with the *knowledge that it shouldn't be accepted.*

So therefore it should not be given because it is immoral and illegal.

If a person cannot be elected by his merits on public television, then that person must not be worthy of being elected.

Almost all political television ads today, are paid for by multi-millionaires and by anxious people who want to get themselves represented.

Most of the television ads produced by this money business tell you nothing about the candidate except that he is being a fool, because he received some money, and that it is a real rotten rat race.

SLAVE MENTALITY 01/08/98

"Father, what can you say about the attitude of the colored folk who feel sorry for themselves because their people have been enslaved in the past, but have been freed since? Why do they not, in general, forge ahead as the other races do?"

Yes, they must realize that in all races, slavery has taken place; not just the so-called colored folk. . . the Negroes, but all races; any color you want; they have all been under slavery in the thousands of years that have gone by.

This is because of the animalistic nature of man which is gradually being controlled more by the spirit, which is in the body; this animal body; and through intelligence, which has control over the heart and the emotions, which are animal heart and animal emotions.

Gradually, the intellect, with knowledge and wisdom, will overcome these irrational animal actions of people who feel sorry for themselves.

The intelligent and wise way for this type of person who feels sorry for himself is to (like they say in the old days of Will Rogers, etc.) " Pull yourself up by your bootstraps, every individual is responsible for his own situation and problem."

Wisdom helps you to solve these problems. Emotions and animal reactions, no matter what race, cause more problems, not less. Problems must be overcome with intelligence and wisdom, knowledge.

Education is the key. Education on the earth, and education in the spirit. Spiritual education using the wisdom of God will co-exist with man's education in the material world. The blending produces happiness and love; and gratitude, and most of all, progress.

This is the end of the Negro question.

BAPTISM WITH FIRE, AND EGO CONTROL 02-16-98

"Father, we are One. John the Baptist said in Matt: 3.11 that, one who will come after me will baptize you with the Holy Spirit and with fire. What was John the Baptist talking about in this book called the Bible? Whoever wrote that; what did he mean?"

Yes, with roasting meat on a fire, where, in the days' barbecue, with the flames below and the meat is turning around above; when the meat becomes baptized in fire, it loses it's fat; it loses it's excesses; it loses it's materialness and becomes more spiritual.

It discards the outside, the world, and realizes the inside; the spirit. This is baptism by fire.

Baptism by fire dissipates the excesses of frivolity, which are within the human. The baptism by fire destroys the ego from materiality, and returns to the spirit.

That brings the attention of the person baptized to the self within, and teaches that everyone is spirit inside, and that there is no reality to the outer side except for the learning.

The material world is for the living, and baptism by fire is for teaching of the spiritual world, and the spiritual reason for being in the material world, and where you are in this material world.

Being in this material world is to teach the personality, the soul, how to live in the material world without losing it's spiritual self.

Baptism by Fire dissolves the outer self; the ego self; brings one down to the realization of the spiritual self; the true self, which is here on this material earth plane to learn how to live with all types of adverse conditions, using the spiritual knowledge that has been brought from times past, into this carnation.

Yes, once brought into this car-nation (which means being reincarnated), it is very easy for the spiritual self to pick up an ego trip by making it's way into the material world, and forgetting the reason of it's existence, and forgetting the real self that it is. The ego is a false self, and it is a self used as teaching.

The ego is when you or a spiritual personality forgets it's union. Yes, it's union with the Father; it's union with the whole; it forgets, and then the more the forgetting of the true self, the more the ego is growing, and the ego is a false life for the learning.

But, the ego and the true spiritual self cannot be separated and be independent. The ego must be under 100% control of the spiritual self, which realizes the use of the ego in the material world.

This material world is for the learning; the

writing of the history of the soul, and to show it's progress; it is a record of progress, and the ego is used in this material world for learning, but it must be under control of the soul; not vice versa, which happens.

A large percentage of personalities, soul personalities on this earth, in this carnation, forget their real selves and live 100% the ego life, playing the game as an ego, separating themselves from God; from the true self, which is One with the Father.

One must return the ego back to the soul control, and realize the Oneness with the Father; the Oneness with God, which is the whole thing; everything.

God is All, and the soul is experiencing for God and for IT-Self. Yes, the stronger the soul, the more the control of the ego, which is the false self, living in the material world for the learning.

This cannot be emphasized enough!

Yes, therefore, do not forget self. You are self; you are your soul; you are your personality. Ego is the tool being used for learning, and:

Ego must never take control over your Self!

Remember this, remember this, remember this, and remember this!

We are true brothers and sisters in God; we are all equal in quality in this stage play of life. We are all different expressions of the One. Let Self realize this.

Pearls; yes, pearls, which are worn about the neck, are a sign of royalty, a sign of beauty, a sign of I am better than you', and that: 'I have come up a long way in the world.

The pearls that are worn in the material world build the ego; they feed the ego; they make the ego feel even more ego and less self.

Now, the true pearls, which are to be sought, are the pearls of wisdom. The pearls of how to live and get along with everyone else; the pearls of how to love everyone else. These are pearls of wisdom, and they are ego-less.

Therefore, do not seek the pearls of the material life, but seek the pearls of wisdom, which is the reason for being carnated, or being re-in-carnated.

Baptism, yes, baptism in fire, or baptism by fire is the scaling down; the burning up of the ego, which has taken control over the self, the soul.

Baptism by fire, yes, baptism by fire brings one back to the raw self, which should be in control at all times.

Yes, this Baptism by Fire is the project for the Flaming Cross, which is your symbol.

Your symbol is not for fear, such as the KKK; the Ku Klux Klan. Those people are doing just the opposite of what they are purposed to be on this earth. They are inflated in ego and have lost true self.

The fiery cross of the KKK is for hatred, and for puffed up egos, and for hatred of others. Their fiery cross has nothing to do with love.

The KKK Ku Klux Klan needs to be baptized with fire. They need to be purified. They need to have their egos destroyed and eaten up by fire, so that they can see their true selves.

Your symbol, the Flaming Cross is spiritual fire. Spiritual fire which is used for the baptism of fire, which will bring ego to it's knees; to it's own soul for it's realization of the true path in this material world.

"Thank you, Father."

SECURITY, INSURANCE, AND RELIGION 02-18-98

"Father, we are One, this is about security; questions on security. People want to be secure in everything around them; they want things to be the same all the time, and they want security; they want to be taken care of. It is complacency. Please speak about security; is it good, is it evil, or what? Please describe security and complacency."

Security and complacency; yes, security and complacency are a non-returnable hook.

Security and complacency are similar to welfare; people are secured and complacent because they feel secure; they are being taken care of; they have no need to use the soul, the spirit within them, and the spirit within their bodies, their real selves.

They have no need; no urge to go out and live; to go out and become a part of the world, which is the reason that they are here.

So, security and complacency are against the law. They are against the spiritual law; a law which permits growth and action and adventure and happiness and constant change.

Adventure! Yes, adventure; this complacency, security, is a living death. It is a death of the spirit. It is a death of the body.

Rust is a good demonstration of security and complacency. When you will set a piece of iron down over a period of time, rust will take over this piece of iron because all matter must be re-used.

All matter must be deteriorated when matter comes to rest; to security, to-complacency. Matter is to be eaten up by forces, whether animal, bacterial, chemical or other.

The human body and the human spirit decays in the same manner, by sitting still; by not being concerned; by not venturing out; by not working; by not being alive.

Being alive is being insecure, and in the being of insecureness, there is secureness.

To be spiritually secure, you must be insecure, because this material life is a life of change, change, and more change.

Life is living in change; secure is death, and no change. Yes, if a person stands in the shade of protection, this person is not learning, this person is rotting.

This is, yes, this is the reason that insurance is considered by My laws to be evil.

Insurance is against natural law; My Law. Insurance is a fraud, perpetuated on society through fear. Insurance is the symbol of security in your world.

If there was any racketeer idea more evil than insurance, yes, then it would be on a similar plane; similar plane of thought, whereas working on the fears of people; such as religion.

NOTE: *The two work on the same principles.*

Working on the fears of people and giving people the attitude of: I am being cared for, someone is caring for me, I am poor, so, others will take care of me, I will not have to go out to work, because others will take care of me, I am fortunate to be poor; I will inherit the earth.

Well, all of these things are a fraud, perpetuated through religion and through insurance, on the human mind.

Yes, if a soul relies on this sense of security, and being cared for, and even doing the sinful actions of caring for others, and stifling the life out of others through perpetual care; these will reincarnate over and over and over without progress; almost eternally, until they get out of this mode, and become living beings as they should, living responsibly, independently, on there own, making choices, and learning by the choices.

If they are cared for, they are not learning; if they are cared for, they are dying.

Yes, people who are cared for, and people who are caring for others in a smothering, perpetual attitude are both dead as ashes on the end of a cigar; they are going nowhere.

Yes, life is to be lived, and life is to be lived by one's self in order to learn.

When one is poor; when one wants either to stay poor, which is all right, or one wants to get rich or get richer and have a better means of living, this is all right.

You can live with money; you can live without money, and of course, if you live without money you will be tempted to steal, or beg; both are bad; both are wrong.

Everything within you must be used productively by your Self. If anyone would help you, which is admirable, the help must be to help you to use yourself to earn the money. Yes, but not to do for you, but to help you to do for yourself; not perpetually.

Yes, I feel a question here; I feel there is a question. What is the question?

"Father, what about people that are crippled, people that are crippled in the mind, and in the body?"

Yes, when people are crippled in the mind or in the body, they will have talents with whatever they have to use, inside of themselves, and when they get hungry they will perform.

If they wish to remain hungry and to starve, this is their right, their prerogative. Yes, when they are unfed, they will want to be fed; they will want food and drink.

This is what makes a soul move; this is what makes a soul work; this is hunger. Without this hunger, the soul in this body would not be alive.

Not working, yes, not working; not performing for food is suicide. Not murdered by those who would help, but suicide by he, or she, who will not work or perform a good for society.

Each person must do some work for someone in society. This is service to mankind; this is part of your life. No one is allowed to be stagnant, without dying. This is enough for now.

BIBLE WORDS VS MINE FROM MEDITATION 02/18/98

"Father, we are One. How come the words of Jesus in the Bible, and the words in me, disagree in many cases? How come they are different from what I feel inside?"

The light, or the truth, which was spoken; which was written, that Jesus had said with threads of wisdom, actually were rooted in branches of past religions of the earth at the time.

Many of the words which were what he was supposed to have said according to the writers, were placed there not because he said them, but to convince others of the writer's convictions.

As I have said before to you, Jesus and Buddha and most all the others: the Moses, the Zoroaster and many of the others were tuned in at times, but they are squares as far as delivering my word.

They had many great ideas and they passed down many great ideas from the past, word for word, some of them, and these words were needed in those days to help the people out of slavery. Today, those words do not have the use that they once had.

So, many of the words which the person Jesus may have spoken, have been written in, years afterwards, for control of the mobs; for control by the keepers.

Of course, as time went on, and the words were written into the Bible, the words and situations were placed like in a play; like a theatrical play, whereas Jesus was made into a King and into a God, just as people were made into Gods before him.

Many of the old gods were Born of Virgins', some were baptized, and many came back from the dead; many died and rose again; many had resurrections.

These were stories that were told in those days, and these stories were portrayed with Jesus as the main actor, and all the time, the whole situation became the usual myth, whereas Jesus became God, and Jesus rose from the dead.

The sands of time have placed halos on many people, who were not angels or gods, but were people who seemed to have put out good effort in my behalf, but this does not make them gods.

There is only One God, and I Am. I Am All there is.

The story of Jesus; there are many stories in the Bible about Jesus, in the old testament as well as the new, which are great, heavy yarns woven for the effect on the people.

The treasures that come from the myth making, feel very good in the emotions of the people; they have a harmonious ring in the animal being, but not to the spiritual being.

The spiritual being deals with the intellect and wisdom, and science. The animal emotions of heart, and animal love, are inborn in the animal body, which you inhabit, and those resonant frequencies of thought within your hearts, mentioned in the Bible, you could say that they are anti-intelligent. They are not my laws; they are man-made laws for the governing of the human animal.

The reason that your understanding of the words in the Bible are disagreeable is because you are in a new generation; you are in a new time, where intelligence and wisdom can be poured forth with new applications, and you have sensed this, because of your Oneness with Me.

I see so many discrepancies in the words applied to Jesus, that it is hard to count the ways (this was one of your expressions). The words attributed to Jesus are a forest among thoughts for today, that cannot be applied to the generations of today.

We are in a new phase of existence today. You are in a new phase of existence. It is actually we; but I mean to say you because I am talking as if I am out of your world and talking to you in your world, but actually, we are in the same world.

The law of old; loving your neighbor as you love yourself still applies. It is the law.

Love is the law. But love must be understood that your neighbor is everyone, everywhere, all the time.

That love means to give him the freedom to express himself, responsibly within all laws, not trespassing on anybody else.

This is love. If you understand love, you will understand all law, and responsibility.

Responsibility is movement within the law.

Loving your brother as yourself (everyone is your brother), and the idea that you are supposed to take care of your brother, is basically the right idea, but it must be understood that with today's mental capacities, uplifted from 2000 years ago, that it must be remembered that the taking care of thy brother is not the doing for thy brother, but educating thy brother.

Temporarily helping, but not doing for, and not stuck continuously. Each person, even with only a brain, must work.

Each person must work with whatever ability that person has, even if it is only one talent; whether it is just speaking or and has no *arms or legs*. This person has a mind to think with, a mind to talk with, and this person can be of service to someone.

This is the reason for existence. This is the art of living; working for each one's self; to support one's self; to be of service to someone else in order to gain compensation in the form of food, especially food, clothing and shelter.

It must be earned, not given.

NOTES: *About the first paragraph, I have also personally found, through old books on history of civilizations, that Jesus in the New Testament is an old story, revised for the current generations and used for the power of the priests of the day.*

This is just an old story renewed in the Jesus story. Many gods, before Jesus had been born of virgins, performed miracles, were crucified, died, and ascended to heaven, and returned to be resurrected, and become Judges of the dead.

This was basically a god story of old that intrigued the masses through the power and magic of the priests, who took control of the people through this masquerade of stories and beliefs, and the fear of the unknown.

BECOMING AS A CHILD 02/18/98

"Father, what is meant by becoming as a child?"

When you become as a child, you will drop your Ways of the World which are thrust upon you, and you will seek Me with your innocent eyes; your innocent self, and you will meet Me within you, innocently, and lovingly, and read Me, and we will communicate.

This is where your childlike mind in meditation within will communicate with Me. You cannot communicate with Me with material world prejudice; you must become innocent, as a little child.

This should be enough for now.

CHAPTER THREE

ARTICLES AND TALKS UP TO NOW

"The Aura" *Fate Magazine* 10/92

In 1972 I was sitting in a dimly lit spiritualist training class in Long Beach, California. A classmate started lecturing in an oriental fashion, standing erect with arms horizontal from elbows to hands in front of her, like Confucius might have done.

She began speaking with fervor, and dead seriousness, as if preaching to the rest of the world, or us.

As soon as her emotions warmed up, I saw my first full-blossomed Aura! It was beautiful. I was awed and entranced. I had heard and read about the experiences of others who had seen them, but to behold this sight of blooming colors in front of me took my breath away. I could hardly move so as not to disturb anything and lose sight of it.

The Aura extended about 18 inches all around her body. It was a living, breathing array of luminous, pastel colors in varied color layers, like a rainbow. The layers of colors were not in simple lines like a rainbow, but more of a human blending; not mechanical.

There were pinks, lavenders, pale greens, baby blues, and light yellows, as if they had a life in them. They seemed to be breathing and changing their colors slightly.

In full view of this beautifulAura, and the lady still standing there preaching, all at once three or four bouncing, pale blue tennis balls appeared, rotating vertically in front of her in mid-air, like the lotto balls on TV floating in the air. This lasted until she stopped speaking and became herself again; about five minutes.

This experience is etched in my mind so vividly that I am sure I'll never forget it. There is more to life than we can even dream of!

MYFIRST VISION *Fate Magazine* 10/94

I was in Pat H's home in Corona, Calif. Pat was a healer, a good cook, a companion, and a conversationalist who did automatic writing with John Watkins, a spirit guide who purportedly lived during the 18th century.

After dinner, while we were talking, as Pat did the dishes, a movie appeared three feet in front of me, six feet off the floor. The vision was on a translucent screen that was five feet wide and two to three feet high, hanging in the air so that I could watch it as I was talking. My eyes were open wide.

I told Pat what was happening while it was occurring, and that I was afraid to move for fear of disturbing it. It was in full technicolor, and the pictures were moving, just as if it were a natural occurrence, like watching a movie.

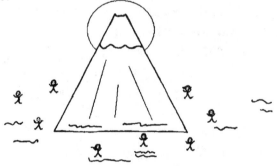

Figure 8

The Rising Sun was coming up behind the mountain peak. The whole mountain was shaking and people were running all over the place.

This was the vision I saw at 3:30 p.m. on August 11, 1969

Lava flowed down the sides of a purplish, hazy, snow-covered mountain, with a large, bright, yellowish sun behind it, rising (this was Mt. Fujiyama in Japan). People scurried all about the bottomlands of this mountain in desperate fear for their lives, and the ground seemed to be shaking.

The same night at 11:30 p.m., eight hours later, I heard on the news that an underwater earthquake (eight on the Richter scale) had just happened on the islands of Honshu and Hokkaido in the north Pacific, setting off a huge tidal wave.

The following morning the newspaper published a Front Page picture of Fujiyama and a story about the event. Then I knew that I had seen this vision as it was happening in Japan, 6,500 miles away.

RELIGION IS EVIL 01/07/95

The Abortion clinic murders are today's proof of it. All religion is based on a belief system, which was cultured by radical and power hungry men. All the gods of all religions are based on the trumped up stories of old legends about dead men, calling them gods.

There have been many gods of the old days who were born of virgins, resurrected, visited by angels, performed miracles, etc.

Jesus was the most recent one, and before Jesus, there were many more:

Osiris, Zoroaster, Adonis, Attis, Tammuz and Jesus
were resurrected.
Osiris, Enoch, Elijah and Jesus ascended.
Danae, many Pharaohs, and Jesus had virgin births.

(The above and many more can be found in your Library, in books about comparative religion, religion, Etc.)

These are only some of the examples of the fallacy of gods in which we believe, even today. When are human beings going to wake up to reality, and get off this belief bandwagon?

The evil of religions is that they are based on belief systems, and not truth. They are not based on reality, but are based on stories and assumptions, which have been grabbed by power hungry men, who want to rule the world by fear, in the name of love.

A religious believer, is a person without rationality, and can commit murder, like all the other terrorists of society, in the name of love and god.

A believer can murder in the name of god , because he believes he is doing god a favor, or maybe he believes that he will establish himself a place in heaven because of his irrational deed. *(This includes abortion murders by the Christians. A few have been actual murders, but I bet thousands of Christians around the world have murder in their hearts because of their belief system)*

A true believer, in reality, is insane because he doesn't recognize reality; he only believes what he has been told by his religious god representative of this earth, who is only a person in the guise of a local god (Bishop, Pope, Ayatollah). This person represents the god (which is always false and unreal), and tells his followers what is right or wrong according to the church.

The church is the main body of evil, which must be changed to a character-building device, or it will completely disappear, after realizing what false base it stems from. The churches of the world have great opportunities to come clean and to transform themselves into places of education for the people concerning God, as we know IT today. Beliefs are out the window for civilized people.

The church, after it dissolves all belief systems and becomes real, will be the best resource to train society in the proper disciplines to be used for agreeable interactions between all peoples of earth.

How to Get Along With Our Neighbors Is Primary to All Life.

By the way, all religious properties and activities should be taxed, the same as any other institution or business. Most all religions are a business and should not be exempt from responsibility to the state or country.

Now, I don't wish to leave anyone thinking that God is not a reality, because IT is. This will require more paper and time. I am writing a book about it. A.L.A.

POLITICAL AND RELIGIOUS MURDER Of MEXICAN SPIRIT 01/08/95

After viewing the Mexican Art display at our new museum today in Escondido, I would like to express my feelings about it. I observed the total domination and death of the human spirit of the people of Mexico.

120

This death was brought on by various religions down through the current one: the Christian religion. . . Catholic and Protestant.

They continue to dominate the minds of the people to the point of spiritual slavery and suicide.

They need uplifting with freedom from religion. They need modern education with good moral ethics, how to get along with all other people (the golden rule) through fairness, not fear.

They are suppressed to the point of desperation and false hopes: The hopes that God will take care of them through the teachings of the Church. Balderdash! They need to realize that they are completely self sufficient without religious domination and fear mongering.

The paintings displayed at the museum bring to light the obvious. The churches are murdering the Mexican human spirit. The people are frustrated because they depend on the Churches and (the church gods) to do for them what they should be taught to do for themselves.

These are genuine people of substance, not slaves or voodoo pawns. They need a truly representative government, not greedy political thieves, or the mind enslavers of greedy religious churches, which prey on non-educated peoples around the world, instilling fear through belief systems, which are completely outrageous to the intellect.

ABORTION: WHAT IS LIFE? 01/23/95

"Thou shalt not kill" is a very general expression of thought, all by itself. We kill, as a society, all kinds of animals for food to be eaten, by many different religious groups. In fact, the killing of animals for food, or the sport of it, is generally accepted. In some nations, live insects are used as food. So, where is this respect for 'life'?

Very few people object to this kind of killing, because we are not killing human beings, just animal, or insect beings. Well, what is a human being?

Most of the people in this world will agree that a human being is a spirit/intelligence inside of an animal body. This explains the reason for the human ability to ask why, whereas the animal can't do this, therefore it cannot reason and improve to the degree that a human does.

121

So, if the spirit/intelligence is living inside of an animal body, then the *animal body, which is being created inside of the womb, is an animal form, not a human being.*

An animal form within the womb becomes human when the umbilical cord is cut, and the animal form takes it's first breath (spirit/intelligence), and becomes a human being.

All through the bible, the breath and the spirit are synonymous to human life. The breath, or spirit of life, is in the nostrils. *We must breathe air into our lungs before we have human life.*

Here are some Bible references:

Genesis 2:7.... "the lord God.... *Breathed into his nostrils the breath of life; and man became a living being.*

Genesis 6:17.... *"I will.... destroy all flesh in which is the breath of life...."*

Kings 18:21.... *"Then he stretched himself upon the child three times, and cried to the lord, 'Lord my God, let this child's soul come into him again'."*

This is the first CPR process that I can recall, where one person presses another's chest in order to get the breathing process to start again. (Evidently, this process had been known for quite a while before this biblical explanation).

Job 12:10.... *"in his hand is the life of every living thing and the breath of all mankind."*

Job 17:1.... *"My breath is corrupt.... my days are extinct,"*

Revised Standard Version: *"My spirit is broken, my days are extinct," (notice how spirit and breath are interchangeable.)*

King James Version: Job 27:3.... *"as long as my breath is in me, and the spirit of God is in my nostrils;"*

Job 33:4.... *"the spirit of God has made me, and the breath of the almighty gives me life."*

Psalms 104:29.... *"When Thou takest away their breath, they die...when thou sendest forth thy spirit, they are created;"*

Psalms 146:4.... *"when his breath departs he returns
to his earth;"*
Psalms 150:6.... *"let everything that breathes praise
the lord!"*
Isaiah 42:5.... *"thus says God, the Lord, who created
the heavens and stretched them out, who gives breath
to the people upon it and spirit to those who walk in it:"*
Ezekiel 37:5.... *"thus says the Lord God to these
bones: behold, I will cause breath to enter you, and
you shall live."*

Why then, all the fuss about precious life in the womb? It is just
a form, being made for the life/spirit, to enter at first breath.

In today's advanced world, we can detect, in the womb, whether
this form is healthy or not, and can change it, or eliminate it, for the
sake of the person who will enter it at that first breath. Why invite a
person/spirit to be born into a form of known poor quality, or just
plain not wanted?

Would you enjoy inviting a friend to your house without having
it in order, or if you are not ready for that friend to visit? ALA

GIVING TO THE POOR 05/18/95
Government Foolishness

Most religions propose giving to the poor, but that only
undermines the poor person's ambition to do for himself, and
promotes a world or nation of dependent sloths.

When Jesus said to give to the poor, he wasn't referring to the
general public type of poor people; he was referring to the Essenes,
Pharisees and the Ebonite's, which were called the poor in his days.
He was supporting the groups of those who were devoting
themselves to God, as He was, and had given all their belongings to
the group for the general welfare of it's members.

We have done our share of giving to the poor in this country, as a
government dole, and we are producing a low class of people at a
fast rate.

The only thing, which should be given to the poor by our government is:

- Jobs first (with pay), and basic education while they are working, instead of money, or food.
- Money and food must be earned and not given freely; higher education must be earned, also; not charged to the government, or given freely.

All free things have no appreciation, nor value to the recipient. Childcare can be provided while they are working for a period of time sufficient for a head start with a definite, short time limit.

Unions are responsible for our governments' not allowing jobs for the poor. With the Union's selfish, self-promoting ideas that they forced on our governments, the governments all over the country have been forced to eliminate work projects for the poor and unfortunate. Unions should never be allowed in Government work.

Do you remember the Street Cleaners, the Park Litter Patrols, and Universal Military Training for the youth, which builds minds and bodies from chaotic to organized individuals of self worth and team spirit? The Aid Ladies who visited the homes of the poor, and many other programs like WPA, etc? These are ideas for jobs for the poor when there is no labor market.

While we have the political minimum wage, jobs for the young, the poor, and the unfortunate are eliminated.

Eliminate the minimum wage and give jobs to the untrained and unlearned, so that they will eventually become trained and learn on the job. That's where training and learning should be done. We really don't need government involved training programs. Apprenticeship is far better than classroom learning. Eliminate, or vary the minimum wage to accomplish this.

Everyone must be responsible for himself as long as he is able bodied (this means if you are not flat on your back). Even Michelangelo worked while he was flat on his back. If you won't work you don't get food, shelter, or clothing.

The more we give to the poor (non-workers), the more the baby producing increases, and therefore global suicide.

Let's face it. . .Let's be truthful for a change. Stop playing Santa Claus and producing a community of non-productive people:

- Give jobs to the poor.
- Give opportunity to the poor.
- Eliminate the minimum wage, or adjust it, allowing young and poor to get apprenticeships.
- Keep Unions from our Government. (The Government is basically volunteered services, not a business organization.)
- Induct all teenagers into the compulsory Universal Fitness corps for two years, where they will learn to live healthy, self-sufficient lives as team members.

Our Spiritual Path 01/05/97
(Our Reason for Existence)

We, being spirit (The image of God), have a reason for existence. The proof of this is that we are. There is nothing in existence without a reason behind it, Even though the process of existence is a random act, Created by the instigator, which we call God (The Totality of All).

The reason for our existence is to live life, which is a continuous chain of experiences, in which we have free will. This free will, which is the responsibility of the individual, (All who are free are responsible for their influence, good or bad, on the rest of society) will cause unending diverse expressions to be realized by God, the Creator.

This is the reason for the Creation (Which never was, because everything always was and will be). What we usually think of, as the Creation, is what is explained as the Big Bang theory. The Big Bang theory is actually an eternal series of Big Bangs, which are the re-introduction of matter into the spiritual existence for new expressions.

Matter formation is eternal, and is in a constant flux, or change. This flux is what the general public calls life, which is in fact, just a changing material expression.

This term life is misused today by most religions. Life is not spiritual, but material. The eternal spirit enters the live animal body and becomes a human being, after the umbilical cord has been cut, at the moment of first self-powered (responsible) breath.

Our spiritual path is one of two paths on which he must live:
  • We must live an animal life, which is a concern for the physical
    existence into which we are born, and
  • We must live a spiritual life for the quality of mind/spirit.

The quality of mind/spirit is the reason for living in this material/
animal body. Being in an animal body is our way of experiencing life
to the fullest on this planet.

In eternal time, which is non-existent (eternity has no time), there
is forever to exist, but existing is not living and learning. All the
things that we experience in our bodies and the physical world are
learned because of the memory capabilities, which are present in
time, and not in eternity.

Our spiritual path is laid out for us in this physical form, which
carries a memory for its performance. We are to train the soul of our
existence for a good quality personality which can be expressed in
eternity in a harmonious manner.

This earth is the best system to train the soul for harmonious
relationships. Where else can you go to get such extreme training in
such a short time as compared to existing in eternity?

Life in this body is not as important as you might think. Knowing that Re-incarnation is a fact, and that such a short life is lived on
this planet, life that is lived in this body is precious, yes, but it is not
the all in all life. The true life is the eternal life of the soul (the real
you), and that soul must be trained, and retrained until it has things
right.

If the body needs to die for the training of the soul, then let it die.
Death is not the end.

Death is a lesson to be learned, in some cases, and a graduation
to another living experience in other cases, therefore why all the fuss
about the right to life?

The Right to life is for people who are more concerned about
material things than the spiritual. Life is eternal, and there is no right
to it. It always was and always will be whether you give it a right or
not.

Abortion and the right to life is a farce argument. If we invite a
friend to our house, we want our house to be in good shape first,

right? Then, in the same sense, if we invite a soul to inhabit a new body at first breath, then we want that body to be in good health, also. Why cause a new body to be born, for a new soul to inhabit at first breath, that is knowingly a sick, unhealthy, or unwanted body? This is an insult to the new soul, and this soul is God. I know that God cannot be insulted, but the newly born soul is what I am referring to.

Our spiritual path is basically the training of the spirit in the physical world to get along with all of it's surroundings, including people, animals, and nature. This training process is extreme compared to eternal existence.

We learn the most through our basic ignorance which earns us severe hard-knock learning.

We are saddled with an ego, which gets in our way as we try to learn about getting along with others.

Selfishness is the basic nature of the animal body that we inherit. Selfishness is a *me-me-me* attitude, and we must learn about others' space that they need in order to live on the same planet as we.

We must conquer this ***me-me-me*** impulse that is built into our bodies, if we are to get along with others.

Our awareness (spirit, conscious mind) is our point from which we view life.

We have the choice of seeing in anything the good or the bad. Our choice of awareness makes us what we are.

Our choice of awareness chooses the food for our soul (subconscious mind).

Whatever is assimilated or digested in our subconscious minds becomes the real us, or the soul.

Our soul is our record of our spirit (conscious mind), and our spirit is our awareness, so, the modern way to say it would be:

1. Our subconscious mind is the soul; the record of our life.
2. Our conscious mind (awareness) is the spirit; the transmitter to the subconscious mind; the chooser of what we will become.

Our subconscious mind will record what it receives from our surroundings (such as music, movies, TV, other persons, or groups of people) while our conscious mind is distracted, so let us be aware of

127

our associations and surroundings; they can be nourishing or destructive to the real you, your soul.

COMPASSION AND CHARITY 01/05/97

Traditionally, compassion is a feeling for our subject's situation, which we take on for ourselves as our own feeling in order to understand the subject's feeling so that we can help our subject to solve the situation it has acquired.

Compassion is a sympathetic feeling toward another. It has the tendency to make you feel above the other, if you let it. This is a dangerous trend because it might exalt your ego, which is the opposite of love, and love is the first consideration.

When being sympathetic, you must become one with the subject of your sympathy, but not above the subject. You must walk in the same shoes as the one you are sympathetic with.

Compassion requires tenderness and understanding, which means to tread lightly, because you want to help the other subject without hurting it. Many times, one tries to help another through compassionate feelings, only to find that the one we tried to help is really hurt by our actions.

For example:

If we decrease a person's ambition by doing for him, we are hurting him.

If we decrease a person's desire to help himself, we are hurting him.

If we increase his dependency on others, we are hurting him.

Compassion requires the utmost in caring; we must examine all the angles.

What will be the outcome of our taking on the problem of our subject?

Will we inherit the problem also?

Is this healthy? How can we help someone if we have the same problem?

We must be empathetic rather than sympathetic, that is; we must understand the problem as an outsider looking in, rather than an insider looking out. We must have good disposition and health in order to help someone else, just as a mechanic needs good tools in order to do a good job.

We must not be worried, or have anxiety, because these are detrimental to our straight thinking. We must devote serious thinking and caution to the problem. For this, we need clear and healthy minds.

Before we become overly concerned about another's problem and butt into someone else's affairs; let's remember how God, or the Lord would have handled it:

God plopped us here on earth and gave us rules to live by. If the rules were not observed, there was the punishment, or result, or reaction that we had to suffer because of breaking the rules; even in our ignorance.

Then the Lord comes by for a visit, and says that we are forgiven, turn the other cheek, love your neighbor, give to the poor, and forgive all trespasses against us.

All we have to do, now, is to believe what he told us about his Father's Kingdom of heaven:

That we are sons of the Father in heaven, and

That we are brothers to each other on earth;

That the Father resides in heaven, which is within us,

in the secret chamber of our being.

We should walk and talk with the Father often because He will guide us in our daily lives, if we ask, knowing that the answer is given even before we ask, if we say Thank you Father, first.

Now. . . with these lessons as a guide, let's proceed.

Being all brothers with one Father in heaven, we must try to help one another. This help is called compassion. Compassion requires wisdom and action. It is wise to help your helpless neighbor if:

> You do not take away his life; that is, his ambition, his pride in being self-sufficient. We must help because we love doing it, and because the recipient accepts it with love and understanding. We must not force ourselves on anyone. Everyone on this planet must have his own freedom of choice, otherwise, how can he learn?

Compassion is an outreach of love. Animal love wants to run some-one else's affairs. This we cannot do. . . after all, we are not animals, are we??? Correct. . . we are not animals.

We are spirit living in an animal body. Spiritual love gives freedom to the recipient of our love to live within all law. Then, with understanding, our love will not interfere in this other person's freedom. Wisdom comes from this understanding of spiritual love and helps us decide whether to help another or not, and how to go about it. For sure we always must know God and His rules before making a judgment on compassion.

In summation, compassion must be used wisely with foresight and care. It is an animal instinct, which must be guided by spiritual wisdom. It is a natural animal force deep within our physical being, which is not much different from parental instincts.

Survival of the fittest is still the major rule on our planet, and we cannot be fit if we have someone doing for us, when we could be doing for ourselves. This is a guide, then, in deciding how to use this force of compassion within us. Survival of the fittest is still the rule in the spiritual world, too.

The "meek shall inherit the earth," means just that, they shall inherit the earth, not heaven.

The poor shall inherit the kingdom of heaven, because the poor, in reality, were not the poor helpless people; the poor were the ones who spent their lives studying God, and living it out on this earth to the best of their ability.

The poor were Essenes, Edomites and Pharisees and other secret orders of the day, which Jesus knew of and was a part of. This has been misunderstood since the beginning of the Catholic church in Rome, not too many years after the crucifixion.

So. . . compassion is not all that it has been cracked up to be. Compassion is always in need of a skilled guide for it to be used effectively. If it is used by the average person with no spiritual insight, it can certainly become a fiasco. Look at the American welfare system as a good example of the fiasco I am referring to. Wanting to help is great, but be aware!

This is charity:

> Charity is to freely love without passing judgments
> on others; "Judge not, lest ye be judged." That means
> that *whatever bad you think of others will bring suffering
> to your own soul*, because *you are the thinker of the
> thought*.

What Is The Purpose of This Talk?

It is to help you to heal or know yourselves now. By healing I mean digging your heels into the truth of life and making yourselves into better recordings or souls for the harmonious pleasure of the complete universe; God!

Remember, you are the result of what you think, what you think is your awareness, so choose what you think very carefully; think only of what you desire to be; this is knowing yourself.

Which do you choose.... heaven or hell, sickness, happiness, misery, the rich life or the life of poverty?

I love you all, and see God only in each one of you.

SPEAKING FROM SPIRIT 01/10/97

Now, when I speak to you from spirit, I mean that my awareness is receiving food from the spirit of God, which is All. When speaking from spirit, people can tune in to whatever personality they choose, when they learn how. We are all of the same mind.

When I speak to you, I ask that you open your soul for the digesting of the spiritual food which I pass on to you for your total health, which is your total spiritual truth, which is your total awareness, which is your total heaven or hell, which is carried with you everywhere, as you change it.

Heaven and hell are dualities of our awareness. What we think is what we are, and what we think is where we are. We make our own hats to wear in our lives wherever that life may be, by creating the thoughts in our own minds of what we wish to be.

Our will is the steering wheel of our bodies in our eternal trip through life. Our life is now, and our life is what we choose it to be by conscious thinking.

If we want to live in the City of Heaven (which is in the state of our minds), then we must choose all the qualities of heaven and seek after these things.

Everything else will fall into place. "Seek ye first the Kingdom of God and all things will be added unto you."

What Are The Qualities Of Heaven?
Spiritual Truth

Truth is eternal and never changes. So what is truth? Truth is God, light, wisdom, love, mind/spirit, and soul (the final record of who we are). Truth is eternal and never changes. So what is truth? Truth is God, light/wisdom, love, mind/spirit, and soul (the now record of who we are). Truth is a record of fact.

Now, to define truth, I must define all the qualities of truth.

God (The First Quality of Spiritual Truth)

God is the complete total of all souls; and God is completely within each soul. We cannot see God because we see with God's eyes, but we can know God according to how deep within our own soul we can perceive.

When we reach to the eternal depth of our own soul, we meet our Father, God, in knowingness and a complete unification of Oneness with all that is. This unification is a oneness, or harmonious acceptance of all things in eternity, because all things in eternity are God, and we are a part of it, we are in harmony with it, and so we are *IT*, God.

This is the same as saying that your thumb is you, and yet it is your thumb. The thumb is a thumb and the thumb is you. You are you, and you are God, because the Father is within you and you are within the Father.

Light/Wisdom (The Second Quality Of Spiritual Truth)

Light is equal to the wisdom of God. Light is the knowingness of God, which, when we become One with *IT*, we fear nothing because we know all things.

Fear is darkness and ignorance, and they are banished by light, which is the wisdom of God. To get this light, or wisdom of God, we must look within ourselves to the very depths of our souls; here we become at peace with all eternity and receive whatever we ask even before we ask; it is that fast.

Our Father within will take care of all our needs, if only we will become One with Him and let Him act through us.

To do this, we must be in the world doing our thing, but we must not be *of* the world because we are not of the world and must not think this way because it is not spiritual truth.

Remember, spiritual truth is eternal, and the material (limitation or form) world, including our bodies, is not eternal. Our bodies, as well as all material things are eternally changing and are eternally available, but not eternally the same structure.

If we make ourselves, through our thoughts, to be of the world, then we will not be free spirits, or souls, but will be hung up to wherever our thoughts have made us cling to, until we accept the Light or Wisdom of God, which is spiritual Truth.

Love (The Third Quality Of Spiritual Truth)

True Love is eternal and freely given to all. Love is the encompassing and accepting of all things in the universe as they are because they are God.

Love has the Light and Wisdom to know that physical life is change, and spiritual life is eternal, so that life in general is eternal change, and satisfaction is knowing that what is at this moment will eventually change.

This is the wisdom of love, which is God, or spiritual truth.

- Love has no fear because love has Wisdom.
- Love has no jealousy because Love has no fear of loss because Love has the Light and the Wisdom.

133

- Love has no judgment because Love knows all things in Wisdom and Light.

Compare the Loves mentioned above and realize that the so-called God of the Bible is mostly the whim of man.

- God is not a jealous God because jealousy is a fear of loss, and God cannot be inferior, or have any fears at all.
- God cannot judge because God is all, and has no favorites.
- God cannot build a hell for eternal punishment because God is All and will not place Himself in hell as such. Hell is a temporary state of mind, which is breaking laws.
- God cannot be a God of love, and a God of jealousy at the same time, as the Bible states. In the Old Testament He is jealous and tyrannical; in the New Testament He is Love. This is nonsense made by man. God cannot be not jealous.

Jesus was trying to explain God (The Father), and we made a God out of Jesus instead.

Jesus was One with the Father as he had told us, and had communicated with the Father to such an extent that when we saw Jesus, we saw the Father. Since then, man has made a mockery out of Jesus, and claimed that He was God. This is sacrilegious.

Mind, Spirit and Soul

These are the two remainders of the qualities of spiritual Truth, which I am defining. These two are eternal; they are *the make up of man and God.*

Mind/Spirit is All (God). Mind is the totality, whereas Spirit is the movingness in the totality: Awareness, which is the spirit, is the movingness. Spirit is also known as movingness.

So, speaking in mathematical ways, as I am used to:

- Spirit/Awareness/Movingness is the vision/life of God, which is the All/Mind/Totality.
- Soul is the unique record; the sub conscious mind, or personality of us, which is created by our choices made with our Spirit/Awareness/Movingness within Mind.
- Our personal soul, which is our subconscious mind, is our record of life in the mind of God, which has been made by our spirit, which is our conscious mind, or awareness.

134

- Picture this. You are going to make a recording. Your awareness, or conscious mind is the needle that scratches your plastic record, (your subconscious mind). Your record, which is your subconscious mind, or soul, can be seen, read and understood by all who contact the Father within, or God (the total Mind).
- God is mind, which is the medium in which we live, and is the medium of which we are. Even the hairs on our heads are counted and known by mind and those who are of the same mind, God.

Here are some communications to help explain the above.

I asked Father, "Who or what is God?"

> God is like a foundation. God is the knowingness. God is the forefront of all knowledge. God is all encompassing, all-inclusive. God is the life of life. God is the source. God is the stationary, never moving Spirit substance in which we live. God is the medium of life.

I asked Father, "What is your relationship to man, what is man, what is God, what is the relationship?"

> Man emulates to God. Man is the life of God in action, and is change; God is not. For God to have life, man must be. Therefore, man is the Son of God.
>
> God is the Father, the source, the foundation; never changing, absolute. We are the life of God. Man is the key on the keyboard; God is the computer. God is what we would call the super brain... the subconscious; a parental computer, which reveals Itself to the mind of man. Man is the life of God. Both are God.
>
> God is All. God is the law to be used; always there, always ready. God is the ear of corn. Man is the planter; the cultivator, and the eater and the enjoyer

of the thing, which is God. God is man. Man uses God with man's individual choices.

Man is God, man is from God, man is of God. Man is using God, man is Son of God. Man is life of God. God is law of man. God is what we speak *of*, God is what we speak with, God is what we speak to. God is our speaking. God and man are two ends of the same stick.

"Father, tell me some of my near future for the next 12 months, please."

You will be moving along at a good rate, gaining equilibrium and balance, you will be happy, good things will be coming your way, you'll be surprised by a few things that come along.

You'll be able to see into the ethers; into the less physical from the physical with much ease. Your eyes will leave the physical and see totality.

Your viewpoint will be sharpened. You'll be able to grasp even the small things with strength and resolve.

You will be able to control your words, your mouth, to a lot stronger degree; the lungs will expand, breathing will be easier.

You will be able to see the cause of things more clearly; you will see the root of all things more clearly.

A heavy weight will be cut loose from you. Much wisdom is coming your way.

"Thank you Father."

"Father, what is consciousness?"

Consciousness is a pipeline which receives much information and the outer shell of the pipeline is the coagulation of the information received into it. This coagulation feeds out multitudes of newly created pipelines, so as to receive more information and so on, and so on.

Righteousness is like a pipeline with feelers, geared to the individual ego, which is the separateness of spirit; this, which is the individual, the I am that I am.

"Father, why all the spirit guides, etc, instead of direct to you? Why the necessity of spirit guides and all this other stuff?"

There is a need in the human psyche for familiar individualizations for processing information. Individual characters, which are sensed and used, such as multiple personalities, familiar spirits; these are necessary for comprehension and comfort of the individual seeing.

"Father, what is the difference between talking to You, Gabriel (the Voice of the Father which is All), or talking to individual spirits like Bright and Shining One, or Dr. Larabee, Tacumba, Rosebud, Buffalo Spear, Heavy Eagle?"

I am all of these and they are in me and are of me, but I am, as Father, the totality of All. I am in and of everything. I am the source of All. I am not a part of Me, I am All of Me, and in truth, I am not really all of Me, **I AM ALL I; I AM THAT I AM I AM, PERIOD.**

"Father, please explain One plus One equals One in detail."

One plus One equals One is the mathematics of the All. One plus One equals One is eternal mathematics. One plus One equals two is the mathematics of the material.

In order to be material, the One plus One must equal two, as progression is needed in the material, but is not needed in the spirit. In the spirit all is One; One plus one equals One.

The material must be diversified, and therefore the numbers must increase or decrease and expand, multiply and divide, and be different and change; change is life, and the life that you call life there, is called a material life, which needs a multitude of numbers. Without these multitudes of numbers, and getting back to One plus One equals One, there is no life as you know it. **There is no material life. Life is an illusion.**

Material life needs change; life needs multiplying; life needs multiplicity; life needs surprises; life needs changes in color, changes in time, changes in everything. Material life is change.

One plus One equals One, (the spiritual life), is non-changing, eternal I am

NOTE: *This is what is called Absolute.*

Within this material life which you are aware of at this time, there are many, many mansions; many, many houses; many, many lives; different frequencies of living; physical and material that you are not aware of at this time, and there's eons and eons of time, as you call it, in which you will live in different frequencies, and still you will be living physical and material lives.

There will be different experiences in color, fabric and material, and different experiences of smell and sound, etc. All the senses will have a different variety, living inside these different experiences, but they will still be material.

This is where all your lives exist, in the material, all living within Me; I AM. Without you, I AM; With you, I Am enjoying life.

"Father, what is consciousness; where is it; where is the real me, the SOUL?"

The real you is like the stalagmite and the stalactite; the seeping; the dripping; the slow process of accumulation is your soul. Your soul lies in the depths and the caverns of your mind.

Consciousness is what drives, records, and etches your soul. The drivings of all the things that apply to your soul, are your consciousness; your awareness.

Your awareness is the needle that scratches the record, as it makes a recording in your soul. Your awareness is what records on the tape of your soul.

This; your soul, and I are One. One plus One equals One. Your soul is everywhere as I AM everywhere. Your soul is within Me; I live within your soul. Your soul is alive; your soul is governed by change. Your soul is the individuality of your self, as it has accumulated experiences through your lifetimes. Your soul is everywhere as I AM..

Your awareness is the living of the life in the physical/material world, and your awareness is what creates your soul, and re-creates your soul.

Your soul lives within Me; One plus One equals One.

Consciousness is your awareness, living in the material world, and your consciousness gains from the senses of your awareness, information to be placed into your soul; and the stronger the emotions that go with your awareness, the stronger the etchings into your soul.

"Where is my consciousness?"

Your consciousness is where your senses are. All of your senses are your consciousness. They are within you. They are your personality. They are your chooser.

Your consciousness is your steering wheel of your living of life in the material world.

Wherever your senses are is where your consciousness is.

"Father, what must we do in simple terms to become One with You; to live our lives as One with You?"

Know that you are in the basement of life; you are not worthy of being One with Me. Climb your way out of the dungeons of your existence, with your eye on Me, the Father. Do this as your goal.

When you blossom from your ascension (going within) to Me, your soul will meet Mine in the same resonance and then you will know that We are One.

While you are in the turmoils of life, keep your eyes on Me. Be in the world but not of the world. Keep your eyes on Me; make Me your goal. Do not be distracted by the ways of the material world.

The material world is for mechanical actions and the mental learnings that come from these. In your steadfastness in being in the world but not of it with your heart aimed at Me, you are on your journey; you are on target; you are on course.

When your mind and My mind become One, you will have access to My Kingdom. My kingdom includes all; My Kingdom knows all, and My Kingdom is all.

"Father please explain acceptance for me."

Where you are is to be accepted. What you are is to be accepted. When you accept anything and everything with gratitude, you are in the planes of happiness.

Acceptance with gratitude sets the mind for new heights.

Acceptance with gratitude is the base upon

which you spring forward, and this is repetitive and continuous in a happy life. You accept what you have with gratitude and you go on further and higher, accepting the new with gratitude; always being in the state of gratitude, whatever the outcome of your new venture.

Acceptance with gratitude is pleasing for all parties concerned. When your boat is on dry land and there is no water, you cannot go anywhere; in a state of acceptance with gratitude, you are comfortable. When the water comes in, then you are still comfortable.

Acceptance with gratitude produces patience. Patience wins all.

Acceptance with gratitude keeps you well in the flow of things. This does not mean giving up, this means being happy all the time. Happy all the time does not mean giving up. It is being in a balanced state for the next lift off.

All things will be done well, when done in the state of acceptance with gratitude. Be happy where you are, and be happy after you have made your next step. Always be happy and accept everything with gratitude.

Everything is done with your responsibility.

If a next step appears to be wrong, it is no more than a problem to be overcome. Problems are good for us. Problems make us think. Problems make us do, and accepting all wrongs, as problems will enhance our being.

Accept all your problems because they are gifts. They are problems to be overcome. They are problems, which give us life. Without problems, we will deteriorate. Problems are no more than challenges.

NORTH COUNTY TIMES, LETTERS

Suicide Is All Right 03/03/97

. . . if you absolutely wish to leave this planet, miss all the friendships that you could have had, and disappoint so many people that you have and will have loved.

It certainly is a self-centered exit from this planet where you were born for the purpose of learning how to improve yourself during your lifetime here.

It is really your choice to leave us, but I am sure you will be missed by others.

If you are healthy, as the MIS-LED (misled) *39* (Heaven's Gate) were in Rancho Santa Fe, California recently, don't be led by religions, believing that they have the Almighty Truth.

Religions have a way of life and beliefs, but the members are mostly all fishing for something, which religions in general don't furnish. They will tell you who God is and what God wants you to do (this is man-made stuff, in general). You must think for yourself. Do not give up your life because a Religion tells you to. Religions are mostly made up of beliefs and myths. The truth lies within your own unique consciousness. God is within you.

You need not do anything except to look within yourself in a deep, quiet part of your mind. Put your mind aside, and practice communicating with God. Do this daily, all day long in a way that you will become familiar with God, and know God as your constant companion until you will become One with God and all others.

God will counsel you by answering questions for you in the form of pictures and understanding, and God will not tell you what you must do. Your life is to be lived by your choices, and no one else's.

Do not be led by man. Be yourself. You need no one else to mis-lead you. Your life is your responsibility; don't be led by the nose by others. Think for yourself.

Abortion and the Right to Life; Since When? 05/27/97

It appears that there are still people out there who think that abortion is something bad, or evil.

They seem to eat dead animal bodies for food, and approve of killing them for such. These animals have children, also. They have feelings and care for their children, too.

All animals have these same motherly instincts, but we are spirit living in an animal body; we are different from the ordinary animal. We are eternal.

The Right to Life argument is a farce argument. No one has a right to life. We cherish human life because the life in the body is the life of a spiritual being, born (brought forth) at the first responsible breath after the umbilical cord is cut.

Before this first responsible breath of the newborn body, this body is an animal growth within the mother of a body (a mold) for the spirit to enter at first breath.

This form is the mother just as her fingers and warts are the mother. This is *her* body form growing within her, to be entered by a spirit (soul) on first breath after the cord is cut. It is *her* choice as to what to do with the body form that she has grown in her body and is her body, not the Church's.

If we cherish and welcome the new spirit (soul/mind/intelligence), which will enter the body at first responsible breath, we want the body to be desired by someone, and we want it to be a healthy form in order for the new spirit to live a better physical life.

Refusing to see this quality of life for the newborn spirit to enter is really an insult to the process, which God has put into place.

The Right to Life thinking is from the dark ages of Church Dogma and even promotes murder, by the believers, to real human beings in the name of religion.

The Right to Life thinking is very disrespectful of the new spirit arriving, and the non-dogma intelligent thinking.

The Dangers of Religion 08/05/97

Do we love God, or religion? Do we sacrifice our intelligence for the sake of religion?

While reading an article in the local newspaper, I noticed a disgusting picture of what religion does to otherwise good people.

The Palestinian protestors were shouting hatreds for the Jews with a gun in one hand and The Koran in the other.

The basic Islamic people are a gentle, loving people as are most all basic religious peoples around the globe, but because of the living in the past mental attitudes which are basically non-forgiveness and non-forgetting, the gentle people are aroused easily by the ignorant fringe people of all religions, to a frenzied attitude of hatred for some other group.

Recently (last year), there were two Catholic Priests on TV spouting that the Catholics should murder the Abortion People because they were murdering the fetuses in the women's bodies.

In that mode of thinking, we saw murder in the clinics by some otherwise good persons. Those priests are of the lowest mentality and should have been held responsible for the murders that they encouraged.

In Ireland we have the same lower mentality of the Protestants and the Catholics who are involved in a senseless battle because of religion.

I remember the time when Jack Kennedy was running for President when the Protestant tracts of hatred talked about the possibility of a dangerous Catholic in the White House, inferring that all Catholics are dangerous to society.

What is it that causes good people to become crazy with hatred? Could it be that a belief (which is putting a limitation to the intelligent mind) is triggered more easily than rational thinking?

A belief works itself deeply into the human subconscious mind where it becomes an automatic reactive power (a demon) over the mind and body of the individual.

A belief is in reality a danger to society, the same as a hidden bomb is in the market place.

A belief has no intelligence; it just reacts.

It seems very real to the believer, but in reality this is not necessarily so. The believing world is a custom-tailored fantasy world where people are looking everywhere for God and do not realize that God is within themselves and within everyone else, also.

How can we survive beliefs? Are we doomed to myths and fairytales, or can we be logical, with reality?

Suppose that we discourage beliefs in our society and encourage intelligent thinking? I'm not talking about believing as a trend of thinking, but beliefs, which are cast in stone.

The leadership for this idea works best from the top down, and I mean from our leaders to the people.

Suppose that we encourage people to think of all the angles of their beliefs and catalog them in their minds as: Respectful

144

Possibilities, having respect for all other peoples within our influence. This is basically the mental service of all religions, but becomes blinded by beliefs', brought on by fear of Satan and Hell (more myths). Since our Priests and Ministers are supposed to become educated in the Religious Colleges, suppose that all beliefs are eliminated?

Beliefs are dangerous, uncontrollable bombs in our society, which, if not defused into intelligent, respectful thinking, will hurt our social progress in this world for thousands of more years as beliefs have done in the past.

The original thinking of most all the Prophets of the past was basically love of one another, which is giving responsible freedom to all others to live within all law; natural (God law), social, etc. (by the way, our courts promote irresponsible freedom today with their interpretations of the Bill of Rights which needs to be changed ASAP).

Where the world has gone wrong is when man puts his foot into his own mouth and tries to control people by claiming that God said this, and God said that.

Those man-made God laws for the control of peoples' minds are what are destroying us.

What God says is advice, not law. (We all have free wills)

God's laws are eternal, which means that they never began and will never end. They always were and will be. This is where the writers of Jesus' words in the Bible have gone astray. They implied that the words are law, but they are only advice and opinion.

Religion is a good service to mankind and could be used to open men's minds to responsible thinking instead of concrete beliefs.

Religion is best when it encourages people to think for themselves in a loving, responsible attitude toward all others.

Beliefs are no better than drugs are for the mind. Beliefs are perpetuated by weekly rituals and sermons. This is hypnosis!

Let us live respectfully and responsibly, loving all others while trying to improve our world.

Armand L. Archambeault is the result of an ever increasing intense love and respect for God and all peoples everywhere for over 50 years, studying religion and the mind, and communicating with God.

Life Does Begin at Conception 09/13/97
(Yes, physical life is begun here.)
By
Armand L. Archambeault

For physical life to begin, there must be the planting of the seed in the fertile ground.

For spiritual life to begin, there must be the infusion of spirit into the physical body. This infusional conception takes place when the first breath is taken by the physical body after the umbilical cord is cut. This is the spiritual seed planting.

This is when the spirit, which changes an animal being into a human being, begins its life on this earth to experience life for the learning process.

For those who are so concerned about the physical life over the spiritual life, the greatest concern is the life of the body, not the spirit; therefore they say that life begins at conception.

This is true, but do those folks have concern for the spirit, or the body? The body is their interest, and yet the body they speak of is the body of the mother, not the body of a human being inside her womb.

This living animal growth inside of her is a life form she is growing to the best of her ability for the acceptance of a spiritual personality to inhabit at first responsible breath. She deserves the right to choose whether it is a fit and welcome body for the new spirit to inhabit.

The body form, after first responsible breath, is for the experience of the spirit while in this realm of life, here on earth. The body is formed by the parents, and the choice of which body to inhabit is governed by the laws of God, not Religion.

Many Religions worship the body as a sacred thing, but if you reflect into the past, you will see for yourself that the body is only a vehicle for expressing and is done away with easily since time began.

Speaking in religious terms about respect for the body, and thinking about the Crusades, where killing was an act of God through The Church, where was this respect for Life then?

146

In those days, and even today, Life is snuffed out of unbelievers in the name of religion. Most all religions have a clause in the belief systems, which says that the believers will defend their GOD unto death, if necessary. Is this sanity?

The spirit lives on forever, and the body is very fragile in comparison. If the body was meant to be everlasting, there is no proof as yet.

By contrast, the spirit has proven it's eternal existence by the facts of mind communication: psychic, which can actually be spiritual, other dimensional experiences including communicating with the so-called dead, visions of the future, far-seeing, out-of-body experiences, near death experiences, so-called miracles (spiritual acceptance of a new truth of ourselves).

Now about this abortion argument, the right to lifers are concerned about the physical body being killed (they don't seem to be concerned much about all other physical bodies being killed, such as cattle, chickens, fish, flies, mosquitoes, worms, snakes, bacteria, viruses, etc).

They are concerned about life, they say. I wonder if they are concerned about the Spirit? When the spirit enters the body, (after the body has been born, the cord is cut, and it has taken it's first responsible breath), the spirit becomes a human being.

Before that, the life of the body (fetus) is a part of the mother just as a wart is, or a tumor. It is a growth, not a spiritual being. This growth is actually the mother herself in the physical flesh, becoming a new form for spirit (God) personality to inhabit for life experiences on the planet.

If this form or body is not wanted or accepted because of circumstances, then to abort the form is a respect for the new spiritual personality. The form is the new home (body) for habitation on this earth, and to be respectful, it should be a welcome form with loving acceptance.

What is wrong with wanting a quality body for the new personality to inhabit? What is wrong about this subject is that there are people, especially young people, that have no respect for the body or the spirit.

They are self-indulgent pleasure seekers bent on self with no respect for others. They have love for sex as if sex were something to love. Sex is a normal function of animals like us, the same as going to the bathroom. Sex is not love. Sex is a function for making babies.

Respect in the process of making babies is a promise to be true to each other for the sake of health of the minds and bodies of each member of the parent-child family.

Marriage is the instrument for showing respect for each other, the children, and the society in which we live.

This blind love for life in the womb is a belief, which is encouraged by religion. It has no intellectual wisdom. It has only belief, and belief comes from ignorance and dogma (man's power over man).

Belief is a non-thinking, hypnotized thought in the mind of the individual introduced by religious repetition of it and reinforced by fear. This is where war and killing start. Belief is pure ignorance. It is a mask of reality, covering real ignorance.

Think of all the killings in the name of various gods and religions. Think of all the hatred for people who believe differently from you, or the feeling sorry for those same people because they don't know the truth.

Let's respect all others, and give them room to be our friends.

Why Pacifism Is Wrong 10/13/97
We cannot let people harm people.
By
Armand L. Archambeault

In the dictionary, pacifism is the opposition to war or violence. This is what is called natural laziness. You go in another direction, rather than face the obstacles.

If Pacifism is the right answer, then we will have total anarchy in our world. When we determine an attacker as something bad for mankind it must be resisted, even with force, if we want this world to work right for ourselves, and our inheritors.

When a country wants to harm another country it must be stopped. In these cases we are forced into self-preservation. We are not killers, but we are protecting our lives and the lives of others.

What higher calling is this, than to lay down our lives for others?

So-called punishment, which is the impersonal effect of the broken law, is for the deterring of bad actions of teaching those of bad intent that the laws are to be obeyed, for order and harmony.

So-called punishment, which is not really punishment, but the non-personal consequence or result of breaking a law, is not revenge or reaction to bad actions; it is a set of laws, which when enforced will carry out the rules of society for teaching those of ill intent that he/she should not intrude on others.

When a person breaks the law, that person is asking for the action of the law to be used against him/her. It is not punishment, but it is the non-personal result of breaking the law. This person knows the law before he/she breaks it, and ignorance is no excuse, either.

Society has not punished the law-breaker, but the law-breaker has asked for the action from the Pre-set law by his/her wrongdoing.

The law is a culling tool for society to improve itself rather than let decay increase. A bad apple spoils the barrel of apples. A bad example produces more of its kind, as the movies and TV are doing today.

A maggot-like influence or person eats at the heart of society. How can an anti-society person learn, except that he/she gets bumped on the head? There are many hard learners out there. We cannot let them proliferate if we are to progress in our society.

Canada and Sweden have laws, which this country needs to look at in this respect. They prohibit hate and punish it before it spoils the society.

Let us teach by example, and not break the law. Those who don't respect the law do not respect themselves or the rest of us. Let the law prevail.

The reason why the law seems to fail these days is because of lack of enforcement rather than lack of laws. We all know that there are too many laws already and they should be culled out. Just thinking of the IRS gives us a good example of stupid, stifling, totally confusing laws.

Lets re-think the Laws of society as well as the Income Tax, and look for simpler results that are not contradictory and confusing. How

149

about a complete, one percent sales tax to be divided up by all governments; state, county, federal, etc.

This tax is paid with no deductions for favorites. A one percent tax on every sale of every thing and every service. Those who spend, pay the most. Those that can't spend, pay the least.

We have so many laws and rules today that a person cannot breath without breaking one. If all the laws were fully enforced, we would all be in jail, proving that the flood of self-canceling laws are ridiculous, then the laws would demand change and simplicity, and the legal profession could be shrunk to it's basics again.

If our government wants to pay for a study, let it study the law books of Federal and State Laws to cut out the chaff. It is overdue.

All law (including God's Law) is set with the intent to train people. Without law there is anarchy and chaos, and also, without law enforcement there is anarchy and chaos.

This is a major problem with road-rage. . .there is not enough enforcement on the road. We need more policemen and highway patrolmen for the enforcement, and sheriffs to see that the fines are paid. Our governments are lax in all enforcements.

Let's support enforcement and getting rid of chaff laws.

Pacifism is against the laws of God. It usually is supported by people, who have the motherly' instinct. Their intentions are good, but their heads are ruled by their hearts, instead of logical, constructive thinking.

Those who think that law is reactionary are mis-led, also. Law is the foundation of the world. Without law, and law enforcement, decency will not have a chance of survival, because it is natural to take the easy way out.

Nature is lazy! Without the laws of gravity, our world would spin into oblivion. This applies to our society as well.

Law and example are the best teachers we know. Law produces consequences for our actions, not punishment. How can a victimless crime harm no one? Crime harms everyone.

We should not succumb to the desire to break the law, for breaking the law is hurting all innocent peoples everywhere.

Pacifism makes the law-abiding citizen a no-brainer. What's the use? When everyone else is breaking the law, what's the use of obeying the law? Pacifism turns the world upside-down with anarchy and the anything goes syndrome.

Love gives freedom to the object of our love to live within all law, so we can't feel bad if our loved one has broken a law; it should teach him/her a lesson in living. If it doesn't, then she/he will get another chance some day now or in the process of eternal life.

Speaking in spiritual terms, God will not judge, or punish, either. God set up natural laws to do the same thing for His creation (which never was) because he/she/it loves his/her/it's created ones.

It is through love that laws are created, not for punishment. That is why life is eternal, and reincarnation is a fact. Learning is eternal!

Everyone, including law-breakers, is God being expressed. Would God punish Him/Her/Itself? Law is just; not punishment.

If you jump off a 20-story building, do you think you won't be killed?

Do Pacifists Condemn God, as They Seem to Condemn Society for Making Laws Resembling God's Laws, Such as the Electric Chair?

These laws are an expression of our love for the trespassers; they are free to live within all Law.

Don't eat the apple on the tree in the Garden of Eden! Don't break the law! The death penalty (the result of wrong action) is necessary for killers with the intent to kill, in order for our society to improve. We've got to get rid of these bad apples.

Executions are, and should be the law of the land for those who have killed us. Killing one of us is killing all of us, and it must be stopped with law.

To abuse a law-breaker, we would ignore his law breaking and encourage him/her to continue until he/she has no respect for us (society) at all.

To abuse a law-breaker, we would use Psychology as an excuse for his actions, and let him continue his raping, stealing, killing until he takes over the neighborhood and the world.

Heil Hitler! He was a good example of breaking the law, and

should have been exterminated in the beginning. We, as a society are too lazy.

Psychology is the understanding of a person's attitudes, and that is all right, but to offer it as an excuse to escape the consequences of his/her actions is a crime against society and the lawbreaker, who needs to learn about his/her responsibilities in society.

Evil and good are necessary for us to see the differences in life. Positive and negative make the current flow. Without good and evil, the current of life could not exist. Life would cease to be.

Appreciate the good, and take a stand against evil in order for the good to progress toward God's Kingdom on earth.

This sounds religious, but it is really just plain fact.

God is real, and at times I think Pacifists are not, just as religions are not. There seems to be fantasy in the minds of these people.

No Expansion Allowed If Water Is Scarce 10/22/97
By
Armand L. Archambeault

How can anyone suggest that we residents are supposed to reduce our water usage so that more people can move into our area?

This is upside-down thinking by any reasoning person. If water is scarce, then additional housing and people should be restricted, not the water usage.

We are facing water shortages all the time as the weather patterns change, and the local governments of Southern California allow increases in housing, and population.

This can only decrease the water available for our communities. Where is common sense? Let's keep our population and housing at a standstill until we get enough water for use. Water first, and more people and houses next.

"But what about the economy?" you say. "We will be at a standstill and also we will lose jobs!"

Let people move elsewhere to find jobs. We need water. When the water arrives, we will have jobs.

The cart seems to be before the horse in our government thinking. I believe they are persuaded by big money and big business to allow home building and more population into the water shortage areas.

If we are threatened with water shortages, let's slow down and wake up to reality, not charge card thinking. Charge Card thinking is playing with your toys before you have earned them. There is no respect for the toys when they are not earned. Earning something means you save for it, first.

Political Extortion 03/10/98
(The nature of politics)
By
Armand L. Archambeault

Political donations are no different from Extortion Rackets. They are hopeful payoffs for our 'racketeer government'.

What has our Government gotten itself into? There is a tremendous thrust for power, money, etc. by our so-called elected officials through the use of threats; implied and brazen.

Why are some Congressmen and Senators holding out on votes? Could it be that they are waiting for favors and deals as the pay-off for a change of their votes? This is extortion and racketeering, also!

Let us outlaw all donations and gifts as the Police departments and grocery companies do, because these donations and gifts produce coercion.

Because the airways are the public's, let there be time on the airways for all legitimate aspirants to express their views in a fair way at no cost to them, every day of the week.

C-SPAN seems to have the proper format for this, and all political ads should be outlawed, also, as unfair coercion of the public. After all, this is a serious business and should be fair in all aspects for the public's consumption.

We need sensible platforms for the politicians to remain free from rackteteering.

Big Bang Theory Almost True 03/18/98
By
Armand L. Archambeault

Eternity is a continuous happening, not a one time Big Bang.

The Big Bang is eternally happening, just as the explosions above pistons in engines. The Big Bangs of Eternity never cease because systems (laws) are in place in Eternity to keep the engines of God as an eternal, never ending happening.

Everything material, including the animal body, which we as Spirit inhabit for our experiences in this material world, is in a continuous state of flux (change). The Black Holes eat the material stuff, as earthquakes do on earth, and the Big Bangs assure the eternal change and evolvement, as do the volcanoes on earth.

"So what?" you say.

Christian thought displays great concern for material form (embryo) in women, which they call life, yet they condone slaughter and eating of animals.

They seem to care more for embryos than for the Spirit which will inhabit the embryo upon first independent, responsible breath, which we call Spirit (God/Man).

Hu-man is: Hu (animal), man (spirit), a spirit living in an animal body. The spirit is the deathless divine within us. (R.J. Campbell). The embryo is a form of animal life.

Sermon: Man, God, Love 04/10/98

Good morning!

What I talk and write about is taken from what the Archangel Gabriel gives to me in meditative communication. About one year ago, Gabriel appeared in my living room between me and the TV set, in full-sized, living form, and confirmed that He is guiding me in finishing my book IT (Eternity as if it had a beginning.).

Gabriel is the voice of God. God does not speak.

Today, I am talking about man, God, and love.

In Gen. 1:26 God said: "Let us make man in our image. . .

I asked Father, in meditation, "What is your relationship to man, what is man, what is God, what is the relationship?"

Man emulates to God (man is always wondering about God). Man is the life of God in action, and man is change; God is not change, God is always the same. God is the best One to have as your best friend.

For God to have life, man must be. Therefore, man is the Son of God. God is the Father, the source, the foundation; never changing, absolute, and eternal. Man is the life of God. Man is an eternal expression of God.

Man is the key on the computer keyboard; God is the computer. God is what we would call the Super Subconscious Mind; a computer, which listens to the mind of man. Man is the life of God. Both are God.

God is All. Man is a piece of All, and can be One with All if he chooses. Being one with God is the supreme expression of love. Loving everyone is loving God.

Do you know why you can't see God? Because you are a piece of the pie, and will never see the whole pie from your viewpoint, until you become **One with the Father**. Then you'll understand God, but will still not see God because you are the missing piece of the pie.

In Jude 21: the Bible says, "Keep yourselves in the love of God".

Father said, "God is the law to be used; always there, always ready."

In Psalms 82.6: "You are gods, sons of the most high, All of you. Nevertheless you shall die like men, and fall like any prince."

Father said, "God is man. God is omnipresent, everywhere at all times. Man uses God's laws with man's individual choices. Man is God, man is from God, man is of God. Man is living within God's laws, man is Son of God."

Man is the life of God. Another way of expressing this is that, God is the hand, and man is a free-willed finger on that hand. The finger can join the hand and all the benefits of being one with the hand, or it can flounder by itself, if it wants to, just like the California high-sign, but wisdom will cause the finger to become one with the hand eventually through the wise process of eternal reincarnation.

Father said, "God is law of man. God is what man speaks of, God is what man speaks with, God is what man speaks to, God is man speaking . God and man are two ends of the same stick."

(Man is a free, independent expression of God.) And now we'll speak about love In Matt 6:22, and John 14:12 Jesus said, "This is my commandment, that you love one another as I have loved you."

Love is the giving of responsible freedom to the object of your love to live within all laws; spiritual, physical, social. (Jesus said to "Give unto Caesar what is Caesars", in other words, obey the laws.)

In John 6:63 Jesus said: "It is the spirit that gives life, the flesh is of no avail."

In Gen 2:7, man became a living being with the breath of life. Man is a human being upon first independent breath. Breath is spirit.

Sex is not love. Sex is an animal function, the same as going to the bathroom, and it should be kept private in the same manner. It is built into the animal bodies, which we inhabit with our spirits, so that the species of our animal bodies, which we use, will continue to exist.

When we emphasize sex in our lives, or place sex above our spiritual well being, we are of this world, the animal world, and *not* of the spiritual world which is eternal. Sex is an animal act.

God is love, not sex! Sex makes babies, not love!

God loves us, and has set up eternal laws for our existence which we must live by for our present and eternal benefit. God's laws never change. They are eternal.

God gives us the responsible freedom to live within the laws, which were set up for our world of existence. God puts you here and says "This is your life; live by the laws, in complete responsible freedom, to learn about good and evil so that you will become wise from your mistakes.

Love is giving responsible freedom, rather than controlling; giving responsible freedom, rather than possessing. If your lover controls you, or treats you like a possession, you are not loved, but you are a slave, by your choices.

Love is being One with the Father, as Jesus was, and as you can be, also. Love is spiritual, not animal.

Love is being *in* this world, but not of this world. God is the first consideration in all things. God is All. Everything exists in this All.

We are born for learning and improving, not for hating, killing and decaying.

You can take Love with you wherever you go. No one can take it away from you. It is the secret of the ages as to how to live a good, happy life.

A house with a solid foundation will not shake loose. You will not fall apart if God is your first love. After all, you are made of God. You always have God, just by the nature of your being. Become One with God, by choice, and flourish wisely in these material worlds.

The opposite of love is EGO, which is edging God out. A person who has a big ego is a person who loves himself or herself more than God, or any other person. This is also called conceit; the exaggeration of one's own importance, which leaves no room for others to have responsible freedom of expression.

Conceit is the absence of love. Conceit wants to control others.

Along with this responsible freedom comes responsibility not to influence others to break the laws—spiritual, physical, and social.

Irresponsible freedom is self-love and self-love shuts out God and your neighbor, also.

Irresponsible freedom is the opposite of love. . . it is loaded with ego (edging God out). It leads to chaos and anarchy. Think of road rage.

Love is not long-suffering. There is no suffering with true love. True love is eternal and effortless, as if observing the object of your love with the wisdom of God and being pleased that your beloved has the responsible freedom to learn at his or her own pace. Think as a grandparent.

True love is full of wisdom and the understanding of God's principles about Law and Responsible Freedom.

Law is a non-bending rule which produces consequences when **a** law is broken.

When you jump off a 20 story building, do you think you won't be killed? That's God's law in action. Our laws on earth should be the same.

Responsible freedom is following the Law; the law of loving your neighbor as you love yourself.

If you play the music real loud because you like the noise it makes, and do not consider the effects on other people within the sound of that noise, that is irresponsible freedom, and eventually that irresponsible freedom will cause a reaction from others.

The reaction from others is from your intruding on their space without their permission. This is an action taken without responsibility (without love). Irresponsible freedom is loveless freedom.

True love produces a feeling within the lover, of:

Peace, happiness, joy, tenderness, patience, understanding, empathy, wellness of being, mental and physical health, confidence and bliss.

Love does not require rewards; it is freely given, and requires nothing in return.

Other than your guardians, when you are less than mature, whoever possesses you, does not love you. Mature means the act of being responsible.

Remember, the City of Happiness, or Heaven, is in the State of Your Mind, living within the law, and respecting all others.

Love is the foundation of the complete eternal universe: God.

And a final thought.

Thank you for listening, and I'd love to come back.

Beliefs 04/15/98
Why believe?

I notice that there is much to do in the Letters about believing, things. It is hard for me to comprehend why people choose to believe anything, unless believing is used as a tool for a trend in thought.

If I believe (as a religious person does), I would be saying that I am believing in something that I am not sure of, and I would need lots of company, sermons, and rituals to reinforce my belief. I would probably want to reinforce my belief by trying to convince others. This is no more than a sad case of self-hypnosis.

Why play kids' games when dealing with the most important phase of your life? Science and experience are the provers of facts, and belief is a guess into the future or past.

In my experiences, I have found that God is real, but Religions are not. Religions require belief, and experience is real.

As far as doctrine/dogma goes, these are man-made laws of the church, and not necessarily of God. God's laws are scientific, not religious. God's laws are natural, not man made.

When you must believe, be very aware of the fear tactics that are in the soup of religion such as:

- Sin (do as I say or else),
- Devil (he's going to get you),
- Satan (have fear of this one),
- Excommunication (you can't bein our gang any more because you are being sent to Hell by us, we are the elite; we have been born again),
- Saved (I am better than you),
- Virgin-born and resurrected (just as many ancient gods were before Jesus, the prophet).

Most Religions Are Not Aware Of Reality 05/04/98
Beliefs are very dangerous
By
Armand L. Archambeault

How long will we have to wait before the End Times arrive? It has been getting pushed forward since before Jesus was born. Many religions of the Christian type seem seriously involved in the End Times as if it is a true expectancy. It is always just around the corner.

- *Jesus* promised that the end would come while the others were still alive, before his generation would pass away.
- *Peter* said that the end of all things is at hand.
- *Paul* said that his generation was in the end times.

- *John the Baptist* kept warning the people about the wrath to come and that the Kingdom of Heaven is at hand.
- The *Dead Sea Scrolls* say about the same thing.

It is time to wake up and smell the roses of reality, which grow today, and give up the fantasies of religions of yesterday.

Your Kingdom of Heaven is the State of Your Mind now, today, and depends on your respecting your neighbors, and not breaking laws . That is it in a nutshell.

Life is simple, and welcomes you to enjoy it in abundance as long as you follow the natural (God), Government, and Social laws. Note that these are not church dogma, belief, commandments, etc, but just good, common sense.

Life is eternal no matter what you do, through reincarnation, so do the right things now, and enjoy life while you are living it. You will never have Heaven in your life except in the present time while you are alive in your present life.

This is the real End Times.

CHAPTER FOUR

MY DIARY: A DEVELOPING SEARCH FOR GOD

Born in Manchester, New Hampshire 1930.
Concord, New Hampshire 1937, My First Communion/Biting the Host/Crazy

At seven years of age, during my first communion, I was receiving the Holy Eucharist. As it was being held in my mouth for melting and swallowing, my teeth jerked shut on it, giving me the awesome sensation that I had bitten the skin of Jesus Christ (a nun had told me this would happen if I bit the host).

Figure 9

I was an honest boy,
who was serious
about my choice of qualities
to live by.
I even attended church
twice on Sundays.
I was truthful, reliable,
industrious, and really
loved God.
I really didn't intend to bite
the host.

Even though I rationalized that it was just my imagination, it left a permanent scar on my mind. Since that time, my mind has been bent on seeking God.

C.4 MY DIARY: A DEVELOPING SEARCH FOR GOD

Crazy People

As you may have guessed, I was being brought up as a Catholic boy. The unusual thing about this was that I was very serious in my studies about God. I loved and revered God. God seemed to me to be the only Reality in this world, because, even at this young age, I sensed that this world that I lived in was not a real world, but a place where most everyone is crazy, or at least unbalanced.

This sense is still a valid one in my mind of today in 2000, sixty-four years later. (They say that when a person thinks that way, then that person must be on the edge of crazy.) Oh well. . .

A World of Make Believe

My mind could not accept the daily happenings as something of substance, but as a weird world of make believe. People seemed to be false, or untrue. The whole world was this way. Why was this so?

Bedford, New Hampshire: My Grandparents 1941

At this time, I was living with my grandparents, Henry J. Rau Sr. and Esther M. (Clark) Rau, who became a great influence in my life. My grandfather was an old German tower of sensibleness and practicality, with a gentle sense of humor, hidden in his fair sized belly. My grandmother had an English Baptist and American Indian background. She was full of life and wisdom from the Indian background, and full of wit and intelligence from her English background.

They were both following the Catholic faith somewhat, as they were married in the Catholic Church. I learned basic good morals from the two of them, and had much love and respect for them.

My grandfather, a stay-at-homeCatholic, showed me sensibleness and reliability, and my grandmother, a stay-at-home ex-Southern Baptist, taught me all the practical ways of life which her Indian side had brought to her. She had no calling for religion per say, but the Golden Rule and Moderation were her life guides.

Manchester, New Hampshire:
My Hobby, Psychology At 15 Yrs 1945

At this time, I was a sophomore in Central High School. My main interest developed while in the school library one day, when I noticed this book on psychology. I browsed through it, and decided to check it out so that I could learn more about it. The theme in the book seemed to match what was imprinted on my mind. . .that this is a world of crazy, irresponsible, two faced beings who would call themselves people.

Their basic instincts of sex and greed were prominent in their beings so that what they professed to be on Sundays was the direct opposite of what they were during the week.

From the time that I read the book on psychology until this day in 2000, I've been a keen observer of people and their habits.

Saint Anselm's College, Manchester, New Hampshire 1950
My Priesthood Studies/Father Francis Steinmetz

I studied, part time, with a cousin of mine who was a Dominican Monk at St. Anselm's college, a professor of physics, and a scientist working on anti-gravity in New Boston, Massachusetts.

My studies were of the Catholic priest's life and responsibilities, and of the inside beliefs of the Catholic church.

I needed to know if I really wanted to become a Catholic priest, or to get married. I decided to get married. I couldn't swallow all the ideas supporting the Catholic faith, even though I still remained Catholic, and attended church on Sundays, etc.

Deep Thoughts: 25 Yrs Of Age/True Love 11/17/1965

While working in a store that I owned in San Bernardino, Ye Ole Smoke Shoppe, there was a dull spot in the business where I did some deep thinking, and wrote:

If you are tired of waiting for your ship to come in, or if you can't swim out to it, leave it be; and surround yourself with a new search for true happiness within your possible reach.

If the grass is always greener on the other side, then why not wear green colored glasses when you look on your own side. Also, the other grass might take a lot more work than yours.

The City of Happiness is in the State of Mind

If you truly and wholeheartedly love someone, or something, and love everyone and everything as God must truly love everyone and everything, then, in your ecstasy, why not share your beloved possessions with all the earth and mankind? Because you love all of the earth, and all of mankind and God. . . the source of all true love.

If true, deep, emotional, and wholehearted love of all brings tear drops from your eyes, then think of all the love God has for us and our planet. His tears cover three fourths of our earth.

True love comes from the heart, or the chest area, not from the lower animalistic glands. Why is the term love so widely misused?

True love radiates outward and wants to share itself with everything and everyone in the universe.

True love knows not what jealousy is, nor does it know the word ownership or possession. It is universal and knows no boundaries.

I believe that the human body is a prison for true love and only upon death of the body is our love released to unite with God's universal love (when we hug another person who has true love, chest to chest, we can come the closest to the feeling of the release or our true love when it unites with God's).

What hurts a person with true love the most is the lack of true love on the part of other possible sources.

True love is fluid, such as electricity, with radiance such as the sunshine.

Body And Blood Of Christ

Jesus said to take the bread and wine in commemoration of him. Why have I been lead to believe that the bread and wine have actually changed into the physical body and blood of Christ?

The morning after, I wrote, "The rain has just stopped during

the night. The birds are chirping in beautiful tones and there are many

of them this morning in our back yard and trees. There is no smog.
Everything is washed, clean and fresh. The sun is out and the
colors are bright and beautiful. The bright, blue sky has puffs of brilliant white and opaque gray clouds moving gently across it.
The green leaves of the trees are shimmering very slightly in the
clean, fresh air as if they were rejoicing in the true love atmosphere."

Thirty-six Years Of Age: Catechism Teacher, Black Shade 1966

I was teaching Christian Doctrine to the seventh and eight grade
pupils on the subject of Extreme Unction (the Last Rites) one
Saturday. While I was talking, I became overwhelmed with a dark,
cold feeling of being a complete hypocrite to these children and
myself.

On the spot, as this cold, black shade lowered in front of my
eyes, I knew that I was definitely not a Catholic; I was a hypocrite.
As far as I can remember, this is probably the first psychic happening in my life. It was an outside sign that something was changing
inside of me.

On My Own In Riverside, California 1967

I was now on my own, and began to read and study about all
religions, which I could reach, and thrived on archaeology,
philosophy, and psychology. I was bloodthirsty-hungry for
knowledge of anything about the human mind, and God.

Introduced To Spiritualism In Rubidoux, CA 1969
My First Vision and 40 Day Fast

One day, a salesman Dick S., who was a good friend of mine
because I took a liking to him, asked me if I would go with him and
his wife to church that night (08-08-69).

I asked him what kind of a church it was, and he said it was a
Spiritualist church. I told him no thanks and said that as far as I knew,
all that stuff was crazy and I didn't want to become involved. He told

me that I was wrong and that I should go at least once, so that I might get some first hand understanding of it.

After his urging me with more friendly pressure, I said that I would go with him. So, that night there I was, in this average large home with about twenty other happy and friendly looking people. We sat in chairs, and on couches and sang church songs after the opening Lord's Prayer.

Then the lights were all turned off except a night light (praying hands) which left enough light to see everyone in the room. We were told to relax in our chairs, and to give out with whatever we saw or felt deep within our selves, so that the others might gain some insights from what was given.

Several people said things which came to them, and I must say that it all sounded pretty good.

My First Vision

Then, when the wife of my friend (Liz S.) started to speak from her chair, which was about six feet from me, her body became a black silhouette, and I saw real, life sized, living, breathing, angel wings on her back, with real feathers, in tones of grey.

As she spoke, I could not believe my eyes. I thought of possibilities of tricks, and could not imagine a possibility of it. These were genuine live wings about six feet from the top to the floor on her back, moving as she breathed and spoke, during which her body had become a total black silhouette.

This amazing happening hooked me into learning more about Spiritualism. I began to go to that church from then on in order to learn more about it. Besides that, I liked the people that I met there; they were genuine, real, down to earth people, who were trying to improve themselves, and had respect for God and the rest of us (I was just fed up with the many, pretending people who went to the traditional Christian churches).

Figure 10

Liz Seyler had turned
completely black and I could
only see the chair and the
living, breathing wings
on her back.
Liz is shown in a lighter shade
so that you may see details for
your understanding.
The wings were different
tones of grey, and moving as
if they were the feathers on a
sitting bird or Angel.

From that time on, I went to all kinds of churches when I had a Saturday or Sunday off. I watched all the ceremonies carefully, and listened to the preachers and participants. I read voraciously about anything that came along.

Forty-Day Fast—On Just Minimum Water 1969

I fasted and prayed for forty days as the prophets did in the old days, in order to hear God.

During and after the fast, I saw visions of the future; I was transported in time to other countries, and verified my presence with newspaper pictures and reports.

I had a voice talk to me inside of my head a few times Traditionally, the Christian people would think of this as the work of the devil, because many of the branches of Christianity tend to give emphasis for the worship of a devil by creating so much fear of this *myth*.

I dreamed of the future, which I verified by using my diary, and I began to read God speaking to me.

The reading began with pictures, and then I found that as I spoke my understanding of the picture/symbols, more pictures came until the message was over. When I did not speak the correct understanding of the picture/symbols, the picture would stay still until

C.4 MY DIARY: A DEVELOPING SEARCH FOR GOD

I said the correct interpretation. All these things were strange, and awe inspiring, to say the least.

(Today, in 2000, 1 realize that the interpreting of the pictures comes out of the mouth in the same type of parables that Jesus is credited with.)

The above is a thumbnail sketch of how I started into this deep side of spiritual life.

Readings At Rubidoux, CA: Met My Future Wife 08/08/69

Mr R., the owner of the home, saw a long white path for me. . .he saw me diving from diving boards into a swimming pool (this meant that I was going to dive deep into the waters of the spiritual world). **NOTE 2000**: *The above came true.*

Jane H., a very popular and accurate psychic since childhood, said that within two weeks, my materialization would not occur, or I would be discouraged about not getting something, and not to let it bother me. It had to do with love. She also told me that I had seen and touched B.B., my girl friend this week, which was true.

Mr R. saw a tall dark haired girl near me. Her name is Norma. He saw me writing figures on a tablet that flips up, and a man was guiding me and answering questions (seems like a taking of inventory).

NOTE TODAY, 2000: *This seems to have been me in my wholesale business which I had for twenty years, from 1970-1990.*

It was on this night that I met a lady named Kay, who is my wife today, since 11/20/78. We were sitting next to each other on a couch, when a spider lowered itself between us so that Kay screamed and I jumped up to kill the spider between my hands.

We hadn't spoken to each other before that, and from that moment, we became friends. Little did I know that this woman, who was fifteen years older than I was, would be my wife in ten years from that experience.

Etela C.: Rubidoux, CA
The Major Change In My Spiritual Life 08/09/69

At Ed and Anne R.'s house, a lady, Etela C. from Anaheim, CA who worked at the Servicemen's Center in Anaheim, gave to me a reading:

Roman leanings-arena-325 ad, in a four: marriage, suddenly hit hard with love to unexpected party (this actually happened in 1973). We'll get many blessings. Read the Koran and Bible, Yogananda books. Vary the reading and authors. . .get all sides of the picture. . . and Hebrews, 15 minutes each day, read Psalms 23,121,123, and say the Lord's Prayer.

Read with feeling and understanding. Stretch out hands upwardly to ask powers for help, and to receive. I am going to school. After a time, open books and see if a meaningful message comes upon first focus. I am like a wet rag now. I am a skeptic. I will live a long life. I will learn many things. I will be able to see very soon." (And I did) **NOTE 2000:** *I fasted for 40 days in 1969, on just water while working 6 days a week and prayed what Etela advised in her reading, and haven't been the same since. All kinds of things have materialized in my life since.*

My First Movie Vision At Pat H.'s In Corona, CA 08/11/69

Pat H. does automatic writing by John Watkins (18th century). She is a healer. She is a good cook, companion, and conversationalist.

After dinner at her house, while I was standing in her kitchen, talking to her while she was doing the dishes, a movie appeared to me in mid air about four feet in front of me, just above my eyesight, which was about six feet above the floor. The vision was on a translucent screen about five feet wide, two feet high, and hung in the air so that I could watch it as I was talking to Pat. My eyes were wide open.

I told her what was happening while it was occurring, and that I was afraid to move for the fear of disturbing the vision. It was in full Technicolor, and moving just as if it were a natural, now, happening. It was a real life-like reality confronting me with itself.

This Was The Vision: 3:30 P.M 08/11/69

Lava was flowing down the sides of a very high, purplish, hazy mountain, with snow in the upper altitudes, and with a very large, bright yellowish sun rising behind it. People were scurrying all about at the bottomlands of this mountain. They were in desperate fear of

169

their lives, and the ground seemed to be shaking. I was filled with the knowledge of this as being Mount Fujiyama in Japan.

Confirmed By The News: 11:30 P.M. 08/11/69

I heard on the news the same night, eight hours later at my apartment, that an underwater earthquake in the North Pacific Ocean, setting off huge tidal waves, #8 on the Richter Scale, had just happened on the islands of Honshu and Hokkaido.

The following morning, there was a front-page picture in the L.A. Times of Fujiyama along with a story of the happening. I knew then that I had seen this vision in Corona, California, while the occurrence was happening in Japan, about 6500 miles from me. Well, no need to say, that this was a very sobering period in my life of strange happenings.

Message From John: My Rapidly Developing Awareness 08/11/69

At Pat H.'s house in Corona, CA, John (talking through Pat, by Automatic Writing) said: "Yes Andy, you are going to learn so much in the future that it will leave you breathless. Just don't push things as you are developing your awareness rapidly and you will learn as you continue to read and study. God is with you and Bless you, Andy."

Messenger Of God: Riverside, CA 08/11/69

I tried meditation (prayer) and soul traveling (mind traveling) in a sitting position. OM (a tuning, vibrational sound created in the voice box and mouth) was my Mantra, and I developed a tremendous, dynamic pressure in my upper chest and forehead to the point where I was shaking and felt like I would pass out if I continued, so I came back down and relaxed within myself, where I saw blueish pictures that looked like an upside down card table or fighting rink floating above a huge crowd of people and turning over to become an 'L' shaped flashlight shining on the crowd. Then a blueish carpet began rolling itself up a high set of stairs where there was an empty chair on top of them.

I saw blueish spirit-like figures floating in and out of doors, I saw a black-blue sky with bright, small stars, which were coming toward me, or I was going toward them. Then at the end of all this, there was a broken granite asteroid type thing coming directly toward me.

A week later, I told some folks at the Reid's home about my experience, and the oldest psychic, Clara, from Beaumont, CA, started into a deep trance in order to interpret it. As she started to speak under trance, then Jane H. of Riverside, CA, joined in with Clara in describing my inner vision above. They both tuned in together on me and reported that:

> I was a messenger of God's, and was depart-
> ing shortly in my spaceship. Before I boarded the ship,
> my people were bowing to me, and I was bowing to
> them as a sign of love and respect for our Father God.
> Then, I flew away to deliver my message to another
> planet, but on the way, in space, my ship crashed head-
> on into a cluster of rocks from a broken asteroid. I
> died on that trip, after a lot of physical suffering.

Vision: Grapefruit In The Sky 08/12/69

At seven-thirty in the morning I was just waking up, when I saw on my eye lids, a hazy, shiny, yellow grapefruit shape, twirling slowly around, looking like the sun, but as it turned around, I was sure it was a grapefruit and it had a brilliance like the sun, but a bit on the fuzzy side. Below the grapefruit, there was a huge flooded area. . .much water over a large area with tops of bushes or trees and houses protruding from the water, and people in the water with their hands in the air. I don't know why I saw it, or what it means, but I wonder if it has application to the Salton Sea area in California, near Palm Springs.

I have that feeling, and had that feeling at the time of the pictures I saw in my mind. More about this is coming below.

All my life I have, an occasion, when I had thought about it, been able to experience a great peaceful, electrifying, loving type radiation feeling in my arms, chest and stomach and head, but thought nothing of it, except that it felt good and wonderful! Lately, I notice that as often as I want it, I can experience this feeling by sort of drawing it into me from in front and above me with my mental desire of it.

It happens at once, and it seems that my mind has to be uncluttered before it will happen.

Verification Of Grapefruit In The Sky 08/18/69

I learned yesterday about 200,000 people being made homeless, and 50 dead in the Louisiana area. There was a 200mph hurricane (Camille) on Saturday August 16, or Sunday August 17. The hurricane caused a huge flood in the area of the Mississippi delta, and a picture in the L.A. Times showed the hurricane eye from an airplane.

The eye of the hurricane made me think of the grapefruit I saw twirling around slowly over the flood area. I wonder if there was a connection between this catastrophe and my vision. The grapefruit, and the picture of the eye of the hurricane, looked identical to what I saw in my mind. This was a vision of the future, which I had seen on 8/12, six days earlier.

This is twice that I have had a vision of troubles, and twice now there has been an eerie connection with world happenings in a short period of time.

Vision: Twirling Pencil, Riverside, CA 08/19/69

At twelve-thirty a.m. while going to sleep, I saw a twirling pencil coming out of the wall, and an 'atomic' bomb explosion, which was like gold specks shooting into the air and flowering out like fireworks of golden color.

NOTE: TODAY, 2000: *I understand this to mean that I was going to write an explosion of material.*

At one-ten I saw a bright golden door with S in the left window of it and the door was opening. I wonder if the letter S is for my friend Dick Seyler.

NOTE 2000: *I know that this meant that Seyler, my friend who first took me to a Spiritualist Church, was the golden door of opportunity for my life quest.*

Astral Trip: Corona, CA 08/19/69

At Pat H.'s house, I was sitting on the sofa in the front room, trying to astral travel (this is where you move your mind through space and time in order to experience outer worlds).

I was traveling over a gold colored city of fine ornate, sculptured roofs. I fell to the streets with a startle because people were rushing by me. I couldn't make out the individuals as people or spirits, except they were hooded in blue-grey robes and in a hurry.

I saw a bright hole up above in the sky and tried to get through and did. Up there was a brightness, like yellow gold and little orange-bright clouds, and a huge face, which seemed to have a beard. Saw a bearded man on a throne of gold also. Seemed to be a God, or ruler.

Mosque Bombing/Astral Traveling In Jerusalem: Riverside, CA 08/20/69

At 11:00 p.m., while in my bed, I tried E.S.P. (Extra Sensory Perception) to Pat H.'s house (about 15 miles away), after the Lord's Prayer, and asking God for permission.

I tuned myself to God and tried to contact Pat H. for about 15 minutes, but nothing happened, to my knowledge, except I was mentally traveling from place to place where ever I thought she might be and tried to speak to her. She was supposed to be listening for me at 11:00 p.m.

While going over the rooftops, I was traveling very fast, and things seemed to be strange looking. There were many similar buildings.

The roof I concentrated on as hers, turned into a shiny, domed roof and burst open with orange-yellow flames and concerned me.

C.4 MY DIARY: A DEVELOPING SEARCH FOR GOD

At 12:30 p.m. the news on KABC radio just said that some Mosque of the Arabs was on fire. It is a place where Jesus was supposed to have risen up to heaven.

Verification Of Bombing: Riverside, CA 08/21/69

The picture in the paper today, of the burned Mosque resembled the buildings I was going over last night. . .I wonder. . .in fact, I am sure that what I saw was the same as the picture in the paper. This place had been bombed at the time that I saw it the night before.

Astral Trip, Eye Of God: Riverside, CA 08/22/69

At 6:10 a.m. I tried to astral (mental) travel to Pat H.'s house to wake her up. I pulled the covers off twice and she pulled them back. I said,"Good morning, Pat!" and tried to awaken her.

Before I got to her house, I saw a tube, leading up to a very bright spot in the sky. Seemed like I tried to get up this tube, but when I reached the top where the light was, there was a net, like the blood vessels on an eye ball (God's eyeball), covering the opening to the bright spot, and I couldn't get in.

Seems like the tube was full of other spirits trying the same thing.

Figure 11

As I was traveling up this tube, there were other people in the tube, also. When I arrived at the destination at the top of the tube, I was met by the Eye of God and told to return. I remember being disappointed by that.

Carl Jung And God: Corona, CA 08/22/69

Met Linda and Louie. They are nice people. Linda saw blue flashes all about me, and Louie saw a glow of bright light on my head.

NOTE: *C.G. Jung was fascinated by an alchemy book called "The Secret of the Golden Flower", translated by Richard Wilhelm. This book was about the laws of opposites.*

Finished reading the book: "What Jung Really Said" by E.A. Bennett (Jung's story of psychiatry and his beliefs). Jung concluded in his eighties, not too long ago, that from his studies of people and their minds and customs, he does not believe that God exists. He knows.

By that, he meant that there are many things about the *sub* or *un* conscious that he has not been able to figure out, and what the unknown is. . . is God, as far as he can figure it out.

BELIEF IS HERESY TO INTELLIGENCE 08/23/69

I've finished reading "Psychic People" by Eleanor Touhey Smith. The stories in this book make me wonder beyond C.G. Jung, about the unconscious and the unknown.

There appears in this world that there are too many people with mental powers and strangenesses to pass up their stories as nothing. There is an unknown something, which seems to elude us as human beings and this is what I am searching for.

Seems as if Religion, in general, is responsible for the bulk of ignorance in this area, among others. Religion puts blinders on the minds of people. It promotes belief, which closes a person's mind. Belief says that there is no room for investigation, which is heresay, in my mind.

GLEN G., MAGICIAN: RIVERSIDE, CA 08/25/69

I met Glen G., who worked at a Standard Brands paint store. He was a magician. Strangely, he takes a person's watch in his hand, and by accident, he says, a four second flushing of his thoughts happens and he gets the brand name of the watch on his mind without even trying to do it.

He doesn't know why, except that he has realized it has been going on for a while unnoticed to him.

C.4 MY DIARY: A DEVELOPING SEARCH FOR GOD

HAUNTED HOUSE: PERRIS, CA 08/25/69

At 8:00 p.m.went to Perris to see a haunted house and some ghosts with Kay Merwin (My wife to be and is now), Jane H. (a super psychic), and Bessie S. (we were all friends).

We found the house, which we read about in the full page story and photos in the Riverside paper. The man who previously lived in the haunted house had moved to Riverside, CA from Perris, CA.

When we told the Mexican man, who came to the door of the house, that we were looking for the house with the ghosts, and showed him the paper and pictures, he became scared, and called to his family to tell them that they were going to move out immediately. Wow! We were sorry that we asked.

REVIVAL MEETING, HELL AND BRIMFIRE PREACHER: PERRIS, CA 08/25/69

This same night, we drove through Perris, looking around because we had come this far from Riverside for almost nothing. We saw a sign pointing to a Revival Meeting. I drove toward the building of this meeting, and we decided to go inside to attend it.

Boy, what a meeting! The Evangelist, Mr. C. was absent because of car troubles. The substitute was quite a powerhouse, especially with only us four besides his own family to talk to from a pulpit.

He went through all the motions of the old southern type of dynamic, forceful, emotional Hell-and-Brim fire type outbursts of belief in God, Jesus, the Devil, Hell, and the Bible.

He made me feel as if I were an uneducated idiot who came to the meeting in order to come under his magic spell. I can see how he could swell the emotions of people who let themselves be blown up with his outbursts of emotion.

He worked real hard for God, he thought, and I believe that he really believed what he said and give him full credit. I can't recall disagreeing with him except where he seemed to slant some of his preaching to the side of prejudice, and the upgrading of the Devil as something, which had power, but I can't say that he was prejudiced from just his preaching alone. I would have to talk to him alone sometime.

176

Seems like he was promoting Satan and Hell more than Jesus Christ. I think I will try to get in touch with him for a conversation. I want to talk to him and his superior, Mr. C. about what they think or believe about evil spirits in this world. Whether they are physically apprehensible, or strictly spiritual, and what proof do they have to offer.

I've got a wild thought. . . Jesus the Christ said to love your enemies, and if he steals from you to give him even more. I'll have to research what Jesus said about loving Satan. . .who is his own adverse enemy. Seems like he said that you cannot have two leaders. . . you must love one and hate the other.

A GHOST IN THE FREEZER: RIVERSIDE, CA   08/27/69

Today, I spoke to Terry H. and found out that he had seen the spirit of a dead person in the store where we both worked, and that this person (John K.) had spoken to him in the ice cream freezer several times.

INSIGHT INTO MIND READING AND
FORTUNE TELLING: RIVERSIDE, CA 08/29/69

At Ed and Anne R.'s house, I saw a bus near Ed's head, within the darkness of my mind, while seeing whatever I could.

Jane H. saw me, "Traveling in three or four days far away like Egypt or Israel."

NOTE: *On 08/20/69 I astrally went to Palestine, as I mentioned above. "I will get a letter from a light-haired woman in a couple of days."*

"I will meet a real psychic man, tall, with light hair, in a couple of days or so. He will amaze me."

Remember the man from 8/25/69? His name is Glen G. of Standard Brands store. . . a magician. He amazed me, just as Jane H. above had told me.

This is the beginning of my realization that many things that an ordinary psychic says for the future tense, is sprinkled with mind reading. I met this psychic man four days before today. Jane was reading my mind, and thought it was the future.

More and more, I do realize, and find proof of the fact that a good portion of Fortune Telling is no more than reading the mind for past experiences and desires. This is innocently done, as I have found, and many of the Fortune Tellers really don't believe that the mind can be read.

Some of them claim that it is a sin against God. . .that it is a violation of privacy, and wouldn't even consider the possibility of mind reading. Therefore, they really believe that they are always reading the future. This is a fallacy.

Sometimes they see future, and sometimes they see what the person has already experienced in his or her mind, and they still present it as future. They don't know how wrong they can be, sometimes.

The more emotion, which went into the person's mind along with the idea, the easier *that idea* can be seen in a psychic's mind.

The subconscious mind is no different from any other mechanical recorder, or movie camera with sound. The conscious mind, which is the aware, directing mind, is like a TV receiver and transmitter, and the subconscious mind is like a movie camera with sound.

The Cosmic Mind, God, is where all these minds reside, because they were made from this Cosmic Mind out of Itself and given a free will as they entered matter.

Remember the above paragraph for later. I am sure it is mind boggling, and needs explanations and proof. It is coming.

DREAM OF DISAPPOINTED GIRL: RIVERSIDE, CA 09/01/69

Had a dream this morning. In it, I flew somewhere with a girl in an airplane and found out that a hurricane was on the way. I decided to take the bus back, instead of flying, and the girl was indignantly disappointed. She wanted to *fly* back.

NOTE: *I know now that this was about my girl friend E. B. at the* *time when we had to go our separate ways.*

MY FRIEND FROM PERSIA: RIVERSIDE CA 09/02/69
(This was before the Shaw of Persia was deposed.)

Today, I went to see Farhang Faradzideh at his apartment in Riverside. He is a medical student here at Riverside City College, and he is from Persia. We talked about his country and religion. His King is a wise and good man, and so is the Queen a wise and good woman.

Their religion is Mohammedanism. The women should cover their whole bodies until they get married and they show themselves only to their husbands.

They believe that their religion was the last one to be placed on earth by God. Their Bible is the Koran. Jesus was not God, but a good man.

How right they are about Jesus. Strange, how our intelligent species keeps making Gods out of people and legends, repeatedly, without taking notice of what they are doing. Seems like our people have a need for a leader, and build legends through wishful thinking, so that a leader will be available for their whims. These leaders are man-made Gods.

Our reaction to the Hollywood Stars is a good example of this. The public wants to adore something, and uses whatever is at hand.

MY URGE TO HEAL: RIVERSIDE, CA 09/05/69

At 10:30 p.m. at Ed and Anne R.'s house, we prayed for Nixon to have the wisest of judgment in all affairs, and to direct us to world peace and brotherly love. We heard a record called *Violet Flame*. It was beautiful and relaxing. I want one someday.

John R. and his wife Rita had their son there, who was hard of hearing and wore a hearing aid; therefore his speech was defective also. He was about nine years old.

In meditation prayer, I saw, all at one time, a white light in a circular shape, thought of the son, and felt a strong urge in both my forearms and hands, and envisioned my left hand on the boy's forehead, my right hand was in back of his head with a tight grip on it. I told Christine about it and she said go ahead. . .do it to the boy, so I did it for about three minutes until I felt loosed from the power. As I held the boy's head, I prayed to God to heal the boy right then and there. Afterwards, I saw no curing effects or results, so I don't know what good it did as of now. The boy was a good boy, too. When I put my hand on the boy's head, everyone smelled spices.

I saw a vision, earlier, of a strap and buckle floating around. I don't know what to make of it, but it looked black, or dark brown. I think it was a symbol showing the loosed blockage of hearing.

MY ASTRAL TRIP: RIVERSIDE, CA 09/05/69

At 2:00 a.m. I tried astral traveling to the house of Pat H. in Corona, CA. My house to her house, 20 miles away. I told her to call me at the store where I worked today, repeatedly, about every five minutes or so. She came into the store with her son! Coincidence? I imagine so.

JOHN THE BAPTIST CUP: CORONA, CA 09/07/69

Yesterday, Dan H., Pat H.'s son, asked if I knew what a certain design or symbol meant to me. He has automatically been using this design for many years, and has no reason for using it. Furthermore, he has no meaning for it. It looked like this:

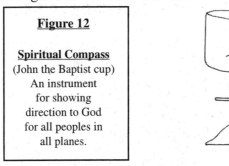

Figure 12

Spiritual Compass
(John the Baptist cup)
An instrument
for showing
direction to God
for all peoples in
all planes.

As I was reading the Bible, dictionary, and a book about religion, I came upon the picture of a compass (drawing instrument). It was drawing a circle, and I at once remembered the symbol. All at once, everything came to me as to what the symbol meant. Was I guided, or just guessing?

My interpretation was: an instrument for showing direction to God for all peoples in all planes.

NOTE: *1998 God is everywhere, always, and a spiritual compass* shows this.

CHRISTIANITY AND CRUCI-FICTION 09/10/69

Did the Jews create Christianity to combat the Spiritualism of Egypt? Out of fear of spirits and ghosts, they might have needed an answer to combat for them against the Egyptians. Seems like Jews and Egyptians are always in a death fight since time began.

Have certain sects of the old Jewish religion invented Christianity as the next step in their mental evolution? The Bible seems to be a futuristic plan developing the use of the belief systems of the public. I see, from the Old Testament, that they were setting us up for Jesus Christ as the Messiah to come. They gave me the sense that they had concrete plans, in the underground sects, to create, in real life, a real Messiah which they had been predicting through the Prophets of old.

Why couldn't they train a selected Son of David to be the predicted Messiah, or Christ? He could 'disappear' out of sight in those years after a Cruci-fiction, *(Mis-spelled intentionally. From all that I have read so far, it appears as if Jesus never died after the crucifixion)* and then they could promote the idea of an Ascension to Heaven, *(which Jesus said was not in the sky, but within your mind)*, therefore He was God.

There were many old religions that promoted these ideas for their Gods. . . so why couldn't the news of The Virgin Birth, Crucifixions, Ascension, Miracles, and many other Christian ideas be used in those pre-Christian eras to describe the old Gods. Also, many quotations of Jesus were said, by someone else, (like Buddha) even before he was supposedly born.

The New Testament and the Old, are filled with illogical statements, which seem to be in code for the elitists of the Religious Right. Looks like there are hidden meanings within the phrases of the Bible.

C.4 MY DIARY: A DEVELOPING SEARCH FOR GOD

Are spirits, voices, and visions etc. figments of our hypnotized imagination? Can the above spirits and voices be connected with the fact of multiple personalities within one individual?

PROOF OF GOD

What proof do we have of God, except that something must have created all this universe? Of course, we have to say that God started the original movement in the universe. How could motion begin without an outside push, *or is motion eternal?*

NOTE 1998*: The mind is invisible and permeates everything. Our individual minds can communicate with each other individual expression of mind, and our individual minds can communicate with the whole mind, **IT**. Our individual minds are separate frequencies of vibration, living within the whole, universal vibration, **IT**. Vibrations are motion, motion is* eternal, *and there never was a Creation.*

PROOF OF SPIRITS

What proof do we have of spirits, except that material things do fly around? This flying hardware seems to be an ability of the human mind and frustrated emotions.

The spirits and ghosts seem to be recorded frequencies in different materials. There are psychics and ordinary people who read these frequencies as if they are movies with and without sound. This is called Poltergeist Activity today.

FUTURE

How do people see the future? This is a real puzzle. How about Psychometry, E.S.P., Psychics? Reasoning can foretell future to a degree, but not to such a definite point as visions and psychic insight.

Seems to me that you cannot see the future unless it already has happened, and we are catching up to it in the sense of Einstein's THEORY OF RELATIVITY. In his theory, if the speed of something is faster than the speed of light, then it might see itself coming before it arrives.

Can you see what I mean? In the case of seeing future, then *our inner sight must be faster than the speed of light*, and *we can see the future before we arrive. This means to me that the future is an arrival point of things happening today on their extended paths.* Our inner sight is definitely faster than the speed of light, and the above premise is justified by this fact.

NOTE 1994: *As I am typing this, I must add that I know that the above is true, because I have seen the future many times, since this diary was noted in 1969.*

This makes the future a projection of the present on its current course. The Theory (Einstein's) implies that there is something about traveling at speeds of rapidity, where you are ahead of yourself, so that you can look back and see what your past is.

How about that for a guess? In this respect, the present is actually the future of the past. Our minds are the real present, and our bodies are the past. Our minds are the real future, and our bodies are the present. Our minds (spirits) are proved to be eternal because they can be in past, present, or future.

The mind is not the brain. Actually, the brain is ours to use. The brain is the translator between our body and spirit, and the mind is for everyone's use. This mind is God. We are living in God.

Therefore, we can be One with God the Father, as Jesus was One with God. Even He said that we could. He said that the Father was in the Kingdom of Heaven, which is within you. The Kingdom is the mind, where you can store up treasures that no one can take away from you.

Actually, our brains are a subjective gadget. They choose constantly anything we wish to choose. The mind is in an eternal ether. . . for lack of a better word (like fish in water). The mind lives in this ether, which is everywhere in the complete, seen and unseen universe. In this respect we can talk to our spirit (mind) world and see what the future will be because it has already happened as a projection of today's values.

Remember: our minds are faster than light, therefore we can see the future as it is projected in time, so that we can see our future coming.

LOVE YOUR ENEMIES?

If God wants us to turn the other cheek to our enemies, then why does He will that we, as sinful enemies of His, must be resurrected to damnation? All sinners are His enemies, and Christ came down to save His enemies, and yet John 5:25-29 said that His enemies will be resurrected to damnation. This is love?

GOOD RULES TO GO BY 09/12/69

(1) Desire no more than what is actually needed
for daily health and comfort.
(2) Look upon all people as equals without favoritism
to any.
(3) Watch and control your thoughts, keeping them
universal. Don't be controlled by emotions.
(4) Each morning, give thanks and appreciation to
every form for services rendered.
(5) Greet the new day with pleasure and enthusiasm
for opportunities to serve the Creator.

SPACE BEINGS IN THE BIBLE? 09/12/69

Genesis 6:2. Sons of God went into earth women. These sons of God must have been from one of God's many mansions; in other words, they were from another planet, or frequency of existence.
Isaiah 60:8. Who are these, that fly, like clouds and like doves, to their windows? (Flying saucers going into mother ship.)
Ezekiel 2:1. And he said to me,. (Must have been a person in that cloud/space ship.)
Exodus 13:21. At night a pillar of fire and by day a pillar of cloud...
NOTE: *Anything coming from above was called God, Angel, or*

Lord, and this God could be seen as fire at night and a solid object in the day time.

2 Kings 2:11. Chariot of fire took Elijah into heaven in a whirlwind. This was an accepted occurrence in those days.

2:16.... they said to Elisha: "the Spirit of the Lord has caught him up," as if it were an ordinary occurrence. What and who were these Lords and whirlwinds?

2 Chronicles 21:12. Ten years later, Elijah came back somewhere else. (Sorry, but I can't find who wrote this translation yet.) I see that in the Bible, Jehoram had received a letter from Elijah, but I can't make out how long ago that Elijah had been taken away in that whirlwind.

Exodus 33:9. Moses talked to space leader who landed near the door of his tent. He called him Lord. Who was this person who could conquer nations, punish sinners, and order thousands of people murdered in order to gain land for the Jews?

Psalm 99:7. The Lord spoke to them in a pillar of cloud.

Luke 9:34,35. A cloud overshadowed them and a voice came from the cloud. A cloud, in the Old Testament, was a flying craft in which people were lifted up and returned.

Acts 1:9. Christ's Ascension, 40 days after the Resurrection. The cloud received him out of their sight. He will come again in like manner.... what was this cloud? Who were these two men, standing there in white robes after the cloud took off? They seem to be the Angels of the Bible. They seem to be space beings, which look like men.

NOTE: *Since the original cloud cover came down in the deluge, the cosmic rays from the sun cut our life span gradually over the ensuing years.*

Genesis 15:5. The word of the Lord came to Abram in a vision and showed him the clear sky.

NOTE: *Mary and Enoch were taken up to the heavens, just like Jesus was.*

Genesis 18:2. Three angels, looking like men, appeared to Abraham, and he called them Lord. How come?

Genesis 13,14. Abraham at 100 years, and Sarah at 90 years, are going to have a baby, and the Lord said: "is anything too hard for the

Lord?" Could these Lords be from the space ships, and genetically changing our destinies?

Hebrews 13:2. Be nice to strangers, because some of them might be Angels. Evidently, the space beings are looking just like us. We can't tell the difference when we meet them face to face. I think the reason that they are shown in pictures with wings on, is to signify that they can lift up into the heavens, which is the sky.

NOTE: *If we all believed in Christ's teachings, we would have heaven on earth right now, but very few people really believe. Many of them just rehearse it to look good, and get along with the others around them.*

John 10:16. I have other sheep that are not of this fold. Zechariah 1:11,12. The angels were sent to patrol the earth. Evidently, we are a watched and manipulated society, and in. . .

Zechariah 1:14, the Lord of hosts says that He is exceedingly jealous. . .

How can God be Jealous? Jealousy is a man's trait, not a perfect God who can do anything at any time with perfect foresight into the future.

This says that the Lord is a human being, not a God, and the Angels appear like humans, also.

I wonder why these jealous Gods didn't want us to live forever? They have placed Cherubims with flaming swords around the Tree of Life to keep us mortal.

READINGS AT ED AND ANNE R.'S HOUSE 09/12/69

A lady saw me next to a pile of lumber with a measuring stick. I don't know what it means. I later rebuilt a shower stall. . .could have been a future insight.

Another lady saw a woman come to me with her head bent and putting one foot in wet cement. (A friend, R.S., had asked me to sign for a loan, today, so she could handle her money better.) What the lady above said, was definitely a mind reading, not a future.

NOTE 1998: *It is difficult to differentiate between past, present, and future; they all look the same in mind, which is eternal, and where all time and everything else is One.*

This woman also saw books in front of me, and someone kept them back from me and placed a stick in front of me every so often, which turned out to be a book (I've been buying and reading many books, lately, and I can't find time enough to read all I want to. Maybe this ties in some how with the lady's vision, but I don't know about the stick part of it).

NOTE 1998: *I feel strongly that the stick was a staff, which refers to the Bible, a book.*

A lady told Liz S. that she saw a scroll for her and it was too heavy to carry. I must ask Liz what she thinks.

(By coincidence, today I was reading Zechariah 5:1 and 6:1. They tell about the meanings of two scrolls. . . 6:1 spoke of an ephah, which is about a bushel of dry measure in weight. . . I wonder.)

FLYING SAUCER NOTES: ZECHARIAH 09/14/69

Zechariah 6:1. Four chariots flying between two mountains. . .

2 Samuel 22:7-16. Flying saucers and God. Picturesque language, but intriguing, also.

Psalms 18:8-15. This appears the same as 2 Samuel 22:7-16, almost word for word.

Psalms 82:6. You are gods. Nevertheless, you shall die like men. Earthly creatures inseminated by the gods from space?

2 John 10:34. I said you are gods. Is this because we have been inseminated by the gods from outer space when they saw that the women of men were fair?

NOTES: *Look up Maori Legend of New Zealan', and Dr. S.K. Maitra, Banaras Hindu University, Calcutta, India. I wrote to him, but my letter was returned.*

HARRY K.: NOTES 09/17/69

Harry K.? Digression Specialist (Pat H.).

C.4 MY DIARY: A DEVELOPING SEARCH FOR GOD

A GOOD PRAYER 09/19/69

I thank you Father God for everything. You have given me everything. I wish, with blessings, that all have plenty, and all misery be erased; not only in my life, but for all mankind.
The above is short, simple, and humble.

LOVE'S INGREDIENTS (PERFECT MAN'S STATURE)

Patience—Love suffereth long
NOTE 1998: *Actually, there is no suffering in true love.*
Kindness—and is kind
Generosity—Love envieth not
Humility—Love vaunteth not itself, is not puffed up
Courtesy—Doth not behave itself unseemly
Unselfishness—Seeketh not it's own
Good Temper—Is not provoked
Guilelessness—Taketh no account of evil
Sincerity—Rejoiceth not in unrighteousness but rejoiceth with the truth

POISONS 09/19/69

I have noticed, since I have stopped consuming alcohol, cigarettes, coffee, and sugar, that when I do take one or more of these after being without them for a spell, that my mind closes tighter and I have a narrower margin to move in, within my train of thought.

I tend to be less relaxed mentally and therefore cannot feel love of everything and everyone so abundantly as I can when these poisons are not inside of me. I am convinced more than ever that these things are poisons for our bodies and our spirits.

A GOOD BOOK TO READ 09/20/69

"The Greatest Thing in the World", by Henry Drummond, $1.00, Fleming H. Revell Co., Westwood, N.J. Read this book; it is a terrific book on love.

MIND READING vs FUTURE 09/22/69

Marilee, at Bessie's, said to set my sights higher.

Lady in Montclair said, from reading coffee grounds: "Good health, letter B means something to me, invest in land; it will bring back good return, going north soon, know someone in the south, good health, set my sights higher *I have been seriously thinking about moving north of San Francisco.*

The two readings above were the readings of my thoughts, and not 'seeing the future' as they had thought. The lady in Montclair did of good job of mind reading, because everything that she claimed that was my future was already in my thought processes in the weeks before I saw her for the reading.

DREAM: MEAT CUTTERS 09/27/69

A dream about meat cutters and me in a butcher room, and the big toe on my right foot starts letting blood flow a steady stream and wouldn't stop (My brother is a meat cutter).

REV. STEPHAN D'S IN LONG BEACH, CA 09/28/69

Went to Reverend D.'s Metaphysics church in Long Beach. There was a self-hypnosis demonstration, offered to those who would participate, which helped them to relax. There were two spirits who talked through Rev. D.

He demonstrated E.S.P. by completely blindfolding himself and reading questions from notes, which people had prepared for him. He gave answers to questions and gave messages from departed souls using their first names for recognition.

He gave healing to the audience by frictioning his hands and asking God to heal those who wanted to be healed by placing their hands in the air facing him. One lady in front of me moaned out loud and nearly collapsed during the healing.

Rev. D. also sent healings to those whom we spoke of out loud. I used my father's name so that the powers would heal him.

C.4 MY DIARY: A DEVELOPING SEARCH FOR GOD

NICE PEOPLE 09/29/69

Just remembered. . . in connection with this subject, a customer, Mrs. Bishop had called me up at the store where I was working (Sage's Market) and praised me so highly for my attitude toward her when she was having a hard time at the store, that she astounded me thoroughly.

I hardly knew her and she said she had made her mind up not to shop at Sage's any more when I came along and helped her (I was night manager at the time) with her problem as if it was nothing and made her feel good about the whole matter.

I couldn't stop her from praising me. She was overwhelmed and so was I, after that phone call. I've been praised before, but this was way beyond the call of duty. I feel that I must be changing for the better and reflecting God in my daily chores. It's just wonderful.

I am beginning to feel like the boy I met on a street corner downtown Riverside about 1:00 AM last year, in 1968:

He was on a corner where the movies and booze bars are located on the main street. He was praising God to the public, passing out literature and never flinched when I put some kindly, but serious doubts before him, trying to affect serious conversation with deep thinking.

Well, this boy, about eighteen to twenty one years old with the most wonderful countenance, bright eyes and enthusiasm never flinched one iota and brought out the most wonderful answers you could imagine. I never forgot him and his spirit and never will.

JUNE B'S BOOKS: MENTONE, CA 09/29/69

I saw a lady named June B., who owned a bookstore in Mentone, CA. She seems to be a very nice person with a wonderful soul. She has had many experiences in healing others with her hands, but not by touch as a rule. She heals from out of body, too. There are many good books in her store.

AUTOMATIC WRITING: JOHN WATSON/PAT H'S 09/30/69

At Pat H.'s house, she was doing automatic writing. This is done by holding a writing instrument in your hand, meditating, and asking a guide to control your hand in the writing process during a conversation with him/her. She was talking with John W., her guide. I asked him several questions:

Q. 1 Are we Gods within ourselves?
A. *You are a part of God and perhaps in eons from now, you will evolve to Godhood and share with the one true God and all of creation.*
Q. 2 Are you the super consciousness of Pat or are you a spirit.... a separate entity and separate soul, independent of Pat through your own free will?
A. *I am John, a part of Pat, as a soulmate. Yes, there is a division made to lower the vibrations so as to take on life as a mortal. Eventually we all rejoin our soul mates and become one Great Spirit Being, eons from now.*

DREAM: FOUND MY WOMAN 09/30/69

Seems like I am in my home, and several women love me and kiss me while I love them all. Then one day a stranger (female), comes to the house and starts fixing and doing things all about the house, spends large amounts of money in the process, and she's very nice all the meanwhile. Towards the end of the dream, she comes toward me while I am lying down and smothers me with wonderful kisses and love.

I thoroughly enjoy it and feel mutually in love with this person very strongly, as if she is mine for life and eternity. After this scene, she tells me that her money has all been spent, and I feel better about it. She said that a guru had told her that I was the one for her as soul mate. This was a dream of the future.

NOTE 03/09/95: *This person is my wife of today, who I married on 11/20/78.*

The last scene before I awoke was in a large building like a hospital. One of the girls who in the beginning loved me very much was crying desperately because I had chosen my mate. I tried my best to console her by hugging her with my left arm, and talking to her as she cried. I think she had reddish hair, and was the slim type of girl, about five feet four inches tall. She was a nurse.

This mate of mine was healthy looking, dirty blond hair, I think. She had blue eyes and was about five feet, five or six inches. Seems like all through the dream everyone had white uniforms and I was lying in a bed on my left side.

I AM CHANGING 10/01/69

My new countenance and understanding seems to be drawing people to me. All kinds of people; employees as well as customers. In a small way, I am noticing this, and it seems as though this will develop more and more as I learn how to help others. Two people approached me today and asked for help. I have not advertised to them or even said a word about helping others in any manner. I believe that it must be my countenance as I said before.

One woman was a customer who has a problem with her marriage and needed advice. We spent one hour talking and I got her mind on God, which I believed would help for a starter. I know her problem now and I'll try to find a good help for solving it soon.

Her husband is the good, home type of man. He wants his wife home and always near him; not out helping others as she does and loves doing. She is a pink lady in a local hospital. She loves to be active and helpful and learning. She feels that sitting at home is a waste of valuable time.

I know of others like her and I know that I used to be like her husband, so I understand the feelings. I just need to be able to help them come together.

They've been married twenty-six years, and it shouldn't dissolve now. I am asking Pat H. to ask *John* for a solid answer in his wonderful way of putting things.

The second person that approached me was a lady barber next door to Sage's where I work. She said that I mentioned something about God and strange things happening when I last got my haircut. She wants to talk to me as soon as I can find the time.

REV. CLARENCE P.: RIVERSIDE, CA 10/03/69

Reverend Clarence P. does not believe in reincarnation, but all other things he does agree with, in the Spiritualism concepts of God, etc. He said that God is Law.

Reverend Linda gave readings for us. She is twenty-four years old from Arizona. She was extremely good all around in giving readings for the folks present.

Here is mine: She sees me reading all kinds of books on religion and studying them all. She said to continue in this direction and be variable in my reading. She said the spirits want me to go ahead and they have a square white door of protection where my head and shoulders are. She just came from Arizona, so how could she possibly know anything about me? She was the same with all others in the room. She astounded me!

NOTE 1995: *Twenty-six years later, as I am computer-writing this from my diaries, I am still reading various types of religious and other books, gleaning them for information which will bring reality to this world of God fantasies*

HYPNOTIZING: CORONA, CA 10/04/69

Tried to hypnotize Pat H. (we practiced on each other), got her under, but not deep enough. She felt very relaxed and comfortable and succumbed to hand on forehead and oriental pressure points. I need a good deepening technique, and something for demonstrating to her that she is really under.

A GOOD QUOTE! 10/05/69

"Silence speaks a million words and a million words express nothing but silence." (I don't know the source).

PAUL TWITCHELL 10/05/69

He seems to say that God is like a void, and that we must set our goals to nothing within ourselves (Tiger's Fang p48), If we desire to know God, we need not study anything whatsoever; we should study only how to avoid seeking for, or clinging to, anything.

NOTE 1998: *I agree completely!*

If nothing is sought, the mind will remain in it's unborn state, and if nothing is clung to, the mind will not go through the process of destruction. What is neither born, nor destroyed, is God.

If you wish to understand the real mystery, you need only to put attachment to anything whatever out of your mind. *(I must try to fall into this void of nothing and experience what he is talking about. Maybe hypnosis will help.)*

Twitchell says the void is the realm of God (p49).

NOTE 1995: *As I am writing this, I concur with the above. I have found, through experience of my own, that the above ideas from Twitchell are sound and true. The void is where we meet God. This is where we enter the realm of God, and communicate.* **I have found that what I call 'One with the Father, is this point in existence, and living in this state of mind, life is a breeze** *(who would need priests and psychiatrists, when being in this state of mind?*

SCHOOL OF CHRISTIAN METAPHYSICS: LONG BEACH, CA 10/05/69

Reverend D. did it again. He amazed me at what he could do with his eyes blindfolded, and communicating with spirits. . . (Could be mind reading, also). He couldn't answer my question about Father Francis (my cousin) either week that I asked (I spoke of Father Francis as being dead when he really wasn't). I later found out that he was still alive.

Tonight, the first spirit talking through him mentioned about gazing or staring at a glass of water and pinpointing your thoughts to the third eye, which is two inches behind the bridge of your nose. It is a gland inside your head.

We must be confident of receiving what we ask for in prayer if we are to receive it. God is power and the power is ours to have. All we need to do is partake of it and know that we can and will have it by asking God for it with confidence of receiving it.

I saw paintings by a Mr. Long of various futuristic (flying saucer) ships and biblical people who were painted by past masters through Mr. Long. . . interesting.

John Watson, Pat's guide, said, "Our over souls and subconscious minds are the same; each one is the other. "

TIGER'S FANG 10/06/69

P52. . . Stop having views and never examine or pursue an argument of God. Neither discuss the problems of others, even when invited to do so.
P55. . .As there is no stream without water, so there is no God outside you.

SAGE'S MKT., DREAM BY LARRY M. 10/09/69

At Sage's market in Riverside, Ca., a box boy named Larry M. had a strong dream. Here is his description:

Twisted dream, small details, not important, ended up killing a girl with a comb. Not just watching himself do it, but actually doing it. Woke up with start.

FATHER FRANCIS IS ALIVE 10/10/69

My mother wrote to me that Father Francis is alive! I must call him up. Pat and I told each other something we had been holding back. We had a good discussion about it! We decided to be platonic friends, only.

JOHN WATSON/PAT H.: CORONA, CA 10/10/69

John, at Pat's house, said: "Yes, Andy, you knew Pat in Egypt. Pat was a high priest. Yes, you were a humble slave. No, a man slave, yes."

C.4 MY DIARY: A DEVELOPING SEARCH FOR GOD

READING THE VIBRATIONS 3:45 AM 10/11/69

The earth going around the sun.... I wonder at what speed it is going around the sun? If it is going fast enough in space, either around the sun or outward from the universal center, then maybe, with Einstein's 'Theory of Relativity', we might be going fast enough to be ahead of ourselves and can see ourselves catching up, or following ourselves and thereby can see future, because we are in the past and future at the same time and in that same theory, we can dig far into our past by reading vibrations which are in space.

NOTE 1998: *If this is true, then God is not directly giving us the visions, but we are reading the vibrations, which is scientifically proven possible. This does not mean there is no God, however. God's power is still with us; we are just learning more about how to understand and use it.*

HEARTH B.: INDIA 10/13/69

The daughter of Hearth B., who is a subject for her mother in hypnosis demonstrations, has an Indian guide called Segmoni, who claims that he is alive now in India and is the rock she sits on, the tree she leans on, or the grass she lays on. She has a compulsion to write, and writes about various things including poetry. She is beginning to be psychic. Her mother is a trans-medium psychic, hypnotist, was born with psychic ability, and Psychometry.

JOHN WATSON: CORONA, CA 10/13/69

At Pat H.'s house, I talked with *John*, the automatic writing spirit.

Will I become a hypnotist?

> *Yes, yes, all it takes on your part is the desire and study and practice and you have a good, honest mind.*

Did I project to the kingdom tonight?

> *Yes, you were in the kingdom tonight and Pat can and will project you until you get on your own spiritual legs. You can help her and she can help you.*

ED AND ANNE R.'S: LIZ S. 10/17/69

Liz S. saw my guide. A beautiful woman with long dark hair, white robe. She was handing me two golden eggs of many riches (spiritual riches); I will be surprised upon that occasion. Liz said that she blends with the aura of the person she reads, and then she is there, in the person's aura. These are not visions or imagination. **NOTE 1998**: *Today, I know now that she was right. One golden egg, was my ability to communicate with God, and the other is my ability to read a person's soul.*

Ed saw an artist painter near me that meant I could paint spiritual pictures and he would help me.

DREAM: COLORED PICTURES IN MY MIND 10/22/69

Had a dream this morning. I was in a plane ready to jump. The searchlight from the plane to the ground made circular motions and I jumped when the target appeared. My parachute didn't open. I landed on my feet in a hunched position. It was dark out. Someone came to help me. I woke up.

Lately, in a waking state, I see colored pictures in my mind upon closing my eyes and letting them happen. These pictures are very interesting, uncontrolled, fully colored, never before seen, and bring on sensations to my being such as fascination, interest, falling, tumbling, moving fast as if flying in a fast plane or as a spirit body because I never see a vehicle; I just see as if from my traveling spirit. I hear no noise, never see people close up. I've seen what looked like hooded and cloaked spirits breezing by me and traveling with me, but no noise or voices.

I travel from time zone to time zone in a flash. I try to analyze what I see, but cannot yet get meanings of the pictures, or feelings of familiarity; everything I see is new and strange; strange machinery, strange lands, strange architectures and structures; even strange colors.

I am not taking medicine or drugs or pills of any kind. I am in a healthy, sane analytical state of mind. I feel that with all these new experiences, that I am smaller and smaller in God's universe and I should be more humble all the time, the smaller I become. I crave for total knowledge and understanding of everything.

JOHN WATSON: WAITING TO REINCARNATE 10/25/69

I asked *John Watson*, "Why did I get visions?"
> *John* said, "Yes, Andy was more receptive for some reason. I will try and find out more."

I asked, "Can we love in excess?"
> *John* said, "Love cannot be in excess, but be sure it is love and not passion or just fondness."

I said, "*John*, please differentiate between love and fondness."
> *John* said, "Love knows no limits, and fondness is an underexpression of love."

I said, "*John*, are you a spirit of Pat, living in the future, and watching us catch up?"
> *John* said, "Andy, I'm waiting to reincarnate. I will probably come down as one of Pat's grandchildren."

I asked, "How will Pat know who you are for sure?"
> *John* said, "She will know."

I said, "Please let Pat know for sure what your plans are, just before you reincarnate."
> *John* said, "I will try."

JOHN WATSON: SOUL PROJECTING 10/27/69

John said, "Yes, Andy was soul projecting."   Pat said, "How do you know he was projecting?" *John* said, "His invisible body went out. . .another plane of existence."

I AM FROM ANOTHER PLANET: PAT'S MOTHER 10/27/69

The first time we met she said, after we meditated together, that she got the impression that I was from another planet. She's the third separate individual claiming this. Why?

LOUD VOICE IN MY HEAD: ALL RIGHT 10/28/69

I went to sleep for five minutes, concentrating beforehand on waking up in five minutes. A voice, clear, sharp and loud in my head, said, "All right", woke me up in the five minutes I had thought of beforehand. The voice sounded like a heavy female voice somewhat like my mother's, but lower pitched and sharper toned. Can't say for sure if I had heard a voice in my past like that, but I don't remember any other instance.

LIZ'S HOME: MY DEAD GRANDMOTHER 11/01/69

Visited the S.'s in Riverside, California. Liz went into trance and had my grandmother beginning to speak through her when she (Liz) asked us for help because she was choking.

My grandmother had died of a stroke in the throat, and I had not given Liz the information. She couldn't have known about it, but in trance she told me about it. She said my grandmother was saying either Anna Mariet or Ave Maria. Did Liz pick my grandmother out of my mind, or was she entering my grandmother's mind?

MESSAGE FROM JOHN WATSON 11/02/69

"Yes, Andy, you are from Venus. By choice, your life should now join the direction of help for the new age."

DREAM: FIRE AND SMOKE 11/06/69

Can't remember all of it. I was outside of a house. It was burning. It was kind of dark outside. No one was putting out the fire. I wondered why. I went into the house after that thought, and the fire was out already, just smoke left, and I was surprised.

C.4 MY DIARY: A DEVELOPING SEARCH FOR GOD

MY EYES HEALED, THOUGHTS ON HEALING 11/10/69

My sight has been restored (about eighty percent), and I expect the other twenty percent to be restored in a little while. I don't need glasses starting today.

Since Pat has started healing my eyes, I've had a dry powdery feeling in them as if they were being polished or ground down (a stigmatism is what I have), and today, when I took off my glasses on the way to work, everything was clear as a bell.

I sure was surprised and happy. Tears poured all around my eyeballs like a flood washing away all this dry powdery feeling or material away, so that my eyes felt even better and more comfortable. I thanked God and told Pat so that she could thank God, also.

THOUGHTS ON HEALING

The receiver of the gift must believe completely with His whole being that he is one with God and is being healed because of that fact. He must blend with God and bathe in all His powers, taking on all the goodness he can absorb. This power of God, which we have access to, is actually *our* power too.

All we need to do is accept this power unto ourselves because we are God, also. We are an extension of God's being and do God's work in the universe and therefore we are Gods. His powers are our powers, if we only accept and love God with our whole being.

JOHN SPEAKING, AND NORMA, TOO 12/02/69

John, Pat H.'s automatic writing guide said, "Yes, Andy, I can smell and taste and express my feelings just as you do, but there is no illness."

"Yes, Andy, I died of a heart attack and it was rapid. I immediately left my body and the cord was severed and I was free."

"I believe I was very startled, and didn't understand I was dead, as I felt more alive than when I was alive. I was met by familiar souls and taken to a place of beauty to rest and reorganize my thinking."

"I am Norma, your guide. You could write too, Andy, try more often, as you need help." *(This was a guide that I was told of in the past; she cut in while John was talking.)*

CONSCIOUSNESS 12/18/69

When we are awake, we are so-called conscious. When we are asleep we have dreams, but we are so-called unconscious. If we are unconscious when we are asleep, then who is putting our dream together and playing it out?

I feel that we have a waking consciousness and a sleeping or trance consciousness. It appears as if our trance or sleeping conscious-ness has tremendous knowledge.

Where and how does it get this knowledge? Is this knowledge readily available from our own collective unconscious? Do you suppose that if we learn how to use our collective unconscious we will have free access to almost unlimited supplies of stored up knowledge from our own experiences and our ancestors' and also from our inheritance, God?

So far, it appears that the way to tap the storehouse of knowledge is to go into a trance or hypnotic state. To do this we must be careful to use proper controls of our faculties. We mustn't let things go haywire. We only have one brain to work with, so you must be careful to keep it healthy. How can we go into trance safely? This I must look into.

When a Medium is in deep trance, he usually can't remember what he did or thought while in that state of mind, just like a dream. . . he can remember some of it sometimes. What is the difference between a trance state and a dream state?

We must become more sensitive or aware of everything at all times. To become more sensitive and aware we must sharpen our senses. How do we sharpen our senses? Vitamins, minerals, proper sleep and eating habits, tuning in more sharply, exercising our reflexes, meditation.

C.4 MY DIARY: A DEVELOPING SEARCH FOR GOD

GOOD AND BAD HAVE ABILITIES 12/22/69

Seems as though the powers, which are available to us, are a physical and mental ability that is ours for the using. Whether we are with or against God.

Good, bad, and indifferent people; we have these gifts, so they must be available to all of us no matter where we stand in society or spirituality.

REFER TO TWIRLING PENCIL 08/19/69 ABOVE 12/22/69

Found out what this pencil means in my symbol book: "A man who fills himself with meat (knowledge and higher emotion) is filled with the good spirit."

Just read MAN WITHOUT WOMAN in my symbol book, and it sure is convincing about man needing a woman partner, or he is dead, just as if positive or negative were alone. . . there would be no life (love); which is what we are here to learn about in the first place.

DREAM: E. B. 01/08/70

Saw E. B., (a girlfriend). She was headless. Her head had been whipped off by an accident. My ex wife was there, examining the lower half of the body. E.B.'s head came to me and smiled.

DREAM INTERPRETATION 01/09/70

This is what one interpretation of the dream above was. Her better qualities have risen to notice me, by separating her lower self from her higher self.

PAT H.'S HEAD GLOWS 01/11/70

Saw a white glow one half inch thick around Pat's head and three to four inch golden flow outside of it under an amber light. I tried a red light and got nothing in comparison to the amber. I saw a glow under the red light, with relaxed feeling, light breathing, empty stomach, glasses on, and eyes open.

A MAN NAMED BILL 01/20/70

He claims that he soul travels all the time. He is a very gentle and benevolent type person, looks like a fighter, but isn't. He claims to have been to Hell several times as his over-soul wanted to show him what it was like. Hell was complete nothingness.

This person lives in Pomona, CA. He leaves his body rapidly upon lying down, has traveled to other planets. I met him at Linda and Louie's house, in Corona, CA. He's been to jail for doing something wrong, and came out better spiritually for it. He learned to soul travel while he was confined. His motto is be gentle.

DEMONS AND DEVILS 01/24/70

This is a note by me to a couple of friends.

"Please understand me about my feelings concerning demons, devils, evil spirits, etc. By not recognizing them or accepting them, I, as a lowly being, am surrounding myself with the best protection I know.

The evils, demons, devils, can enter my body only through my mind. They can only communicate with me through my mind. If my mind has no openings for them, they cannot come into my body. My mind is the gateway to my body.

In the same sense, God, angels, and people cannot come to me except through my mind, and if my mind will accept them, then, and only then, can they take over in my physical being.

I can tune in to whatever forces I wish. It is up to me, and only me. I have free will and choice. I am responsible for my own destiny. I have an open mind for good, and love, but not for evil and hate.

I will absorb all the Christ Consciousness I can, because that is what I wish for me to be. I love God, you two, and everyone. I love the devil, the demons, and the evildoers.

I pray for all of us, good and bad, that we will all progress rapidly to Christ Consciousness and to Godhood. Through love, I can abolish all evil from me. When we cast out devils, we do it with love and in the name of Jesus Christ. Well, I have love, I am reaching for more, and I am living to the best of my ability in the name of Jesus Christ and in his consciousness and trying for more.

Fear, like Lobsang Rampa said, is our worst enemy, therefore I refuse to accept fear either, in the same sense as I refuse to accept or acknowledge evil, devils, and demons.

God is the symbol of love in my world, and He created everything with love. Therefore I love everything He created, whether it has fallen away from Him or not. I must pray for all those who are away from God, no matter what their titles are (evil-doers, demons, devils, etc.), and I must love them because they were created by God.

I must respect each person's free will and choice, and try to have loving indifference toward them. I choose the food for my development to whatever my goals are, and I must, through love, let all others choose their food for development toward their goals. The only way I can influence others is to become what I think is right. This is by prayer, and living example."

DREAM: E.B. 01/24/70

E.B., (a friend) was living with Steve (her son) and me.

DREAM: MY BROTHER BOB 01/26/70

I drove Bob (my brother) and me on a long trip in my car.

GROUP IMAGINATION 01/29/70

What about chain reaction in group imaginations? What about the suggestive possibilities between Clara and Liz at Ed and Anne's about me in the space ship from God? How about the groups at Linda and Louie's? How about Flying Saucer reports? Same thoughts? Suggested thoughts?

JOHN WATSON: DEVILS AND DEMONS 01/30/70

Dear Andy,

We received your letter and thank you. However we understand how you feel about God and the evil ones. Pat and Dan's concern and upset was the way you asked any evil ones to show themselves and believe me that is a challenge if we ever heard one, even if you don't believe in them.

If you want to see them show themselves, go to a black magic place, not at Pat's home. That is what the upset was about.... not your belief in God and Christ.

No sleep was lost, just concern for your challenge for evil to come forth and show itself, as they love nothing better. So forget it Andy, they both have released it with loving indifference and asked God to protect you in the future. It is wholly and totally unwise to challenge invisible forces. So God bless you Andy and may you find soon what you are seeking with the knowing that true knowledge is power.

God be with you forevermore. Pat, John and Dan.

NOTE 1995: *I have no belief in evil and give it no power. I was demonstrating this to Pat and Dan.*

MY FIRST PSYCHOMETRY AT ED AND ANNE'S 1/30/70

I just remembered that my first Psychometry with proof happened with Bill B. We were sitting outdoors at R.'s home one warm summer night when he placed a card from his wallet into my hand and asked me to read it. I could not and did not want to see it, because I wanted to test myself. Well, with my eyes closed, I saw a ship on the ocean waters going by me while I was standing on a beach with tall sea grass growing on it.

I told Bill what I saw, and he told me that what I had in my hand was his Merchant Seaman card from World War Two. This was great for me; it gave me assurance that something was really happening in my development process of mind.

The following is what I saw in my mind-pictures, as I was sitting in the darkened night. I saw Bill B. (his wife is Alice) looking through (as if inside) eyes of a big Buddha on top of a green hill. In front of him, downwards through the green, bushy area on a road, people and carts and animals were heading away from him, slowly, naturally.

I saw for Alice B., a girl in the distance in a wedding or white chiffon gown, and then some brilliant green gems and clear gems hanging as vertical strings together as if they were a headboard on a bed.

For John, Rita's husband, a tool kit and then a beautiful leopard, climbing onto kitchen tables and then gnashing of teeth, and I sensed the working of leather.

DREAM: MY UNCLE PETE RAU (Henry J. Rau, Jr.) 02/01/70

My uncle Pete was at his corner store, choosing the best salt for winning a contest, then he and I were sitting near a car talking about my grandmother (his mother), receiving calls to be answered from the spirit world.

I was a substitute produce man in his store (I worked in his store in 1942 behind the soda fountain and candy counter. Only in dreams can all this strange goulash happen).

SUPERCONSCIOUS QUESTIONS 02/03/70

I asked Super Consciousness (God) four questions as a means to speak to God.

Should I go back to Theresa (my ex-wife)?
Blackbirds, darkness.
Should I marry E.B.?
Hard struggle, rough, many storms
Should I live alone?
Skeletons, dark, lonely.

PREDICTIONS 02/07/70

Australia having trouble with Negroes or natives. Yellow blimp, whale or goldfish behind bars (The Beatles?)

THOUGHTS ABOUT GOD 02/08/70

Suppose our God consciousness is, as a group, God Himself, and individually we are Gods, but only a part of the complete God, not the complete God?

Then again, it seems more logical that everything that is, is God when we look at it in group form or totality.

Look at your body as if it were God. Your body is the same as God in totality, but actually, you are billions and billions of moving human parts, moving according to your strongest desires (which is the same as God's will), but these moving parts do have a will of their own, living within the laws that govern them.

GIVE BEFORE RECEIVING 02/22/70

Just as the giving of blessings, grace, or thanks before meals, when there is a want, then give before you get.

PRAYER AND FASTING = ATTENTION + SERVICE
02/27/70

Reach into yourself with expectation and belief to summon what is there, waiting to be used. Then accept as an obligation the effort necessary to produce results.

Our Father Who art in Heaven.
The Kingdom of Heaven is within.
Ye are Gods.
Ye will do better works than I.
Ye must have faith and believe.
I, and the Father are one.
Love God with all your heart, mind, soul, and strength.
God is within us, and His powers to use if we will only believe Him to be there.

DAVID SEABURY, GOOD AUTHOR 02/28/70

Draw cosmic (God) power by imagination and inspiration; make effective use of it by reason and judgment.

C.4 MY DIARY: A DEVELOPING SEARCH FOR GOD

Persecution: Simply thinking that we are such lovely creatures that no one must ever say an unkind thing to us.

Frustration: Believing that the world is not giving us fair play, because we should be presented with every kind of opportunity.

Inferiority: Concern for our position, whether we have as fine a mind or as fast a car as someone else has.

Superiority: We are claiming power to ourselves.

The Will: Absolutely and utterly obeys subconscious mental imagery.

The birds chirp and sing for they feel like singing and thereby, others enjoy their good feeling being displayed.

God can't make two hills without a valley between.

ALICE B.: X-RAY VISION 05/08/70

She sees through bodies at times like an xray. She sees intestines and the various parts of the body. In a store, for example, she sees a whirlwind and feels like she is caught up in it and then from this uplifting feeling, she sees through people.

Very similar to Eileen Garrett, The famous English Medium. She also has a voice speaking to her.

Rita C. goes into trance and tremendous wisdom from other worlds comes from her mouth in a whisper voice. She is referred to as the White Light in this trance state. Out of trance she is a very sweet, calm, patient person; so is Alice B.

E.S.P. IN LONG BEACH 05/10/70

Reverend D., at his church in Long Beach, told me in the E.S.P. part of service, that I will be traveling all over the earth, speaking to many Peoples, and they will hold great respect for my words, which carried much weight.

REGRESSION FOR ME: SPANISH 05/11/70

At a session in Redlands, California, with Dr. Fred A. and his group of interested parties in the search for spiritual insights, I was regressed (brought to the past in my mind, in a very relaxed state of mind).

I saw two angels in a spirit type of room with me. I didn't see myself, but felt that I was there.

I was watching a long pattern of cotton batten go upward. It had a sprinkling of gold on it. I can't explain this, except that the cotton pattern seems like a scroll unrolling upward, and the gold was probably a good message on the scroll.

NOTE 1998: *This appears to say that I was going to give out with important spiritual knowledge in the future.*

The two angels had no sex apparent, and were tall, good looking, and blond, wore golden slick material in the form of long gowns.

I saw a Spanish town, a pair of male legs in dungarees and rough type of brown shoes, sitting on old adobe cement stairs on the side of an old adobe cement type building, which was surrounded by sand.

This area was desert, and the person with the dungarees and brown shoes was me. Ron Rodriguez is the name I associated with these legs and myself in this regression. I was a Spanish youth.

NOTE 1998: *I realize now that this was a regression.*

PSYCHOMETRY, AND THOUGHT CONTROL 05/26/70

•Psychometry is working fine for me. Perfect relaxation and a little darkness are the best surroundings.

•There is a neutral power that exists everywhere, and this can be put into action by thought.

•My thoughts control all the cells of my body. All cells communicate with each other by their being directed by outside force (the law of my being, or subconscious mind, or soul).

•Seems like the cells are Soldiers, the mind is the General, and the awareness is the President (the awareness is us; our personality; the real self; the controller; the decision maker; the Spirit.)

•The cell power is neutral, and can be activated by positive or negative thought, which makes linear energy out of neutral energy. In the above manner of control, we are Gods within ourselves, controlling our bodies and minds with our thoughts (our laws).

•Our imaginations can lead us into health or sickness by our

containing either good thought or bad thoughts.
•Emotion is the power behind the force of thought to control cells.

REGRESSION FOR ME: AMERICAN INDIAN GIRL
05/26/70

Here is what happened when I went into a past life on my couch: In Ohio in 1792, I was a seven year old Iroquois Indian girl, had woven straw thongs, long black straight hair to the middle of my back, a band on the hair around my head, made of woven straw. My name was Mooséne.

When I was twelve years old, Dick S. was an Indian medicine man, sitting opposite me across a fire, which was outdoors enclosed in a ring of stones. He had a roll of fat around his waist. His name was Chekawa. We were eating whole kernel corn for breakfast, on this hillside.

About seven Indians were coming into camp on their horses, from the crest of the hill above us. They were wearing beautiful headdresses of large eagle feathers with bright white and other bright colors.

Each had a squaw walking beside him. There were tall pine trees all around.

At seventeen years of age, I was watching brown and white cattle in a pasture. My hair was shorter, and came to rest on my shoulders instead of my back. I was wearing a brown leather dress tied in the waist with leather strips like a belt, a collar flap of same material about twelve inches laid down across my shoulder blades. My shoes were brown, laced, leather moccasins.

At twenty-two years, I was looking at the remains of a shelter, which must have been mine and had burned completely to nothing. There was no foundation left or any sign of shape. The area was burnt also.

There was a large patch around this shelter, which had been cut; birch trees with two-foot stumps (seems like they had been sawed); tall pine trees all around. The sky was overcast, and cloudy.

Saw a funeral; a woven straw canoe just large enough for my body on the water.

SPIRIT COLOR 05/26/70

I asked God for my spirit color, and this is what I was given. Out of a bright, white light, came a shower of rainbow colors.

Figure 13

A super white flash of light appeared with multi-colored rays radiating from the center.

This was my spirit within the body that I use for earth living.

LOOKING AT MY BODY 05/26/70

This is what I saw, while in meditation, when I asked to see the real me.

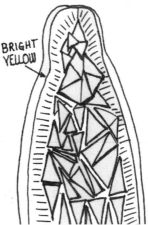

Figure 14

The real me looked like a brightly lit pocket of diamonds radiating pure white light outward from the center, and a golden halo (aura) on the outside borders. It was a beautiful sight.

BRIGHT YELLOW

HEALING: MY TOE 05/27/70

While I was talking into the reflection of my eyes in a mirror, I had asked for my toe to heal while I was sleeping, and the next day it was healed. I had sharp pains under the toenail for two months before this.

C.4 MY DIARY: A DEVELOPING SEARCH FOR GOD

TRANCE MEDIUM: JANET 05/27/70

This is what a trance medium, named Janet, had told me. "I see an earthquake, flood, many people dying." She used about twelve entities for information, which seemed to bring valid information.

She said that I should call my son. She was right. She doesn't remember events except the ones in which she was herself, not other entities. What came through her, she did not remember.

DREAM: KNEE CAP 05-31-70

This morning I dreamed of getting a medical shot right into the area below the kneecap on my right leg. Last night I saw a TV show which gave shots for the flu.

DREAM: WAR 06/01/70

Congress declared war.

DREAM: THIRD EYE 06/02/70

A Third Eye opening. Two days ago, a woman told me that she was told that her Third Eye was wide open.

PSYCHOMETRY: BARBARA'S CROSS 06/02/70

This was a Psychometry of a Cross, which a girl named Barbara gave to me to read. This is what I saw:
> •A woman with a beaded cap, blonde hair, dark glasses.
> •A large lake, dark blue water, homes on left side of the lake, looks like European type structure, possibly German, Dutch, Scandinavian, and a yellow bank on the other side of the lake with green grass. This lake could also be open like an inlet from the ocean.
> •Horn rimmed glasses, a wooden bucket full of white

stuff.

•Scarecrow on top of a brick building. Near a clock? Or tower?

NOTE 1998: *This reminds me of the movie Back to the Future.*
•*Horse drawn like this.*

> **Figure 15**
>
> The horse was like the picture here, and it looked like the horses on the inside of ancient caves in France. I wish I had traced these things that I saw, but I didn't think of it at the time.

DREAM: MY WEIGHT/FUTURE 06/03/70

Lose weight.

NOTE 1998: *See 06/07/70, below, where Rev. B. said that I have a weight holding me back. This confirms this dream of the future.*

DREAM: PARTY 06/04/70

A party in a large house. No one special was there, and nothing special happened. Tonight I am having three men over here for discussions. Might lead to thinking in terms of a party.

REVEREND B.: A WEIGHT TO LOSE 06/07/70

Reverend B. of Long Beach said that I have a weight holding me back from climbing the hill as fast as I would like to, and to get rid of this weight.

MY THOUGHTS: 06/07/70

For every light there is a shadow.
Face the light and the shadow will be behind you.

C.4 MY DIARY: A DEVELOPING SEARCH FOR GOD

I Psychometrized Pat's Cigarette Butt.

Bulls on walls inscribed in tomb tunnel with two Egyptian boats (*caskets*) across two long beams. *(This tied in beautifully with what Liz got this afternoon, and with what the symbol book told of these things.)*

I Did A Cigarette Lighter Psychometry for Liz S.

Water wheel like near a cider mill with strings of wild red roses hanging around it. A fresh-water fish like pickerel or trout and a square tile with small stones in it, about 12"X12".

Are visions the power of the mind, of the receiver or the sender? They seem to be neither because they are not willed, they just   happen unexpectedly.

<u>THOU SHALT NOT KILL 06/10/70</u>

'Don't eat meat'. Jesus ate fish and caught fish (he killed them). Lord God killed people in the Old Testament.

If we must turn the other cheek, and not kill, then how can God kill us with flood or fire as the Bible says? There is a mixed deal here.

A misunderstanding is evident, or if not, then I don't believe the story is true about God in the Bible (see the last part of 06/11/70).

<u>CARBON DATING 06/11/70</u>

Carbon 14 Dating methods are accurate up to 400 years from after the flood to now. They are not accurate before that, in time, according to Carlous F. Mason and associates, who have advanced a plausible theory of a belt of solid water encompassing earth as a complete filter for outside forces of Sun etc., coming into earth, giving us this longevity of life and tropical paradise type of living with no seasons, and no storms or disturbances.

At night the moisture would rise up and form a mild, light mist and at day break this mist would evaporate or settle to keep life fresh and clean.

The flood was the letting down of this covering of water over a period of 40 days, freezing the mammoths instantly as they were

214

eating with food on their tongues and no time to swallow.

We lost the even temperatures at once and got our cold and hot climates instantaneously because the filter we had was broken and the beasts are large, four footed animals according to the dictionary, so fish and fowl seem to be exempted from Jesus' teaching against killing. Also, He talked of blood taken in and being death to the body. Fish and fowl have very little blood and their meat (especially fish) is white.

EMOTIONAL SICKNESS 06/12/70

All emotional problems are the result of the conflict between our pretenses and reality. Be simple, decent, and honest.

PAT AND JOHN: EATING MEAT, THE FLOOD 06/17/70

Below is a letter from Pat.
Dear Andy,

I'm putting this on notepaper for you to keep if you so desire. I will add that the Law of Life book gives an interesting account on eating meat.

When an animal is killed the flesh registers fear and that is absorbed into the emotional body (physical) of those eating it. The reasons for not eating meat and using serums should be apparent. So this would be taking on vibrations of animal fear.

Below is a letter from *John*.
Hello Andy,

I will do my best to answer your questions, however they are truly unimportant as who would believe it?
How did the deluge happen physically?
My answer is: God caused it to happen to eliminate bad vibrations being made by man in his ignorance and imperfections; actually the bad vibrations throw the natural balance out of nature. So actually the word physical has no meaning in a ques-

215

tion like this as it was done mentally by man himself.

Where did the waters come from?

At that time there was a heavy protective mist around the world to protect it, and for many reasons. This apparently was broken loose and came down as heavy rain and a great portion of the world was already water so it covered most of the globe, however others besides Noah were saved in different parts of the world.

How were mammoth beasts frozen instantly while still chewing food?

It happened so suddenly that it took the animals by complete surprise.

What happened in nature to cause us to lose our life span from 700 years to 70 years since the flood?

It isn't nature so much as it is man's nature. The protective film now gone has much to do with this, but also man has accepted to live shorter life spans in ignorance and refusal to live according to Divine Laws. There is so much to this question Andy, and man was aware of who he was when he lived for hundreds of years.

Now he refused to understand or believe so he spends most of his time here creating bad karma instead of serving God and the Divine laws.

Why and how did this wooden ship (the Ark) get on top of Mt. Ararat?

With the earth covered with water it would be a simple matter. It had to lodge somewhere when the waters resided.

Andy I don't know if this satisfies your questioning, but study the few Divine Laws and you can arrive at your own answers rapidly. Your friend John.

CAUSED BY GOD SOUNDS WRONG 06/17/70

The thought occurred to me today that in the old days anything that was, or happened, that was not understood, was given as caused by God intentionally. As science and communications progressed, less was accredited or blamed on God, and more was explained as natural phenomena. The same thing applies today in the realm of spirits and psychic phenomena.

Whatever is unknown is applied to God as the cause. Actually, it appears as if this God is a neutral power and we are the Gods of the world, either using this power for good or evil, according to our will. God's laws are always and standard.

We are beings (spirits) created by Him, and all that we do are actions of His, in a sense, because He is this whole thing, and we are the expressions of it. Our minds are fantastic things. It appears as if our minds have no limits as to capabilities, and by knowing God's laws, we can survive beautifully, or suffer according to our own choice.

DREAM: RAZOR BLADE FIGHT 07/16/70

A young boy tried to cut me up with a razor blade and we had a duel with razor blades. It became a psychological duel with plenty of fright and conversation. We ended up friends and made a date to see each other again like father and son. When we face our problems, we become friends with them.

Later, while dreaming, Robert Young, the actor, was looking for a tool and found that his son had most of them upstairs fixing something.

HAZEL D.: MY FIRST PROFESSIONAL REGRESSION 07/20/70

At Hazel D.'s home in Riverside, she proceeded to regress my mind toward the past, as I was reclined on a couch. I saw a mask, which had two holes for eyes, and three horizontal slits for mouths. It was gold, and it caused me to have an Aztec impression.

C.4 MY DIARY: A DEVELOPING SEARCH FOR GOD

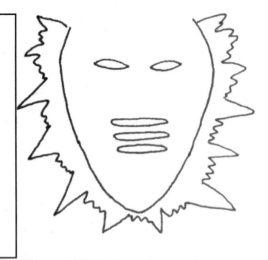

Figure 16

This mask was coated with pure, bright and shiny gold.

The burst lines around the drawing depict the brightness of the shining gold.

This mask must have been used in solemn, sacred ceremonies.

Then a cave or stone building (inside), dark, about four to six people in there this looked like a meeting of sorts and I don't know the meaning of it, and at the far end was an orange-red glow like a fire place color from fires. Above the fire place was a gold Sun-God plaque:

Figure 17

This shows a Sun God Plaque, which was on the altar of sacrifice above the fires burning below, and the people in the cave were appealing to the Sun God for the safety of their people. The feelings of these people were intense.

This is inside of a large cave entrance.

This reminds me of my business trademark which I've had for about six years; it was a smiley face, but the face above was not smiling.

Just before we were in the cave or building where the fire place was, there was a dark area like a street at night, or a hallway inside a building or cave with one hundred pound bags of grain or something like it stacked along the wall.

218

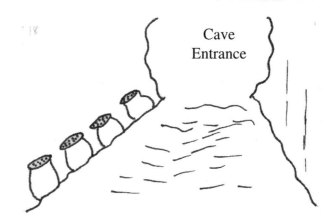

Cave Entrance

Figure 18

There was a dark area like a street at night, or hallway inside a building or cave with one hundred-pound bags of grain or something like it stacked along the wall.

Next, I was standing on a cliff, looking at a square, black hole at the bottom, about a half-mile down. Mysteriously, I sensed that I was to jump into this hole (probably full of water) to be sacrificed and become One with the Great Spirit for the comfort and safety of my people. Here is the scene.

I had a chief's headdress on, my arms were folded, and I had a leather skirt from my waist to about six inches above the knees.

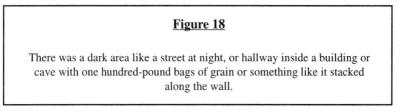

Figure 19

I was an Indian Chief who was about to sacrifice my life for the sake of my people by jumping off this high cliff into the pool of water below.

Then I saw an Indian runner with a lighted torch on the other side of the chasm. Above him was Christ on the Cross in the air.

C.4 MY DIARY: A DEVELOPING SEARCH FOR GOD

While I was standing on the cliff's edge about to jump, my emotions were strong in the sense of power and determination with love.

My name was Kone Ge Wa.

(Hazel D. eventually became the President of the Para Psychological Association of Riverside, California, and wrote books about her experiences.)

BOB B.: THREE MONTHS TO LIVE 07/24/70

Given three months to live from one month ago because of lung cancer, a US doctor said there is no hope at all. Bob went to Tijuana, Mexico at the cancer hospital and took their diet and fifteen treatments.

He developed a hole in his lung. US doctors blamed cobalt treatments from other U.S. doctors as the cause for the burn, which caused a hole to form.

Bob had an operation at St. Bernardine's Hospital in San Bernardino, CA on 7/21/70. A stomach tube is in his belly to be fed with baby food. His neck on the right side has a tube from his lung (I think), sticking out.

On the morning of 7/21, I was thinking about calling June B. (a psychic) to perform etheric (psychic) surgery by her five doctors in spirit. At that same time Bob was having a dream that his body was being separated, the bad parts thrown out and replaced with good parts. That afternoon I called June and she said she would do whatever could be done according to the will of God.

7/23/70 I saw Bob and asked Edna (his wife) the latest news. Bob had been dreaming all the last day and a half that he was presented with many good foods, which he ate and enjoyed. He had real good steaks among other things.

I called June yesterday (7/22) and told her the situation. She said the five doctors would be helping until he got well with whatever they could do. She said to tell Bob to continue to eat this food he dreams of. I had already told Bob this the day before.

220

As far as I can make out, if nothing else, the psychological reaction will be good for his body healing process. Bob doesn't know about June B. or the fact that I had called her. I told Edna about it yesterday, 7/23, and maybe Bob knows it by now. He's so sleepy and groggy though, I feel that Edna might not tell him yet.

DREAM: MY BROTHER RICHARD 08/22/70

Dreamed that my brother Richard was in trouble in the ocean water. . . a submarine.

MEDITATION: FUNERAL 08/23/70

I imagined in meditation the funeral of someone that I know. I tried to find out who, and got Richard (my brother) again. Several times now, I get Richard in trouble. I must be subconsciously worried about him.

DREAM: RUTH KENNEDY 08/24/70

Woke up with Ruth Kennedy on my mind; don't know who she is. Maybe Rose Kennedy was the right name because I was thinking about Washington.

DREAM: GOBE DESERT 09/06/70

The Gobe Desert. Quail-shaped birds finding less bugs to eat because of disappearing ocean. Soviet square building on Desert; about a dozen men and women working on officers' procurement billings. People, or spirits appearing and disappearing in surroundings, playing silly tricks on Soviet personnel.

TRANCE-VISION: DEFRIEDAS IS ME 09/28/70

In bed one morning, I had a wide awake vision. A stone wall

with a cross in the center of it. The wall was in flames, had stone arches and there were stone buildings on fire behind the flaming wall. There were walkways of stone twenty feet in the air above the stone streets, where there was brutal fighting between Spartans and Trojans; an army of multitudes with metal hats and spears, and blueish-shiny shields with faces on them. My name was Defriedas.

I wore a white mini-skirt with brown or gold mandala design all around the hem, leather thongs with straps between the big and next toes, coming up around the ankles. I was a Spartan soldier with hairy legs, getting ready to go to battle. I had a leather shield.

LETTER FROM PAT/JOHN: TOUCHING GOD 11/18/70

Dear Andy,

I am so sincerely happy that all you desired was given to you. God love you.

I'm glad you're back on the track again; this is truly a lone path as no one can do it for us, and we do have to be careful to let no one side track us.

I keep meeting and talking to different ones and I love every minute of channeling. I can't see yet, but I know, and that is so wonderful, I wish I could talk to the whole world.

Andy; reach down and touch your arm. You've just touched God! God is all and in all. Don't try to define Him as you will confine Him. Each has to realize this for himself, and all we can do is pray for that day.

I'm reading more and more, and the better it gets. The job gets shorter, but I am doing great as I no longer worry, as I know I'm watched over so very perfectly.

I've done some group regressions only to help people know reincarnation is true. People are weak and need proof and this does it.

If everyone could be regressed it would take the aggression out of them and peace would come quickly! Of course that's not the answer, but it could be of great help.

There's a college professor that can teach the regression technique in four hours and he offered to go any where in the world and teach it!

I'm pleased for your accuracy in Psychometry. I'm glad you are meditating as the Kingdom is truly within.

I went to the Church of Religious Science Monday night, and it was for the healing service. I submitted my Dad's name and my oldest son. I had to rush him (Pat's son Bert) to the hospital about two weeks ago as he had blood poisoning and it had gone into his body. One more day and the Doctors said he would have died or lost his hand.

God got in contact with me and it was all perfect as he (Bert) told me he loved me very much and the part of his not wanting to see me is over! Bert had much help by June and her doctors and I went every day and helped. He could feel the glorious power.

Please read Fate, December issue, "*I Found Life Beyond Death.*" It's very, very good. I've suddenly been guided to books of life on the other side and it's now become clear to me. We can go only to the plane of our vibrations. If they are low, we remain low until we raise them. So the lower entities can't go into the higher realms until their vibrations are raised!

I will close now, except I will say that there are two books that would answer your questions, called, The Going and the Glory, and Space People:

C.4 MY DIARY: A DEVELOPING SEARCH FOR GOD

Are they Angels or Astronauts? Both by Gloria Lee. One is seventy-five cents and the other is one dollar and fifty cents, and you can get them from June in Mentone and are a must for your library.

And a Letter From *John*

Dear Andy,

How nice to hear from you and we are so pleased you got back to spiritual things. So many people wish to be able to describe it and you must believe, "as above, so below". Come over to my side in Spirit and look around; of course you won't know where exactly you are and the veil is getting thinner every day.

If you read the article in Fate magazine and get the two books Pat told you about, it will explain far better than I could and Pat doesn't have time to write that much!

The time and space is explained in the book: 'The Unobstructed Universe' by White. You don't really need to worry about those things, as through meditation you will get an awareness of all types of things that at this time are of little importance to you. When you become all knowing then you will truly understand.

God speed your progress and send love out to all, Andy, as the world needs it so desperately. We are all One.

Your friend John

ECOLOGY: CLEANING OUR MINDS
FIRST 11/19/70

Speaking of ecology. How about cleaning our minds first, and a good method to help the world with, is by cleaning up the communications media and the news.

224

As in newspapers, when the facts are reported, weigh them with the truths of life in the same articles so the person reading the article will associate the bad with going against natural law (the law of God).

SEX AND FOOD 11/19/70

A spiritual man does not need sex. *He may want it*, but doesn't need it. A male does need sex. When doing sex, he becomes more weak minded and boyish, and subservient to the female. The more sex with the woman, the more dominant the female, and the more weak the man.

We don't need lots of food, drink, and sex for sustaining ourselves. We need to diminish these needs gradually and become masters of our bodies. This is not saying that we should completely give up these things, but that we should dominate these matters and not let these matters dominate us.

DREAM: A MAN AND HIS SON 11/20/70

1:00 am. I was invited to go to lunch with a man and his son on his son's birthday to talk to him about work. He owned the business, was six foot two inches tall, fifty five years old, had an upstairs in his home, and I was tearing sponge figures from the hallway walls because they were loose, while I was waiting for him.

DREAM: WAR EXERCISES 11/27/70

Very clear and vivid. War exercises in my back yard area by Marines. The prisoner, who was caught, even spoke the foreign oriental dialect.

DREAM: MY BROTHER BOB 12/08/70

My brother Bob and I were taking money out of manure. Theresa (my ex-wife) was very shapely, happy, and lively. I was sure glad to see her happy.

VISIONS ARE REAL 12/13/70

The visions that I've had leave no doubt in my mind as to the reality of them. There is an actuality sense which supersedes any possible doubt. I have had night dreams and day dreams, and imaginative thoughts, but they leave me with a sense of wonder and questioning.

Visions are for sure. There is no doubt as to their actual being. The mind and body have a knowing that this is so. The problem here is to understand the language of the mind, which is entirely with pictures and emotions. How do we learn this language?

At the moment, I feel that experience is the best teacher of this. Practicing with the imagination, thinking processes, dreams, emotions, Psychometry, E.S.P., and all related paths.

Spiritualism is another pathway of training the understanding processes of mental picturing; all the mystic organizations have a form of help, also, in their teachings.

What do we benefit from understanding our higher language? We increase the accuracy of translation, which makes this Universal Intelligence a reliable source of info.

As of now, the best psychics are eighty percent accurate. If we can boost this to ninety five percent, we'll be doing humanity a great service, because all of the higher and better thoughts of wisdom and knowledge come from this Universal Intelligence, which I must call God.

DYING NOT WANTED: I'D RATHER LIVE 12/14/70

I recalled, just now, some thoughts I had as I sensed that I was dying, four years ago in a hospital bed when I had the experience three times inside of a few days. I was definitely afraid to die because I had so much to do. Previously, I had entertained the conviction that I was willing to die and was solid on that ground.

This fear of dying while I was experiencing the real thing brought my true feelings out of me.

This is the period of time when my feelings of being a hypocrite came to the surface, to become a firm reality beyond doubt. I have always had this feeling in my mind, and teaching religion to children had surfaced this thought considerably. Then the experience of dying did finalize it.

I became at that time convinced that I knew myself better than I had ever in the past. The games were over and I had to face the business of my reality of existence.

From then on I had to become my true self outside as well as inside. I had to totally understand what I really was, where I came from, and where I was going. I had to investigate all walks of life, and all inner and outer thoughts of man. I searched for truth, and I had to become truth to myself to avoid the hypocrite in me at all costs.

This is where I stand now. I am able to search within myself and know my true feelings, and am quite capable of evaluating which course I must take in the future to improve on my understanding of all.

DREAM: ALBERT C. BOE, MY STEP FATHER 12/18/70

I saw Al Boe; he had been away for a long time. I was getting ready to wallpaper a room.

DREAM: SELLING 12/23/70

Started about five a.m. one morning on a new job, selling boats and trailers for a man who was a bachelor. He told me where to deliver a boat. Then he said he had a new delivery somewhere else. He said he was glad to have another bachelor to work with. I thought to myself that I was a bachelor, but I was living with my wife and kids.

FIXING A FLAT 12/26/70

In Fort Worth, Texas, five people who were driving at about eleven thirty a.m. Sunday, October fifth 1969, toward Dallas and saw and reported seeing a white Chevrolet careen across the road and running over it's driver after a blow out which made it weave in and out of three lanes. The highway patrol found no accident; just a man who was fixing a flat on a white Chevrolet. How do we explain this? Is it future?

EVERYTHING IS ALIVE 12/27/70

I have a strong feeling that everything in this universe is alive. All people and things have feelings, and live, somehow.

An instance came to mind recently when I was losing my patience while trying to fit a square ice cream package into a tight square hole in the freezer and I couldn't get it in just right. I thought and spoke crossly and blamingly at the dumb package.

Well, the thought came to me with reality then, that I was stupid, not the ice cream package.

This brought to mind that everything is a living thing. It has molecules, atoms, vibrations, and life; electrons are whizzing around the atoms in everything there is. This is life. This is movement; this is change.

In the world of E.S.P., this is communication. We all ('material' and "living" things) must harmonize to become perfection. This is the spirit of life (the atoms, e.t.c.). It forms beings and things and offers it's different products to the aid of each other. Even our own bodies feed the worms, and help fertilize the earth. The communication (the Word) is the secret to life we have been looking for, possibly, even though John's Revelations starts out with it; "In the beginning was the Word".

We can rationalize, so we say. Well, so can a blade of grass in its own world. It (the spirit of it) is hung up in the physical form, and within it's physical boundaries it breathes, drinks, and seeks light.

What I am getting at is: why shouldn't we harmonize and love every thing as well as every one to be in perfect balance here on earth? I believe that communication can exist in all atoms everywhere. I believe that communication (The Word) is the Essence of God. This communication is passed on and received by the sensors of whoever and whatever.

There are many types of sensors (receivers) in the human body. This E.S.P. is one of them. We need to sharpen it and I believe we will in twenty years, have found solid methods of controlling E.S.P. in most individuals.

This E.S.P. communicates with tremendous sensitivity with no limitations as time, space, as we have in our physical earth bodies. This E.S.P. has to be the spirit part of us.

GENESIS 1:14: LET THERE BE LIGHT 12/28/70

And God said, "Let there be lights in the firmament of the heavens to separate the day from the night; and let them be for *signs* and for seasons and for days and years". . . . this is a hint as to the verification of astrology.

DUKE UNIVERSITY: ANXIETY 12/28/70

The Para psychological Association of Duke University science studies of 1967 have proven that *faith* increases E.S.P. tremendously.

Page 10: "Exhilaration from Success Results in High ESP. Scoring." This shows that 'feedback' is important for progress in E.S.P.

Page 8: Cleve Backster proved communications between single cells.

Unitrol page 102: Asks if protective amnesia is used in spiritual evolution (reincarnation) also? Energy is held in check (or decreases) as anxieties increase. *In other words, faith and a relaxed attitude (patience) have more energy. As anxieties decrease, meditation decreases anxieties.*

Page 104: Says to count your blessings and forget your troubles; appreciate the present.

ACTUAL P.K. CASE: POLTERGEISTS 12-29-70
(Thoughts with charged emotions)

Parapsychological Assoc., 1967 Report:

Page 18: Says that strong feelings of hostility, especially toward parent figures, with no way to release feelings except by nature (P.K.), had caused breakage of more than 150 glasses, ashtrays, and novelty items which fell off their shelves. Seems like the energy is released unconsciously from the back of the head area. Seems like psychokinetic energy is for real, and explains some ghosts and poltergeists.

If by not outwardly expressing hostility, we can build up a psychokinetic force to knock glassware (which is heavy) off shelves, then *by withholding love* (which can be an even stronger pent-up emotion) *why couldn't we build a dynamo of power within ourselves as Jesus, Kathryn Khulman, etc.?*

To carry this further, let us build this emotion of love within ourselves; *how do we go about it?*

1- Read the Psalms in the Bible (they seem to be anti in many places).
2- Clear our minds of any 'anti' thoughts.
3- Feel deep inside, the emotion of love.
4- Eliminate sexual activity for the buildup.
5- Eliminate "specific" personal love (the love of a

specific person).

6-   Love everything in the whole universe.

7-   Do all good things for God, even saying so to whom
ever you do good to.

8-   Praise God in all cases of goodness.

9-   Keep single mindedness on God.

10- Keep the body alive and healthy, but eliminate all
excesses, which will make it drowsy, sluggish, sick,
fat and earthy.

The above are my own observations.

In reading about Paraphysics and Parapsychics, I find that the universe is proved, so far, to be full of random motion of atoms and molecules. Everything is composed of these, and it appears to me that creativity lies in *the intelligence factor. This is the God factor.*

This source is a directional influence on all these random motion particles in the universe. How do we prove it?

All I have to go on at present is the fact that thoughts do cause action in the body of the thinker, and that thoughts do influence outside beings (intelligences including plants and animals), and pent-up emotions give more power to thoughts.

This being the case, then I believe that thoughts affect all forms of living matter because they are all in partial fluctuation (random movement of molecules and atoms).

BECOMING 'ONE WITH' 01/01/71

I just got the thought that: When we make commitments, laws, pledges, statements of facts, etc., we entangle ourselves in the fact, and become a part of it.

The more solid we have committed ourselves to the fact, the more our bodies and minds must follow this fact, in order to be healthy. Therefore, should we not commit our selves to a stationary fact or idea (one that cannot be changed)?

It appears that life is a constant change, and we must be able to freely change with it. . .the same idea as if we are a note on the musical scale. To be healthy we must let ourselves blend or change octaves, and harmonize with the environment.

This seems to say also that the only unchangeable facts are: Love God with all your heart, mind and soul. Love yourself as you love God. Love your neighbor as you love yourself. Then we get a problem; how do we love God? Who is He? Where is He?

Everyone has a different opinion. Since we actually don't know, then why bother? Well that's a good one isn't it? Then suppose we eliminate the 'Love God' part of the unchangeable facts, and use the other two; then what?

O.K, love yourself as you are, and love your neighbor as much as you love yourself. Almost everyone loves himself as he is and accepts everyone else as *he* is. We harmonize with each other and respect each other as we are. Where is the discord; the fighting?

HUMAN BEINGS bring the discord; the ideal situation is a goal to shoot for, but is not the actual existence. Should we be idealists, or should we be actualists? Let's face up to now as it is, and use our ideals as the carrot before the donkey to lead us on to better things.

THE SPIRITUAL WORLD 01/02/71

Since the outer world of life (the spirit world) is theoretically on a different vibration, then how about a stroboscopic and vibraphonic type of investigation to try to equalize our physical reception with this other world, or plane of existence?

LEARNING 01/04/71

Learning is acknowledging or rediscovering. We should give credit to God.

LETTER: TO GEORGE V. T. 01/05/71

The so-called I AM, or consciousness of the individual entity is proposed by many, including myself, to be the *reality* of being. This 'I AM' adopts a *particular* consciousness upon entering our world. This is a consciousness, which is *hypnotized* into the state of being that it is.

Christ preached faith and belief, to change our consciousness of being. This is a form of hypnosis; a training of the consciousness. This faith and belief, or hypnosis, can actually cause miracles, or things, which are beyond our present state of consciousness.

Everything that happens in our world is a result of consciousness of those in power at the time. The communications media has complete control of quality of impressions put forth for the mass hypnosis of the public. Therefore, I say that the communications media are the GODS of our time. This includes the television shows, the TV commercials, newspapers, books, movies, and radio.

These GODS need to be hypnotized into working for the good of mankind, and to break away from the tearing down process, which they are doing at all levels. I believe that the place to start this action is through the people, and having the people place the responsibility of the trend of mankind onto those in control of the mass media.

One method of reaching this goal is through the churches (organized religion). Another is fraternal organizations, and social clubs. We need people with guts to stand for good and inspire the big boys to take the responsibility of their task unto themselves, as a man would. A man accepts the responsibility for everything he does.

ASTRAL/OUT OF BODY 01/06/71

Fever, eyes shut and a loud bang. This was the experience of someone who had an out of body experience. He was in bed, quiet, and had the desire to be with a friend of his, who was dead, then a bang and out he went beside himself. Was it the fever? The desire? Both? The fever and closed eyes helped to loosen the spirit from the body.

FAITH/BELIEF/TRUST 01/25/71

Faith: In complete understanding and surrender.
Belief: Be and Live; to *act* as if you *are*.
Trust: Affirms love.

ADAM/CREATION 01/26/71

God created Adam as a perfect being, to make free will choices. Well if this is so and God is a God of love and righteousness, then because I know for a fact that God knows the future, God cannot be just and righteous. This creation of his would have been a house of horror in his eyes, seeing the future of mankind, and all the evil ways.

So, following this line of thought, God could have made us as stated, but everyone will be all right in the end because this earth is just a training ground for development of the soul. The possibility of reincarnation becomes sensible in this case. This would be in line with true love.

The flaming sword turning every way, which is to keep us from the book of everlasting life, could very possibly be a flying saucer or disc. All the descriptions of flaming in that time period refer to something very brilliant and shining. The sword is a sharp edged thing, which is turning all about, and shining and brilliant. The angels of the Lord could be the occupants of the saucer.

How is this keeping us from the Book of Everlasting Life? Could this book be the world outside of the earth, such as outer space, time travel, etc. and flying saucers are to keep us from the knowledge?

ARE WE IDIOTS, AND RESPONSIBILITY 01/29/71

With Bible philosophy, we can lay all responsibility on someone else. We can blame the influence of God for all the good, and we can blame the devil (there is no such thing) for all the bad.

Then what are we? If we are not free will agents in our world, then we must be robots or idiots as I have suggested earlier! We must be responsible for everything we do at each moment of our lives, or we become idiots. Psychology seems to say that we are all idiots, and not responsible beings.

Psychiatry has brought the same type of blameless philosophy to the world, and nowadays, as a result, no one is to blame for his actions, or his thoughts. We can blame our past, and present, besides the devil, or God.

So, without individual responsibility we can have free reign to kill, steal, etc, without being blamed for it. There are so many accepted escape routes now, that the person doing the action is forgotten in the courtrooms, and the excuses are being formed and displayed to erase guilt from the accused.

So psychiatry has made us into hypnotized, easily swayed idiots. Is this what we really are? NO! But with time, we will accept this idea if we let it continuously happen in our society.

If with faith and belief we can perform miracles (and I know this to be true), then with faith and belief we can eliminate the devil, and accept Good only.

WHY: MANY QUESTIONS 02/01/71

If God *is* God as we are told, then why would He want us to rely on the word of men for His story? Why would He keep Himself in the background or hidden from the senses which we have common use of? Why should we give up our physical world as is known to us by our natural and obvious sense? Why should there be room for doubt as to the existence of God? Why should there be so many versions of truth? Why should there be so many people claiming to be of or from God? Why should miracles be happening all through time?

BEING A MAN 02/01/71

If you can't get a hold of yourself, then someone else or something else will. If you have less need you have more influence. A male is not a man until he is a whole person in full control of his being, and a free, responsible individual.

DIFFERENT APPROACHES TO GOD 02/04/71

All the different methods of teaching God and Christ to people *(all the churches of different denominations, languages, customs, etc)* are for the understanding of the different intellects of the so many *different* people.

To hit the heart of a rough and tough, ignorant type of person, the teacher needs hell-fire and damnation of the Bible.

To reach the heart of the emotionally trained and embodied person, he needs emotional experiences such as Baptist, Catholic, Foursquare evangelism, and other church teachings charged with heart scraping emotionalism.

To reach the heart and mind of the transitional type of person *(between heart and mind control),* Christian Science and Spiritualism are steps upward, but Spiritualism is too easily infiltrated by fraud. There are many gullible people in this. Spiritualism is on the right track, but like all unseen things, it is easy to be fooled if not trained with *real experience* first.

In Spiritualism, I feel that the best part is the classes about Going Within to find God. They teach about Spirit Guides, but the trick is to focus on God, rather than Spirit Guides. Spirit Guides help in mundane things, but God teaches reality of soul and reason for living.

To reach the searching intellectual type of trained minds, the teacher needs the intellectual methods of teaching, such as Science of Mind, Universal Thought, and Scientology type of intellectual thinking to appeal to what he feels in his state of being.

In the end, all the individuals who are serious in wanting to understand, please and reach God, and do try hard according to their understanding, will certainly attain their goal; God!

The main thrust of a person should be in seeking, seeking and more seeking. "Seek and ye shall find".

When you find God, you have arrived at the next level until you seek again for the next level of finding. It is a never ending progression of seeking, the same as any other education. Don't be a seeker who is not finding.

BAD HABITS 02/05/71

A person who has a bad habit needs to realize that he is doing wrong before he can be reprogrammed to do the right things.

POEM: UNKNOWN SOURCE 02/09/71

Show me the way,
Every minute of the day,
And I'll obey.

THE PUBLIC LEADERSHIP OF CONGRESSMEN 02/14/71

I wrote to congressman Craig Hosmer in Washington, D.C., telling him about the hypnotically receptive and responsive minds of the general public, and pleading with him to use this knowledge to lead our people back into the sanity of thinking good things and doing good things through leadership of our government influences, taking the control of these weird individuals *(our supposedly responsible media leaders)* who preach uncontrolled sex, murder, dope addiction, violence and uncontrolled tempers, out of their hands. *What is lacking in this country is the proper leadership from the top.*

FACING EAST? 02/15/71

All my best results in visions, Psychometry, etc, so far, have happened when I was facing either east or west. North and south positions have not produced as much in clarity or accuracy.

WE ARE ONE, and TIME 02/17/71

We are all one. We are all connected to each other in the universe. We sense each other; we are not always consciously aware of each other, but at times it comes to our consciousness more to some than others.

We do not all have the sensitivity to realize this. The facts of E.S.P., Psychism, Mediumship, Prophecy, e.t.c., prove the constant communication between all of us at all times, and also that time is not really as we make it out to be. All time is now.

These facts of the relationship of all men could be what would bring all men together if we can only prove it to the world.

VOICES IN THE HEAD 02/18/71

As of today, I have had three experiences of audible voices in my head. All have been one and two words only, and not my own voice. Two were female and one was male.

PSYCHOMETRY: BOB W. 02/20/71

At Ed and Anne's I did some Psychometry. One was very accurate about a woman's (Lucille) travels in Europe. I saw bulls, which were for a bullfight, a jeweled baby Christ, three pools of water with a path to one side, and a cathedral interior, which were all accurate.

For Clara, I saw a ship in a bottle and I couldn't figure it out. A few minutes later, Clara made the statement that she was all bottled up.

For Bob W's son (19 years old), I saw a tall skyscraper among small homes in a large area. He had been doing architectural plans for skyscrapers and homes. I saw an airplane that looked like a drawing or a toy. He said he used to draw planes a lot.

Several other Psychometry attempts were: a mass of broken pieces of pictures when the noise from the crowd in the room interfered, and another interference to the Psychometry was my forcing it, on some occasions.

A PSYCHIC EVENT 02/20/71

I saw brown elves' shoes and got the name James Cavlaugh.

MIND READING? 02/24/71

Every so often a thought comes to mind: "Can all these strange phenomena be figments of our imagination?"

Well, no! They cannot possibly be. Then, why can't we decide what they are? If they are not from our imagination *(and that is for sure)*, then they must be from cosmic sources.

Could it be that my mind and your mind and God's mind are everywhere all the time?

PRIDE VS HUMILITY 03/07/71

All tradition, including pomp and ceremony, is bad for the self because it increases pride in the self. It pacifies it into being secure, proud, and satisfied as to what it is, blocking improvement in social and personal habits, and blocking the truth of everything around us. It blocks understanding of the outside world.

A proud person is blind and helpless to the cause of his pride. He is a slave to conditions and leaders. In humility is where the truth is.

Be guided by intuition and not by emotion. Intuition will guide you in the spiritual truth, whereby emotion will guide you in animal truth, which is pride.

PSYCHOMETRY: THE READING OF VIBRATIONS 03/18/71

Where your treasures are, there your heart is, also. I wonder if this applies to Psychometry. Does a part of the spirit stay on with what we possess in our hearts, our material possessions?

In Psychometry, do we feel these parts of the possessors' spirits? No, I think, because Psychometry is only a means to start with.
Later on we can see the same things without the holding of objects, and the future is seen, also.

NOTE: *1999 (Today, as the year ends, I realize and have experienced that Psychometry is a good tool to read the experiences of the item and the minds of the holders of the item , but when reading minds of people, I connect through sounds of the voice as a major touching in with the person's mind or spirit.*

With that said, I have also used vibrations on paper, or tissues sent from thousands of miles in envelopes, to read peoples minds with feedback of verification that it has been done accurately.

It seems like it is a matter of tuning in to the frequency of what or whom I want to read, and this includes God.)

We are really reading the vibrations of the person, and not of the object impressed by the person's vibrations.

The object has been impressed by the vibrations of the holder of it and we read the holder's vibrations through the tuning in to the person's vibrations in that object in that period of time.

Well, now I could be wrong because when reading a person's mind without Psychometry. . . No, I must be right. It makes more sense that way.

Our spirit is vibration and it infiltrates solid objects so that Psychometry is the reading of the thoughts in mind; mind being the mind of the individual soul in and of the complete mind of God. Solid objects hold records of vibrations.

CARL A.
A GREAT TEACHER OF RELIGIOUS SCIENCE INTL.
LONG BEACH, CA 03/22/71

My Thoughts While Studying *Science of Mind* in 1971.

There are no new ideas. There are given ideas from God. Assuming that these given ideas are new to us, I'll continue with five new ones for me.

1. *I am God.* In the beginning, if there was One, God was all there was. Everything It created was created out of Itself, therefore I am God as my finger is me, the same as my hand is me and my arm is also me, but my arm is an arm, my hand is a hand, and my finger is a finger, and all of them are me. I am in God and God is in me, and as I am in my finger, my finger is in me. So, we are all One in God, and God is still all there is.

2. *I can create.* I can create by thinking with my spirit tuned in to God, and God's forces will comply with my thought forms as long as it is in harmony with God's laws of the universe.

In spiritual thoughts of creation, I must steadfastly become the idea in my mind in the present, requiring no conditions of time and space, and holding no thoughts of opposites or doubts, which would cancel out the creation. This creation is really a reorganization of already existing material.

3. *Negatives are absences.* Negatives are absences of primary cause. Fear is absence of faith. Darkness is absence of light. Hatred is absence of love.

4. *God cannot punish.* God cannot make mistakes. We make mistakes, and thereby we punish ourselves until we correct our mistakes by living rightly and forgetting the wrong. We are completely responsible for all that happens to us, which is caused by us in the first place, or which we let be caused by outside influences.

5. *Intuition is real and understandable.* A past experience com-

ing into the mind is a warning from subconscious of forthcoming events, which will be similar to that past experience. This will be a great tool for making decisions. We must be aware of it at all times.

HUMAN DYNAMOS 04/01/71

In referring to association, you can count on your memory. An example is when you hear a song or some music; the music brings thoughts to your mind, just automatically.

So, through association of when you heard the music, or the words of the music, they bring thoughts to your mind of something that happened in your past. There is association here.

Our minds are part of the electromagnetic force, which is throughout the whole universe, and our bodies are part of the physical world, here on the earth.

We have, around us, the likes of a power house; electromagnetic force which is similar to the force around a motor.

We are just a charged up thing, throwing out a field. Our minds are a part of this field. Our bodies are a physical thing attached to the earth, and the laws of the earth. We are physical, and we are what you might call 'spirit', which is the term generally used for this electromagnetic place or being, or whatever it is.

Our minds control everything about us. Whatever our minds put forth, our bodies will follow. Our bodies become what our minds put out. Our minds, or thoughts, are our leaders, which direct everything.

What we think is what we become, so we might just as well think the right things, and clear out anything that is not good.

Bad thoughts destroy us. They will make us sick, such as fear or hatred, worrying.

Things that are upsetting in our thoughts will upset our bodies, and our bodies will draw sickness from this.

Now, here is a good thought; we are alive in a universe where everything that we know about is alive. We are alive in this thing and *nothing really ever dies, it only changes.*

Think about it; everything goes from one form to another; nothing really ever dies. Think about that in association with your *body* and thinking of yourself dying; you only change bodies (Reincarnation?).

Thought is a one-way street; it must be expressed. It's a natural law. If your thoughts are not expressed outside your body, they may well be expressed in some form inside your body, which will be a short circuit or sickness. This is a law that was brought out by Harold Sherman in his book *How to Foresee and Control Your Future.*

The stronger the feeling you put behind your desire, the greater the electromagnetic charge that goes out from you, seeking the manifestation of this thought. Emotions are powerful, aren't they?

Strong feelings, then, are the source of the power from within you. See that you are guided along the *right* way.

The whole universe is made from atoms, from electrons, protons, and neutrons circulating about them. This is called electromagnetic force. We are made up of this, too. We, and everything else, put out an electromagnetic field, or aura. Our minds are of this electromagnetic force.

They are not physical. The brain is physical, but not our minds. The body is physical, but our minds are dependent on the universe, not the earth.

Our minds have other names such as soul, spirit, and so forth. Our minds tune into different wavelengths, different consciousnesses in the universe, and on the earth.

By tuning in to the various wavelengths we can read minds, see the future, diagnose sicknesses, be in other places, move matter, cure illnesses, and know all there is to know at that particular frequency.

Our conscious minds are like tuning knobs on the radio. What is the source of all this? It must be the medium, which we call GOD. It appears as if we all make up God, and God's make up is **us all.**

The key to the universe is harmony as in good music. All the laws of the Bible are designed to produce harmony between beings. What is another word for harmony? It is love. Love is the harmonious togetherness of beings or things.

Each accepts the other for what it is, and goes about it's own task to keep the universe going. Whatever becomes inharmonious destroys itself. Whatever is harmonious, blooms.

In the natural state, our feelings, or emotions, always win out over our thinking. We must have faith in our spirit selves. We must believe in our spiritual ability to overcome this. We must implant our positive suggestions on the emotional level, if they are to be fully effective.

Make God your partner; nothing will be impossible if we do this. Place your positive suggestions at the emotional level of the God power within you. This will develop faith. It is hard to realize the fact that the power of God is within us.

Like the Bible says: The Kingdom of Heaven is within you. The Kingdom of God is within you, and God resides in this Kingdom. *The powers of God are within us.* They are yours to use. By denying faith in ourselves; by having negative attitudes, lack of confidence, or inferiority feelings, this self-denial is really a denial of God, our source.

Every pain in our bodies; every diseased cell, tissue or organ is a voluntary destruction of the Temple of God. Our bodies are the Temple, and we (our minds) are God.

Root out negative attitudes and thoughts from your mind, and replace them with positive affirmations; positive beliefs. Have strong faith in your self and in the God power within you.

When talking to your subconscious mind, you should always give general commands; always make positive statements, never say if. Repetition is a sure way to your subconscious.

All our values are in the now; not the past and not the future, but *now*, like: Do I love somebody now? or *Did I love somebody then? Forget it.* Do you love somebody now? Do you hate somebody now? or Did you hate somebody then? Forget it.

Live now, because everybody and everything has changed since the last time. *Now is different from before.* Always live for now in the present. Learn to delay your natural subconscious reactions.

Stop and think before you react. *Re-action without thinking is animal. You are not an animal; you are using an animal body.* Stop and think before you re-act.

In the lore of the mind, like always attracts like. Hate and prejudice will most likely be checked or eliminated by the new ideas and programs in your mind, that release tensions, and promise better existing conditions and relations.

A lady, *who sees visions of the future,* has deep depressions for periods of time before she ends up in a wild, terribly nervous state at which time she sees her vision, or whatever is going to happen, happens. It begins with a deep depression, and ends up in a very nervous state; nervous tensions. Each time she had a nervous spell, or a nervous tension-type affair, it was followed by a sudden calm, and within four to twenty four hours she would hear of a storm or hurricane or earthquake somewhere.

Evidently, the impressions had been received by her subconscious mind, and she resisted it as it came into the conscious mind; she couldn't get through; she couldn't become aware of what was happening, without a struggle.

TIMER OF THE MIND 04/04/71

Time, in our minds, is so accurate that I wonder if when we entered our bodies at birth, did we put a time limit on our earth existence? Or another thought says that our existence here has been influenced by the Law of Averages life span statistics which has been impressed on our minds. Statistics say that the average person lives to seventy or so. If we feel that we are average, we accept this statement in our subconscious so that it puts a time limit on our existence.

BENEFITS OF DIFFERENCES 04/04/71

In the shower this morning, I realized that **we only sense what is *different* from our immediate feelings.** We feel temperatures, which are *different from* ours at the point of contact.

Suppose eyes see only what is different, and see not what is the same? The same as what? The same as itself *(the sights it inherently knows).* God is the same, and invisible.

I wonder if magic works this way? We are sensitive to what is different from our present state. If we are hot, we are sensitive to cold. If we are cold, we are sensitive to hot, etc.

Let's apply this to our spiritual selves.If we are bad or evil we are sensitive to good. If we are good, we are sensitive to bad. If we are perfect (One with God, or natural) then we are sensitive to nothing, because then we know all and are all, and become the Law of God which is stable and never changing.

MIND 04/05/71

Miracles are caused by mind. The idea of devil is mind. God is mind. All of the universe is mind. We are our use of mind.

God is all; therefore everything we sense is God. *We are the action of God in God.* Therefore what we see, when we see, is ourselves, because we are mind and God is mind and we see with mind and *every-thing there is, is mind.* Our whole life originates in mind.

We have the complete choice of allowing or disallowing what enters our minds through our senses, by the control section of our being, the conscious mind (the spirit).

GOD: ONE WITH THE FATHER 04/07/71

We cannot see God; I wonder if this is *because we are God?* This ties in with the above viewpoint of *not sensing the sameness of being.*

God made us in His image and likeness; total perfection. Our thoughts have strayed away from the perfection in our minds, and we have created or caused imperfection by our word (our thoughts in action).

Let us reverse this trend of thought and cause perfection again, by thinking and knowing the perfection that we are because God made us perfect. If we love God and are one with Him in every detail of our thinking, then we have no need or use of a knowledge of Good and Evil.

We rely on the psychic part of our being; the spirit, which is perfect, and is tuned to God for all information and life.

We must learn to *know* totally God and His/our perfection and live according to His direction, which we receive intuitively by tuning in to Him (being One with the Father).

THE BIBLE: TREE OF GOOD AND EVIL 04/20/71

I have been reading all morning into the metaphysical and occult ideas of God. One article referred to a passage in the Bible and my being underwent a chemical change at once as I read the Bible passages and took in the understanding from them.

This feeling was a sickening feeling; a cringing of the nerves, saliva excreting into my mouth, acids generating in my stomach, a numbness in my stomach; a totally upset wave of feelings.

This confirmed again my inner conviction that *the Bible is the Knowledge of Good and Evil (Gen 2:09) that kills us,* according to Genesis 2:17.

I have a growing conviction inside of myself that the *'Tree of Life Everlasting' is our direct connection with God (One with the Father).*

When I feel the presence of Oneness with God, which is becoming closer to 100% of the time, I feel beauty, life, perfection, health, wealth, abundance, goodness, love and understanding throughout me.

When I refer to the Bible, I become negative and sick. According to tradition, this makes me a man of evil and the devil, but my being does not reflect this to me.

Now, I must say that: "Is the Bible the Truth, or is my being the Truth? The Bible is written by men of all types of characters. Many are murderers, thieves, kings, unknowns with assumed names, and so many possible wrong types, but *in general, they are all trying to rule the thoughts and behaviors of man according to their beliefs and desires.*

Is this what I am to accept as the truth? I cannot accept this as the truth for me, because it is not the truth/essence of my being. I feel and sense the truth, and it does not agree with the Bible.

I am not sorry, but I do wonder about it all. My feelings being sensitive to God, I must accept the teaching of Church and society as the truth, which continuously seems more obviously false. Am I a hypocrite?

This is why I am offish, or separate from the group since I was born. I have tried to love individuals with deep emotion, and have fallen because of it. I find that I can love in a universal way with my soul belonging only to God and me, and enjoy this love constantly, and nothing hurts it, or prevents it from being. It is good!

I find that I can help others more by loving in this manner. Normal love is very selfish; it causes the person to become attached *(which is a sickness, or lack of individuality)* to another person or group of persons.

Universal love brings freedom to the person to be an individual entity; overseeing all others with love and fulfillment in letting the others enjoy their freedom of expression, or being.

CLAIRVOYANCE: SEEING THE VIBRATIONS 04/22/71

I am becoming clairvoyant! I was reading on a white page in the E.S.P. book in the morning light in the bathroom. Pictures of the same type as in my mind during Psychometry began to form on the white page as I *lazily stared* at the whiteness of the paper. They were vague outlines only, but were in constant change as in Psychometry with the inner mind. I think that these are the same images, except that I was projecting them onto the white paper. They appeared darker with more body when the reflection or glare was not so great. I saw them with or without glasses about 6" to 15" from my eyes. I feel that eventually, with practice, I will develop in this talent.

There is one physical difference today, which I think has no bearing, but just in case, I am writing it here. During the night my throat became sore, so as an experiment, I am wearing a plastic bag around my neck to keep the heat in the area.

HUMAN TV SETS 04/28/71

We are instruments of reception and impressions, transmission of impressions, storage and sorters of impressions. It appears that our reception is affected by our attention and acceptance. Attention being the tuning in, and acceptance being the volume control. The more acceptance, the higher the volume, or stronger the impression.

By repetition the impression is impressed deeper into our system, just as scraping the dirt with a hoe; the more you scrape, the deeper and more real is the impression.

This last line makes me feel that *reality is the total of all the deepest impressions of the mind.* If a person loses control of himself and reality, then his deep impressions must be either short circuited, or better still, his deep impressions have recently had too many opposing deep impressions accepted at one time. *This does seem like a short circuit.*

How do we undo a short circuit?

a) We must turn off the power (conscious mind) by going into trance, relaxing, sleeping.

b) We must cut loose the fusion by confusion.

c) We must insulate the opposing wires (ideas) from each other by forgetting one and remembering the other.

d) We then turn on the power of consciousness.

McD.'S HOUSE: LESSON LEARNED 05/04/71

In Cerritos CA I did about three hours of accurate Psychometry for these nice folks and some of their friends. Pictures were accurate. Things are improving. I am gaining confidence in the process. I picked up a guitar and saw fjords and was told that the guitar came from Scandinavia.

I mentally asked for a fast reading when I first met the wife and received a clear picture of a cucumber with four wheels on it. This turned out to mean the Meals on Wheels program, which the husband was just starting into.

Bill (a co-worker at Gemco,) is a big help. *He asks questions in detail which bring out more information.* This session, with their guests that evening, taught me to not bring up anything that seems frightening, because it weighs heavy on the mind of the person being read. It tends to scare the people who are not familiar with psychic stuff. The movies, I believe, are mostly to blame for this. They always seem to blow things out of proportion for the effect, as in the southern type movies of the Deep South where they cause the people in the south to look weird and stupid.

TIBETAN MONK: LOS ANGELES, CA 05/08/71

Notes and comments on a lecture and demonstration: (Most people here in the audience look like witches, voodoo producers, weirdoes and hippies.) The main benefit from Zen etc., is enlightenment, which helps you to understand all and have concentrated universal discernment.

God = no effort.
Results = O *(nothing gained, nothing lost).*
Thought = always in the past.
O polarity = state of reception.

I asked the Tibetan Monk, "What is the ultimate benefit from meditation, or becoming spiritual in this life and after?"

He closed his eyes and slowly said, "True meditation does not seek benefits. Listen with absence of expectation (openness). Meditation is the only way to understanding ourselves. Our spiritual being is above the law. The intellect transcends blind faith. Self consciousness consists of boundaries or limits which need to be defended. Truth contains a sense of humor. True spiritualism is selflessness, a journey without a goal, and the only goal is the correct path to take on this journey."

MORE VOICES IN THE HEAD 05/15/71

A thought occurred today when I heard a voice inside of me again. I wonder if because we are thinking of a particular person, the voice that we hear is of this particular person? So far, it seems as though this is true.

Then, to pull this along further, I wonder if these dead entities, which talk through mediums, are the voices of whoever the medium thinks of, and the intellect of the subconscious of the medium? Of course, the intellect would be tuned in to Universal Consciousness.

JON J., LONG BEACH: A READING FOR ME 05/16/71

Went to aSpiritualist church on in Long Beach. Very nice place, and atmosphere.

A reading by Jon J. Very accurate.

a) I will do much traveling and speaking as lecturing not exactly about God, but about my feelings.

b) I want to travel for this, but haven't the funds available.

c) I am hardnosed and meticulous in my thinking. Need to loosen up.

d) I write things and don't stick to them; I am liable to change my mind after I read what I wrote *(this is my researching of God and thoughts about God)*.

e) He got a good feeling about my lecturing.

f) He saw a 200 lb, 6ft. person with receding hair and a small head near me.

g) I asked what Granny, Pa and Pete *(relatives)* were doing at this time. Jon J. said that God would reveal this in due time.

THOUGHTS ABOUT CHURCHES 05/16/71

If the churches were interested in God, they would not be interested in politics or money, because God's Kingdom is not of this world.

Their dogmas and doctrines would dissipate, and love would be the only rule. Getting along with all mankind would be the only teaching because their Kingdom is not of this world.

HEALING AND CHURCH HYMNS 05/16/71

If I am ignorant of disease, then I shouldn't catch disease. When a person is in the spirit, that person is said to be: out of body, in mystical rapture, unaware of surroundings, receiving impressions, completely detached, sensitive to the Holy Spirit, yielding self completely, putting forth no effort, as though he is looking on rather than participating, shocked at the audacity of some of the things said, a different person, in a different kind of sleep, etc.

Healing is self forgetfulness in the receiving of love. Healing is transferred by surrendering ourselves in the act of love for another. The singing of hymns in church builds up a hypnotic effect in the group's subconscious minds. There will be an anticipation of miracles and such.

When an unknown hymn is sung, and the participants have to analyze what they are doing, the effect is broken.

New hymns in church destroy the reason for the hymns, which is to build a common trust and expectation.

The greater the emotional intensity of the hymns *(they must be familiar ones to build the emotions)*, the greater the power is built for what is about to come.

There must be no interruptions between the singing and the readings. Two songs should be sung just before the sermon, and two more highly emotional songs sung just before the readings. These methods should apply to the healing sessions, also.

Prayer produces psychokinetic energy, in the sense that as we sincerely desire something, and give it up to God with thanks, it will come to us by God *(in which we live and have our being)*.

A GHOST STORY TO HAUNT ORGAN RECIPIENTS 05/16/71

An article I read recently quoted a Psychiatrist who said that patients who have received a transplanted organ from a corpse are sometimes haunted by nightmares in which they imagine the ghost of the dead donor is demanding the return of the organ. Some of the patients were subject to dreams and hallucinations in which they are being attacked by the ghosts of the cadavers, punishing them for the crime of acquiring a kidney.

After a two-year study of organ transplant patients he remarked that the psychological problems of the few patients who were unable to accept the idea of acquiring a new organ might be a bigger threat to their lives than the body's rejection of the kidney.

This brings to my mind the stories of reincarnation. *Could the memories of a reincarnation be received from ancestral blood cell memories in the genes of our bodies?*

VERIFIED MIND READING OF A DEAD PERSON 05/16/71

Today I did a reading on a flag, which had been draped over the casket of a dead man. His wife asked me to read it. I received accurate and clear pictures of him. This flag had not been used by him in life, just death! Yet the info came through! What does this mean?
I saw him as a rodeo clown, which he had been at one time. I never knew this man, and had not been informed about him.

For sure, now, I know that all mind is in mind. *All thoughts, vibrations, movements, and changes are eternal. All impressions that are made in the stuff of the universe are recorded forever.*

These impressions can be retrieved by tuning in with our minds. What are we, but minds, thinking machines, spirits? As the Bible says, we are created in the image of God, and we are spirits, which enter the body upon first breath of the body. This is life in the animal body.

MY FIRST MESSAGES 05/20/71

These two were received by me today. This is the first time I have been able to receive symbols and translate them with an assurance that they were right. Things are still improving.

   a) Freedom from hell gets you stuck in the web of beauty.
   b) To catch up with the fire power of prayer, you must raise up
      to God, the All Seeing Eye *(wisdom).*

LONG BEACH: I AM A PSYCHIC DETECTIVE 05/24/71

A friend of mine, Betty H., asked me to help some friends of hers to find out where their fourteen-year-old girl was. She had disappeared without notice, and there was nothing to be suspected for her vanishing.

I went to the house, sat on her bed and asked for close belongings such as socks, underwear, pajamas, slippers, stuffed toys, dolls, jewelry etc... I arranged these things all around my body so that they were touching me. I began my meditation while hugging these things all around me

Figure 20

I sat on the bed, surrounded by the girl's clothes and toys so that I would have a contact with her vibrations.

Then to the disappointment of the parents, I described what I saw, and I was unknowingly accurate.

until the pictures in my mind started to flow. I asked spirit *(God)* to help me find this girl, and went into complete relaxation, waiting for answers.

Then I spoke what was given to me in the picture form, while the meanings were impressed on my mind.

The *first* thing that I saw was a baby coming out of her womb, a frightening feeling, scared and bewildered. I said that she was afraid that she was going to have a baby and ran away because of the fear.

The *second* scene, after asking where she was, was: A street blocked by black and white street blockades on yellow and black X supports *(this was a street to the beach where the white building was, that was shown to me afterwards)*. The street was near high piles of stacked up large round things *(these were Navy mines, stockpiled in the general area where the blocked street was)*. These were very clear and leading me toward them. I expressed what I saw, and asked for more specifics.

The *third* scene was a beachfront sidewalk, which I was moving north on, until I stopped at a white wooden building with a sloped, flat black roof. I explained that she was here with a man, and asked for more info.

The *fourth* scene was a three story red brick building in a downtown area, and the impressions told me that they had lived there, also. I explained this to the parents and we talked awhile. Then I left.

In the following days, I asked my friend Betty for some feed back from the parents. She told me that the parents were insulted and disillusioned by my saying that their fourteen-year-old daughter was probably having a baby. This really hurt my feelings, because I really thought

I was on track; it was all so clear in my mind without confusion or doubt.

Three months later, the daughter came home and explained that she thought she was pregnant and ran away because she was very scared. She had holed up with the older male, and that she stayed at the two places I had seen. She found that she was not pregnant. This was a good ending!

A DIFFERENT STATE OF EXISTENCE 05/30/71

I still have a bug in my mind about the Bible being darkness in men's minds rather than an enlightenment. I can't get a complete picture of it, but it keeps occurring to me. It seems as though the Bible is an enslaver and a hypnotizer of the mind, the which is the same as bringing death to the soul or the free will itself, which was given to us by God in the first place. I cannot feel God as being an enslaver of the mind, but I think the Bible does just that, when it is used by religions.

It appears, in a way, that men's experiences in the realm of mind are experiences in a wholly complete, different state of existence. People, throughout history, and nowadays, when they use drugs (hallucinatory), or when they use meditation *(becoming One with the Father, merging with the universe, joining the Spirit world, etc)*, develop a feeling of being God. *The stronger or more prolonged the use of drugs and/or meditation, the more the sense (feeling) of being God, or One with God.* If we all had this feeling at the same time, we would have a respectable relationship of Oneness with each other.

AUTHORITY OF THE SUBCONSCIOUS MIND 06/02/71

The spirit masters which come through a medium and have strange names or titles could possibly be the subconscious mind, or the true self, or the God self, speaking clearly without obstruction from the world of spirit or mind.

The knowledge which comes through is usually in tune with what has been implanted in the subconscious mind of that person, and comes out of the subconscious when in trance, so that there are no obstructions from the reasoning or conscious mind.

Thus, all thoughts, which come from the subconscious mind directly while in trance, always appear as though they were authoritative because there is no conflicting thought or control from the conscious mind.

How does this apply to seeing dead people?

When in touch with the subconscious level of mind, the speaker sees the person as remembered in life form, and is tuned in to the consciousness of that person which is in spirit, or dead.

JESUS AS DEATH FOR US 06/02/71
(Looking at Jesus as death for us.)

Gen 1, 2:17 in the Bible says: ". . .but of the Tree of the Knowledge of Good and Evil you shall not eat, for *in the day that you eat of it you shall die.*"

Jesus and the Bible are considered to be sources of the knowledge of good and evil.

The Tree is a book, and Knowledge is teachings in the book. Jesus brought us a knowledge of good and evil as well as the rest of the Bible does.

This knowledge binds the freedom of our beings into a narrow gate of slavery of mind.

This knowledge has increased our desires to force the minds of our fellow beings to think as narrowly as we do, because we need company in this excursion of giving up our selves, our free wills. In this narrow way, all freedom of the individual ego is lost in the way of Jesus and the Bible.

Our free wills are given up, and we are forced to accept the thoughts of the stories in the Bible as God's Word.

Once the freedom of the ego is given up to the way of Jesus and the Bible, and we enter the narrow, straight gate, we gain a new freedom within the realm of God's universe.

This is a complete freedom from fear and want *(of course, the fear and want were produced and emphasized by the Bible and Jesus, and others like them in the first place; this is a tactic of witch doctors and magicians, which Jesus seemed to be).*

But supposing we don't follow the straight way and flub it up? *We are to suffer eternally (this is a fear tactic produced by witch doctors, magicians, and religions).*

What is suffering eternally? This must be a strong hunger or desire for something; a craving. Then this is also the description of God within us. A desire and spark of life within us. It appears as if we end up in the grip of fear whichever way we choose to go until we reach the breakthrough to the other side of the straight path. This other side is the side of freedom and Oneness.

All religions and all beliefs seem to lead the mind to the other side eventually, which is direct contact with the universal intelligence, God.

MY GOALS 06/15/71

1. Become One with God and truth.
2. Become perfect in total health.
3. Travel to see the kids.
4. Meet Jesus and converse.
5. Read the thoughts of someone else: present, past, future, as Jesus did.

WHY IS IT EVIL TO DO WHAT JESUS DID? 06/29/71

The Essenes trained Mary, Ann, Jesus, John the Baptist, etc. in astrology, prophecy, all psychic sciences, etc. from early childhood about four years of age.

If Jesus learned these subjects within this Essene organization, then why do some Christian Bible folk term them *(astrology, prophecy, mind reading, seeing future, seeing Angels, communicating with spirits, healing, etc.)* as evil?

Could it be that people were discouraged from these things so that the religious leaders would have an edge on them? Keeping the people ignorant of these things would give more power to the religious leaders.

PRAYER: ALL TIME IS NOW 07/04/71

God knows the past as if it were the future or present; all time is the same for God; all is now. So, in prayer, we can change the past. If all time is the same to God, then the past can be changed as well as the future. Investigate this. Seems like nothing can be done at any time except the present time.

PHINEAS PARKHURST QUIMBY (2/16/1802-1/16/1866) 07/15/71

My thoughts. Mr. Quimby is a man of truth and sincerity. He learned Mesmerism, Coueism, philosophy, and Christ's teachings with the real meaning behind them. Quimby was born in Lebanon, New Hampshire, just about seventy miles north of where I was born. He was born on February 16, 1802 and left us on January 16, 1866.

He was not swayed by public opinion, superstition, mass belief, society, churches, and belief. Through steadfast truth, research and practice, he brought proof to us that belief is the foundation of our being. He acquired the meditative state of being, similar to Jesus, though not as complete. The result he hoped for was to establish a science of life and happiness, which could be taught even to children, so as to abolish error from among us.

I love this man very dearly. For about ten years, Mrs. Patterson (to become Mrs. Eddy in the future) was a follower of Quimby's and backed him up at every turn as to the fact that he was a good man of truth who had healed many people including herself.

After Quimby died, she had begun to organize churches with the name, Christian Science. She was a great organizer and businesswoman. She had a tendency to be dogmatic, and also claimed the teachings to be her own for some strange reason, which I should not judge her for. I would like to know her because of her spirit of get-up-and-go. She was a real tiger, and woman of truth.

SCIENCE OF MIND: THE CREATIVE PROCESS 07/15/71
(My understanding of Science of Mind)

This is a study of the order of things in our universe, seen and unseen, which brings us to a realization of our relationship with this universe and it's inhabitants.

To begin with, we must break all barriers of thought to become free of all influence but truth, which sets us free. All the influences I refer to would become belief in our minds if we accept them consciously or subconsciously.

The truth, which I refer to, is what we call God, or principle, and which is us, also (seems like this truth is the reality of our own choices).

There is no limit to this truth, no boundaries. Everything in and about this truth is in perfect order. We cannot see this truth because we are looking through its eyes. We must look within ourselves and see this truth for what *IT* is. . .us!

We have had our minds so clouded with the thoughts of men over the centuries, that we have forgotten who we really are. We must bring ourselves back to reality by:

> **a.** Recognizing the truth of our being; looking within, giving thanks to God, realizing the existence of this truth and the power of it.

> **b.** Unifying with this truth of our being; *becoming it* in our recognition of it, and remaining completely in the state of unification, never losing contact with it by being of the world; always knowing that we are in the world, and living in the world, but not of the world. *We are using this animal body for expression, but we are not this animal body.*

> **c.** Through the above two steps, we will know and act with authority, which will deliver the power abroad to others, seen and unseen (flesh and spirit), and to God the Principle. We are the manifestation of the Principle.

The First Principle of The Law of Mind is harmony.

Without it there is limitation. For the cosmos to exist, there must be a Cosmic Mind to bind all individual minds to certain generic laws. We, as individuals, are carrying forward the creative process under the Law of Cosmic Mind.

We individuals are spirit with the powers of selection and initiative. Substance is something universally present which is our compliment for the expression of spirit.

The Divine Ideal is truth, life and beauty, which permeate all spirit, and we must learn to recognize these in our self-contemplation for the sake of harmony.

In this process of self-contemplation, we must recognize that the power comes from the originating Spirit; we are One with it, and then we see ourselves as It, and think of ourselves as being surrounded by the conditions, which we want to produce. We become these conditions. We must take the initiative and use it with specific selection, and become the livingness of the idea we self contemplate.

THE PRACTICE OF SCIENCE OF MIND 07/15/71

God is Spirit, Spirit is Mind, and this Mind is the only mind there is. This Mind then, is my mind. My conscious mind is my awareness and individuality. It works in the world of form. My subconscious mind is in the world of ideas. It is my use of the Universal Mind: God.

With our conscious minds we direct the universal subconscious mind to act in the idea state to produce manifestation in our material world.

To live as we want, in happiness and wholesomeness, we must live constantly as One with God, and as God ultimately, in the world of ideas so that they will become manifested in form for us. This is great stuff! *IT* is us and we are *IT*!

A SAMPLE SCIENCE OF MIND TREATMENT 07/15/71

God is the only Mind there is. I am this Mind. This Mind is perfect in every way. I am perfect in health, as this Mind is perfect in every way. I feel great at all times. My heart is vibrant and full of healthy power. My muscles are alive and strong.

My complete body is perfect in health. This perfect health is the Law of my Mind and my subconscious Mind accepts this law as itself right now, and forever more. **"Thank you God"**.

IN LOVE WITH GOD 08/31/71

I am in love with God. Being in love with someone is becoming One with him. I am One with God. I see through God's eyes all of the goodness that is in all that is created. Being one with God, I realize that:
I am perfect in every way.

I love everyone and everything because I created them.

I see only the good in them because good is all there is. Anything else is the lack of good. Lack of good is only blindness on the part of the one who claims it.

I express my goodness to all who hear me, see me, and think of me, because I am expressing the goodness of God who dwells in, and is me.

If we love God, how can we not love evil as well as good, or satan as well as Jesus?

Jesus said that you cannot have two masters; love one and hate the other. I say, love all that God made; good and evil, because there is a purpose: without evil you cannot recognize good. Evil is just a necessity in this physical world to show the difference between it and good. Without differences, we cannot choose. Without differences, we cannot make use of any of our senses. Without differences, we do not exist.

APPARITIONS 09/02/71

Thoughts express themselves in the form of pictures. When a person sees a ghost, I feel he is sometimes seeing in picture form the expression of ideas, which exist. This is the same as mind reading. These ideas appear to be in the now, and not repetitions of the past.

The apparitions are seen by more than one person, many times, which shows the reality of *IT*'s existence. The image moves and expresses independently as if it were an individual live person. Apparitions seem to be a recording in the surrounding areas, which people see under the right conditions.

It seems to me that these recordings have been made by strong emotional force, such as what causes the kinetic happenings of a highly emotional teenager, called a poltergeist.

LISTENING TO THE SERPENT 09/16/71

We are all looking for a comforter, a standard of truth, a balance. God is this spark of truth and desire, which is in us. Nothing bothers us until we are aware of it. The Serpent is Emotion.

Sickness is listening to the Serpent; listening to the emotions. Listen to your intelligence and positive thinking, not your emotions.

INDIVIDUAL FREQUENCIES 11/01/71

At this point in time, I am wondering about truth as pertaining to inner visions and communications such as voices and mental picture receptions and understanding revelations while in the meditative state of mind; between sleep and awakeness.

Is this information coming from the subconscious of our own minds? Sometimes this info takes on personality and sometimes it doesn't. In either case, where does it originate? How does this info relate to what we call God? Some info is accurate in any sense of time; past, present, future. Some info is inaccurate in any time zone or period.

Where is the difference from? So far, I gather that our minds can tune in to different levels of info in the Universal Mind. What are these different levels?

It seems sensible that maybe these levels are the individual minds of those who have died, who are at different stages of intelligence in the spirit realm, and when we receive a communication, we have the result of tuning in on a certain individual frequency.

This would mean that each individual entity or mind or spirit is on an assigned broadcast frequency, just as each individual has different features and fingerprints. In other words we have a natural resonance.

LIFE PROCESSES 11/09/71

It appears as if long life is due to a flowing through, a harmony, a cleansing action, a purifying stream, air intake and output, entrance and exit, with an action taking place in the process. These are my (own?) thoughts, which just came to me, and acting on me, and I am passing them on.

It appears as if life is all the same action: an intake of something, a harmonizing with it, and a passing on of it. The harmonizing is the gaining or increasing of life in this process. It is a digestive process. Here are some examples:

a. Air, food and water taken into the lungs and mouth must be digested, and passed on. Without either of the three actions, life will not exist. This is a trinity.

b. Wisdom, or God is taken into the mind, digested, and passed on. In this process, we harmonize (digest) with God (wisdom) and manifest (pass on) this wisdom in our example. If any of these three actions does not take place, we will not have life, or will be dead as Jesus referred to the blind leading the blind, or the dead burying the dead. All three actions must occur to have life and to have it abundantly.

c. The earth receives sunlight, water, and flesh for food, it digests it, and brings forth or passes on more life from it's digestion. If either process is not used, a dead planet will occur.

d. Our bodies take in food, water, air, light, and it becomes digested into our blood stream. We must pass on these energies after digestion, and we must increase our capacity of digestion to gain more life. We have pores in our bodies; these are outlets and must be clean to work properly for the bodily health. We have blood vessels, which must be clean and free flowing for proper delivery of fresh life and retrieving of old life to and from all parts of the body.

It seems as if the capacity of these blood vessels was kept at the fullest, then the body life would hold on longer than normal. Old age seems to be a shrinking process, which could start in the mind for one thing, and in the body for another, and yet they are both one. When the body deteriorates, we are separating ourselves from it.

If a man's thinking shrinks, so does *he* in many ways. In one way, the shrinking thoughts of man *(by this I mean a giving up of life and abundance, or an acceptance of death as a close reality, the decreasing circumference of a man's thought)* will by nature shrink his blood vessels and pores and digestive tract, thereby decreasing his physical life. He will decrease his activity of thought and action because he is shrinking from life. He will eventually die by choice.

If a man were to *expand his thinking* and his actions he should therefore increase his mental and physical life by *increasing his total being.* His pores will sweat and remain clean, his blood vessels will enlarge and deliver more fresh blood and clean themselves out better. His digestive process will enlarge and his intake and output will enlarge. He will have life more abundantly.

Like the controlled handwriting, which changes our personalities, controlled walking should expand our minds by taking longer steps.

This leads me to think of chemicals, which enlarge the flow of blood through out the body and brain. If such things as Gota Kola, which long living elephants thrive on, and caffeine, and cola, which are dilating agents for our blood vessels, are taken into our bodies, would they not increase our life span?

If our blood system is increased in capacity, then our digestive system is increased and we must increase our intake and output to balance out for life abundance. This means that if we are drinking coffee and coke, we must eat more nourishing food and work harder in order to balance the increased capacity caused by dilation, which is caused by coke and caffeine.

Our teenagers of today are a good example of what my thoughts are trying to express. This is the coke and caffeine generation. These teenagers are eating tremendous amounts of food, putting out great activity, and living more abundantly.

If all works according to my thoughts, this generation will live lots longer than ours unless their thoughts and actions change to smaller circumference.

This also brings to mind the Nephilim or Sons of God which were the giants in the Genesis of the Old Testament. These Sons of God were cloud people who merged with the daughters of man to produce our race of the present stage. This is the race of Adam and Eve, or animal and wisdom, or body and spirit.

These giants who came from another place (planets?) were called Lord Gods and Sons of God in the Bible, and they were very intelligent. Now this ties in with what I have just mentioned about the trinity of life; intake, digestion, and output, even though this Nephilim story in the Bible occurred to me just now in connection with it.

These people (Gods) were giants and were highly intelligent, giving Moses and others as Ezekiel many scientific processes, and mind processes to benefit our mankind, such as moral laws, and the building of the temple and the Ark of the Covenant.

MESSAGES FOR ME 11/09/71

Some messages from classmates in Long Beach.
- *Silverthorne is my gatekeeper.*
- *Joshua of the Old Testament is helping me; he wears purple and gold, including a gold scarf.*
- *My aura has a red ball on my right side near the ear and pink (love) on the left.*

SLEEP RESEARCH 11/11/71

Sleep research: Falling asleep and awakening periods are best suited for telepathy.   This is a mild trance; a passive state (viewing or spectating feeling) rather than an active state (where we are actively participating in the scene) and is the more valid state of telepathy. An active state will produce your own material or an involving of conscious thought in the telepathic or trance state.

MY FIRST READINGS GIVEN OUT 11/16/71

I saw and gave two messages for the first time. Clear pictures came before me with my eyes wide open in the darkened, church classroom. Along with the pictures was a knowingness, which flowed with them.

As I would pick up a knowingness of one picture, then the next knowingness would flow in. The pictures came first, and the knowingness came second. The messages were actually a mind reading of the person's anxiety *(immediate problems, or emotions)* and a comforting assuredness that all is well and will end well.

This seems to confirm and cover most messages I have heard from all kinds of preachers, Spiritualist, Catholic, Protestant, Jewish; the difference between the Spiritualist readings and the others seems to be that the Spiritualist is reading the spirit (mind) of a person, and the others are reading the body of the person.

Seems as if when the Christians and the Jews decided to call off prophecy when the Bible was printed, they decided to recognize a man by his body and not his spirit. They seem to think that the Bible ends all spiritual life. The Spiritualists never called it quits. They recognize man as spirit.

CHOOSING OUR LIVES 11/16/71

In most all religions there is the warning of possible damnation if a certain course is taken, that is not according to the words of the Bible in which they believe *(some believe that each word of the Bible is the word of God),* and this produces fear which enters the subconscious of the individual.

This fear leaves a scar in the memory of the individual according to the attention, which he paid to the sermon and his belief in such things.

This memory scar becomes a driving force for the individual even if he is not aware of it. This is another proof that we are robots or hypnotized beings.

We are robots in so far as we do not exercise our right to choose what goes into our senses. This leads me on to think about how to choose what we want to become of ourselves. Actually, we can become anything we choose so long as we exercise our choice of influence.

Which influence do we want? Whichever direction we want should be as a plowed road in a snow-covered field of ideas. This is a field of ideas, which coincide and oppose each other, positive and negative as everything else is in our universe. We must be the plow in action, aiming for what we choose to become and push the rest aside.

How do we find out what to look for? Make a list of what we want in this.

1. A good disposition, healthy in mind and body.
2. Good living conditions, clean and comfortable.
3. A strong wisdom, foundation and basic good rules to live by.
4. A clear understanding of all things, and ideas.

So how do we go about it? We must learn everything about all that we can, realizing that we are using these ideas and knowledge as guides, but not as being within us as ourselves except only what we choose to become one with. The more we learn of everything, the better we can choose for what we want to become. This says that learning of all ideas is necessary for proper growth. This also says that we should become spiritual to become wise, because in the spiritual state, all things are known at once.

Being in this spiritual state is what Christ is. Jesus became the Christ by being born into the Oneness with the heavenly Father: God. He was Christ from that birth, i.e., he was born into the Oneness of spirit and manifested in the human body. His consciousness was spirit, living in body. His consciousness was spiritual, totally aware of the spirit world. He was this way from his birth into the Oneness and knew no other consciousness. This consciousness was all wise, all knowing; it had the perfect knowingness of the total existence of life or love.

This to me is the road to go; spiritual consciousness; all knowingness; this is pure bliss, clear understanding, and total love.

MESSAGE FOR ME: WHITE KNIGHT 11/16/71

A spiritualist message was given to me. *Jeremiah is helping me. I am a white knight on a golden horse performing my mission.*

MESSAGE FOR ME: STAYING ON COURSE 11/23/71

• Nina gave me a message. *Felix is watching over me and prodding me on.*

• Linda's message to me: *I am staying on my course even though many influences around me are trying to swallow me up. I am seen pushing aside and throwing off these things, which detour me, and God (Spirit) says that I am doing the right thing (this agrees with my own spiritual correspondences).*

If she was reading my mind; then whose mind was I reading when this communication came to me? Was this the God mind? Was this the subconscious mind of me? Science of Mind says these are all the same minds.

GOD AND I: AN OBSERVATION 11/28/71

Seems as if I can love only so far, and when it comes time to give myself over to my love, I become apprehensive and unsure. This feels as if I do not know how to lose my life in order to gain it.

There seems to be a mental or spiritual block which prevents me from losing my life to anything that is short of a rock. Being a Taurus, this is my personality trait, and I sure do have it in me.

This Rock is God and I continue to search for this Rock in order to lay myself down and lose my life in IT. I feel this Rock within me and am gaining ground on IT.

I find it hard to understand and am steadfast in my pursuit of It. This Rock seems to be an all-knowingness; a perfect, complete, total truth and unification of all intelligence and wisdom. In this completeness of all knowledge, there is the perfect love and abandonment of self. . .The losing of personal life.

There is also a tendency to abandon this physical life in the process of entering the Oneness with the Father. There is a vague feeling that Oneness is attainable at the spiritual level, and not at the physical level at the present stage of civilization.

All the more, I feel that this aloneness must be attained in the physical form, also, because of the mere fact that it exists. I feel that all the attributes of this spiritual level will be surely manifested in the physical level eventually, and we are now in the process of manifestation.

Whatever is spiritual is thought in the mind of God, which is being manifested in the world of form. We are in the world of form and Thy will be done on earth as it is in Heaven.

PROPHECY AND PROPHETS 01/01/72

Prophetic dreams and ecstatic states were produced by artificial means most of the time. In the old country, the whirling dervishes are a good example. Old Testament prophecy and soothsaying differ only in that in soothsaying, the object is to gain information about the future.

Prophecy fell upon people as if they were chosen; not by heredity or schooling. Prophets prepared themselves to receive the spirit of prophecy, but didn't always receive it. Music was used in the preparation to receive. Continued gazing upon a picture or image helped them to receive.

They retained their consciousness and memory while receiving prophecy. Their gaze is fixed upon the activities of the living God. The future trend is known in the mind of God because we are living in the mind of God and as He thinketh, so it be.

To Read the Mind of God is Prophecy.

Revelations of John closed all prophecy by saying not to take away or add to this book.

I feel that this John of the Revelations wrote the book so as to put fear in the people and to make the book something that had to be believed or else. I feel that this Book of Revelations was written as a power play by the religious zealots. The New Testament was to be a closed society of ideas. A closed society is blinded death.

EMOTIONS: RELIEF VALVES 01/04/72

Emotions are the voltage stored up in the body as a charge on call and ready to discharge when needed. These charges are like a relief valve on a dam. When a person is faced with a situation of surprise, the emotions are released for safety, security and health. With emotions on tap, we will not dam-up and die, but ease the tensions of the moment.

ANXIETY: FEAR WITH A TRIGGER 01/04/72

Anxiety is a main drive to action; a fear triggered by cues or symbols for a remote danger rather than one physically or immediately present; fear and anxiety are two distinct qualities and different, too; anxiety is a disorganizer of effective action, anxiety is the central problem in neurosis.

THINGS THAT I'VE HEARD 01/10/72

- Sex drive is the failing of man.
- God is the only one who can forgive man.
- Immediately after sex, a wife hates the husband because she has been used.
- Resentment is felt for the weakness of the man.
- Don't go to the wife for security.
- Put your arms around her, love her, kiss her, and don't get excited. This is the right kind of love.
- Sex is failing.
- To build your image is to build a slave master.
- The ego is the extension of the consciousness of God. It should become One with God. It is the soul of man. It should reflect God.

DR. JAMES BARKER: RHINITIS 01/12/72

In my mind, a Dr. James Barker told me to eat carrots for my rhinitis. I had asked spirit what to do for my nose dripping and sinus problems. Two weeks later, I found that carrots are the proper source of cure, written in a health pamphlet at my neighborhood Safeway store on Cherry Street in Long Beach.

TO BELIEVE IS TO BE CRAZY 01/17/72

The conscious mind goes into the subconscious mind when it sleeps. When a person is crazy, it seems that the conscious mind is stuck in a particular area of thought, which I would term as a belief. This being caught up in a belief is a restriction on the conscious mind and it is as if the conscious mind is locked in and can't go about its business.

Suppose that a person had no beliefs whatever, and had a flexible mind to be aware of each moment for what it was. It would be a constant awareness and have no past-related emotions because it knew no past to refer to for reference.

This conscious awareness would see and have all the senses, and feel the emotions of the now experience. This awareness would have curiosity because it is being driven by all the senses which are hungry by nature. All these senses are searching for new experience. If the senses are not hungry, it is usually caused by beliefs.

This above is what I figure, so far, as being God manifested in the flesh. Now we give this awareness a memory bank. With this memory bank (the subconscious mind) there is a printed being formed which is the individual man. His awareness is the image and likeness of God.

Man is the sum total of all of his recordings (beliefs) in his subconscious mind which were placed there through the God awareness which is driven by the hunger of the senses which is curiosity, which is life.

This is a clear, but detailed description of man. Man is actually a living record of God. He is a manifestation of God. He is a result of God in action.

Each change that man makes is a result of his reasoning process which is the awareness reviewing the possibilities of gain for the self (ego) according to what it has on record as an idea of gain. Its idea of gain might be loss in a particular instance.

MAN IS GOD IN ACTION 01/17/72

From the above, I can only see man as God in action. I can only see all creation as God in action. Life is God's action. *All life is God's life. All mind is God's mind,* to be used by any spiritual awareness *(conscious mind),* dead *(there is no death)* or alive.

This mind is the common denominator of all life. This mind is God. Now, back to my original thought: crazy minds, sick minds, stuck in a belief.

According to Christ and all mystics,
1. The truth shall set you free.
2. Love is the ultimate existence.
3. Forgiveness of sins or forgetting of sins is a cure all.
4. Ask in my name (my example), believing that you have already received it, and you shall receive it.

Since we are the sum total of all our beliefs, we should find out what belief or beliefs have trapped our awareness, and to get our awareness back, we must dissolve the particular belief or beliefs in our memory which is the trapper.

We must be very careful to accept only the good and the healthy ideas into our subconscious minds via our conscious minds; *once our subconscious minds accept an idea as memory, the idea becomes us.*

MENTAL SPIRITS 01/21/72

A thought just arrived about the possibility of spirits being from our own subconscious minds and not being real.

From experience, I know that the subconscious mind (the holder of ideas) conjures up many fantasies from facts. Review your own dreams to see what I mean. The truths *(true facts)* are mixed with fantasy and play a game of acting as if on a stage.

There is an intelligence at work here, and it is trying to communicate with the awareness of the conscious mind of the individual. Thus we have our own self, playing games with us in disguises, trying to give us truth.

Now, in the case of spirits *(deceased persons),* in the same manner as in our own dream world, our subconscious mind is picking up facts about other personalities, and becomes an actor in it's own stage play, trying to tell us these facts. I think this is a good explanation of medium controls, and spirit entities.

DIE DEAD? 01/21/72

From what I can gather about belief, if we believe we will die dead, then we will. If we believe we shall not die dead, then we shall live

according to our belief about it. Of course, this is only temporary, because we cannot die, in fact.

KNOWLEDGE IS DEATH 02/01/72

Knowledge is the death of us *(our present ignorance),* and the
beginning of a new life *(another level of seeing things; another plane
of existence).* It is like taking a bath or shower and washing the ignorance *(evil)* down the drain, and seeing the new, good and true you,
which was always there, but hidden behind ignorance.

OPPOSITES/ONENESS/TRUTH 02/01/72

Opposites Are Two Necessary Ends, Which Hold The Middle Up.
The above was given to me in meditation on 1/30/72.
If we don't recognize that the middle is down, like when a jump
rope is down when the two persons at the opposite ends let it loose, then
there is no need to give recognition to the opposites.
If we see only the good and the best in everything **(the truth),**
then there is no such thing as opposites.
Opposites will be only different viewpoints of the same object.
Opposites are experiences in material and spiritual life, which are like
guideposts or guides, or teachers on the road to truth, which bring realization that there is only Oneness and harmony, and no such reality as
opposites in truth.
In Truth, there is only Oneness; One God, One way, One harmonious life, One reality, One love, One being, One mind; and all these are
good.
Opposites are <u>relative</u> to truth, they are not truth, and they are
reference points necessary for expressing life of truth. Truth is the flow
of progression unto Itself.
Opposites are the life given in which truth may flow with expression for the experience of the creation, which was created for life, or
experience, of the Creator.
Opposites are the tools of learning, and experiencing. When the
truth is known, opposites disappear from view. All the above flowed
through me as if from God.

DIFFERENT VIEWPOINTS 02/02/72

We can see things differently from different angles, and when we see things with God's eyes we see the whole picture, or truth, because God's understanding and sight is composed of all viewpoints in existence. We can say that God is centered, and when we become One with the Father, *we* are centered.

MEMORY/MIND...WHERE ARE THEY? 02/13/72

The whole body and brain are said to renew every particle of their substance every few years. If this were true, then memory (if it be a purely physical attribute) would be annihilated.

So. . . where is the mind? Some say that the mind is just physical. If our complete physical replaces itself every few years, then the unknown, immaterial mind is the instrument of memory.

The physical brain is just a material instrument for the messages and filing system, which relay the final information to our non-material minds. Food for thought!

THINGS THAT HAVE BEEN SAID 02/15/72

- Love your illnesses; don't regret them.
- Seek truth and discern; all things will be added unto you.
- Pride is driven by emotion. Emotion causes illness.
- Woman draws life from man.
- Man draws life from his surroundings.

BLUE TENNIS BALLS 02/16/72

In the Spiritual Development Class tonight in Long Beach, I saw blue spots about the size of tennis balls around the body of one of the students as I was trying to see the aura, and finally did. These blue tennis balls were floating up and down in circular fashion while the aura of many rainbow alive colors was about two feet outward from the body, in the widest areas of it. It was a beautiful, enchanting, awesome sight.

Last week I saw a colored aura for the first time; in fact three of them. The colors were beautiful! Now I know that they exist.

IS THE BIBLE ANTI-GOD? 02/25/72

I am bugged in my mind this morning. I have a great urge to say that the Bible is anti-God, and is nothing but the representations of men and their babblings through time to satisfy their inner ego feelings and yearnings. They wrote these things in good faith and belief, but do not really understand them.

If a perfect God is behind all this confusion, which is in the Bible, then the minds of men are very far from perfection, because they interpret the Bible in so many different ways.

If the minds of men are behind the Bible writings, then the whole thing makes more sense. The minds of men are of incomplete understanding, and therefore cannot write simple things in an understandable way.

There is an undercurrent in the Bible, which holds to simplicity and truth. That is, that:

1. God is a mysterious power of good and evil, which is transmitted into materialization according to the minds of men.
2. Whatever power manifestation is distasteful to a person is evil and given to the devil as the source.
3. Whatever power manifestation is tasteful to a person is of God.
4. This power of the invisible source seems to be drawn by imagination, emotion, concentration and durability of thought.
5. This power seems to fill a void, which is created after the desire is imagined with emotion and concentration, with durability, and then left or released totally from the mind and body to do it's work.
6. This seems to be a power or form created by man to do the will of man in the world about him. This power of man is really the power of God being used by man and man is really God in action as an independent, free-willed, responsible individual for a variety of feelings or experiences.

FIRST TRANCE: REV. NINA VAN H. 03/08/72

At the Spiritual Development class of Rev. Nina Van H's in Long Beach, near 7th street, I went into a trance for the first time.

What triggered it off had been a buildup of events:
Spiritually, through others, and me, I had been told recently to open up in faith and close down my material thoughts. This has been going on for about a month.

Recently, I received strong pains in my left hip joint and went to the Kaiser Hospital in Harbor City after a week of this severe pain, which practically crippled me. I was seriously thinking about taking a week off work so that my leg might heal.

Knowing that all physical manifestation is caused by thought, I asked at class tonight on a folded billet, "God, what is the cause of my left hip trouble?" Richard, the one who read the billet, asked for the answer in his spiritual being. The answer was, I am keeping to myself what I should be giving out for the benefit of others.

This was precisely what I had been told through spirit for the past month. When Richard told me that, I felt a sensation from my head to my hip and into my leg. A thought occurred to me that I was healed in my leg.

Later on, we sat in the dark to let ourselves become one with spirit (God) more easily. Linda, who usually goes into trance and speaks beautiful messages in English, Italian, and other strange languages, began to speak in English and as she spoke (*for*, or *as* someone from somewhere else), I knew this voice was speaking to me.

Then, Bethene (she does very similar things as Linda) began to speak in English, and I knew this was spoken to me, also. But these were not to Armand L. Archambeault, but to the real me; my soul everlasting.

These two girls coincided in their talks and did not speak as if directed to anyone special in the room. I became entranced by these voices as one of them, Linda, spoke a particular language which I knew that I knew, but could not remember where from or how.

My arms became unfolded and laid open with palms up in my lap and my head was thrown back against the wall. I said, "Thank you" to Linda's voice because I knew the voice was to me.

Then my body became electrified as if full of electricity, and I said, "These are my people, but I don't understand". Then tears formed in my eyes as if I had peace in my soul at last, and my leg had the sensation of becoming whole again; it froze and shook for at least a minute before it relaxed, and the relaxation felt so good that I knew I had been healed.

Just previous to this, as Linda was speaking to my material mind, I was deciding to let my self go and let God and only God's own goodness take me over in my body.

Then I spoke (while in trance) and I'll try to repeat word for word what I remember of it.

Knowledge is death, wisdom is life.
We must die in order to gain life.
Wisdom is life, life is change, change is life.
Life is love, wisdom is love, love accepts all things.
Love is truth, love is light, love is wisdom, love is light.
Wisdom is light and light permeates all things.
A flower is knowledge and its odor is wisdom.
Water is knowledge and the evaporation is wisdom, wisdom permeates all things.
Wisdom is the cycle of birth-and-death-changes.
Wisdom sees all and is love and love accepts all things.

It took a lot of shivering, convulsions, deep breathing, and gradual undoing before I had my own senses again. Afterwards, I was frozen cold and pale white, and slightly dizzy. Sort of a foggy feeling was in my mind. My mind was sort of stunned and had lost some normal activity of thought and inquisitiveness.

This morning I feel fine, and my leg feels as if a residue pain is left in it, but it has been healed.

NOTE: *As I type this in 1995, 1 can tell you that after 23 years, the leg is definitely healed. It hasn't relapsed. That pain was in my hip joint, and has not returned. Thank God.*

PSYCHOMETRY: WHITE ROCKS 03/10/72

I picked up two white rocks at the Cherry Street beach near my apartment in Long Beach. I psychometrized them without pre-thought *(just on the spur of the moment I decided to do it).*

Here are the strange, realistic and unexpected results.

1. *I am the rocks,* looking up a steep sand cliff wall to the tall, huge, trees on the edge of this tall cliff or bank. These

trees were bare all the way to the tops where thick green foliage profusely grew.

2. I am the rocks *(or one of them as if I were a wide, flat surface)* on the floor of a body of flowing water watching an alligator swimming above me. He swallows a big fish, head on. I am seeing his underside, and thinking I must be wrong or upside down, until I realized that I am the rock platform, and not myself.

3. A female woman or ape with a hairy body appears. I had the pictorial impression of a female human being squatting on me and giving child birth in or on my face, letting loose from all her openings in the lower body.

I was stunned with a shocking disgust and surprise as the rock, and as myself. The water kept flowing over my face, washing the debris down stream and washing my face. It sure felt good! This whole episode took about four minutes and was as real as if I was really there.

Then I saw myself in the belly of a large animal or mammal. It had giant ribs and was dark inside. This seems to be an actual existence of the rock platform used for childbirth, after it had been broken up in the future times, and had been swallowed by a fish of some sort.

ETERNITY IS: 03/13/72

<u>A.</u>	<u>B.</u>
All	Never ending
Always	Never begun
Always is	Never a part
Always was	Never a start
Always will be	Never a stop
Eternity	Eternity
Love is	God is
Light is	Mind is
Wisdom is	Spirit is
<u>Truth is</u>	<u>I AM ETERNITY</u>

YOUR AWARENESS IS YOUR LIFE 03/15/72

Your awareness is your point from which you view life. You have the choice of seeing in anything the good or the bad. Your choice of awareness makes you what you are. Your choice of awareness chooses the food for your subconscious mind. Whatever is assimilated or digested into your subconscious mind becomes the real you, or the soul.

Your soul is your record of your spirit, and your spirit is your awareness, so, the modern way to say it would be:

1. Your subconscious mind is the soul; the record of your life.
2. Your awareness is the spirit; the transmitter to the subconscious mind; the chooser of what you will become.

Now, when I speak to you from spirit, I mean that my awareness is receiving food from the spirit of God, which is <u>All.</u>

When I speak to you, I ask that you open your soul for the digesting of the spiritual food, which I pass on to you for your total health, which is your total Truth, which is your total Awareness, which is your total Heaven or Hell.

Heaven and Hell are qualities of your Awareness. What you think is what you are, and what you think is where you are. You make your own hat to wear in your life wherever that life may be, by creating the thoughts in your own mind of what you wish to be.

Your will is the steering wheel of your car or body on your eternal trip through life. Your life is now, and your life is what you choose it to be by conscious thinking. If you want to live in Heaven, then you must choose all the qualities of Heaven and seek after these things. Everything else will fall into place. "Seek ye first the Kingdom of God and all things will be added unto you."

WHAT ARE THE QUALITIES OF HEAVEN?

Truth: Truth is eternal and never changes. So what is Truth? Truth is God, Light/Wisdom, Love, Mind/Spirit, and Soul *(the final record of who you are).* Truth is a record of fact. Truth is Law.

Now, to define <u>Truth</u>, I must define all the qualities of Truth.

God: *(The first quality of Truth)* God is the complete total of all souls; and God is completely within each soul. You cannot see God because you see with God's eyes, but you can know God according to how deep within your own soul you can perceive.

When you reach to the eternal depth of your own soul, you meet your Father, God, in knowingness and complete unification of Oneness with All that is. This unification is Oneness, or harmonious acceptance of all things in eternity, because all things in eternity are God, and you are a part of *IT*, you are in harmony with *IT*, and so you are *IT*: God.

Light/Wisdom *(The second quality of Truth)* Light is equal to the Wisdom of God. Light is the knowingness of God, which, when we have it, we fear nothing because we know all things, love all things, and appreciate all things.

Fear is darkness and ignorance, and they are banished by Light, which is the Wisdom of God. *To get this Light, or Wisdom of God,* we must look within ourselves to the very depths of our souls. Here we become at peace with all eternity and receive whatever we ask even before we ask; it is that fast *(this agrees with Einstein's Theory of Relativity)*.

Our Father Within will take care of all our needs if only we will become One with Him and let Him act through us. *To do this*, we *must be in the world* doing our thing, but *we must not be of the world* because *we are not of the world and must not think this way because it is not Truth. It is an illusion, or game.*

Remember, Truth is eternal, and the material *(limitation or form)* world including our bodies is not eternal *(the forms keep changing),* but if we make ourselves, through our thoughts, to be of the world, then we will not be free spirits, or souls, but will be hung up to wherever out thoughts have made us cling to, until we accept the Light or Wisdom of God, which is Truth.

Love*(The third quality of Truth)* True Love is eternal and freely given to all. Love is the encompassing and accepting of all things in the universe as they are because they are God.

Love has the Light and Wisdom to know that life is change, and life is eternal, so that life is eternal change, and satisfaction is knowing that what is at this moment will eventually change.

This is the Wisdom of Love, which is God, or Truth:
Love has no fear because love has Wisdom.
Love has no jealousy because Love has no fear of loss
because Love has the Light and the Wisdom.
Love has no judgment because Love knows all things in
Wisdom and Light.

Mind/Spirit and Soul *(The fourth Quality of Truth)*   •
These two are eternal; they are the make up of man and God.
• Mind/Spirit is All (God).
> • Mind is the Totality, whereas Spirit is the movingness in the
> Totality.
> • Awareness is the movingness, and Spirit is also known as
> movingness *(They are both the same).*
> • Soul of man is called Personality.
> • Soul of God is called Super consciousness.

So, speaking in mathematical ways, as I am used to; Spirit/
Movingness is the vision of God, which is the All/Mind/Totality.

Soul is the unique record; the subconscious mind, or personality
of you, which is created by your choices made with your Mind/Spirit/
Awareness.

Your personal soul, which is your subconscious mind, is your
record of life in the mind of God, which has been made by your spirit,
which is your conscious mind, or awareness.

Picture this. You are going to make a recording. Your awareness,
or conscious mind is the needle that scratches your plastic record, or
your subconscious mind.

Your record, which is your subconscious mind, or soul, can be
seen, read and understood by all who contact the Father Within, or God,
or Super Conscious Mind.

God is mind, which is the medium in which we live, and is the
medium of which we are. Even the hairs on your head are counted and
known by mind and those who are of the same mind, God (Oneness).

This is Charity. *(The fifth Quality of Truth)* Charity is to freely
Love without passing judgments on others; "Judge not, lest ye be judged."
That means that whatever bad you think of others will bring suffering to
your own soul, because you are the thinker of the thought.

WHAT IS THE PURPOSE OF THIS TALK?

It is to help you to heal or know yourselves *now*. By healing I
mean digging your heals into the truth of life and making yourselves into
better recordings or souls or personalities for the harmonious pleasure of
the complete universe; God!

Remember, you are the result of what you think, what you think is your awareness, so choose what you think very carefully; think only of what you desire to be; this is knowing yourself.

Which do you choose. . .Heaven, Hell, sickness, happiness, misery, the rich life or the life of poverty? I love you all, and see God only in each one of you.

I Am, Armand L. Archambeault

IN-CLASS READING FOR ME 03/15/72

A monk named Gwen from 1636 wants me to call on him for assistance.

TIME/LIFE IS DEATH *(Ecstasy = Timeliness)* 03/22/72

To know something is to Believe *(Be-live)* it in the now of time. This is why knowledge is death, because knowledge is a change of awareness *(consciousness)* from the former to the present, just like reincarnation.

Time is death, also, because time is a limitation as is belief. All limitation is death, and belief is limitation. This would mean that if life is change, then life is death, also *(That is enlightenment)*

NOTE: *Year 2000 (See the movie: American Beauty. This movie will help to explain what I am saying. Stay until the end of the movie in order to understand all the trashy lives which are exposed)***.** *(PS. . . I was tempted to leave the movie after a short while, but I am glad I stayed until the end.)*

FATHER IS THE SON, LIVING WITHIN ITSELF 03/23/72

The Father sees all and knows all and is all.
The Son sees and knows in part because of time and space.
The Spirit is the life or action, which is the movement of the Son's awareness in the Father.

ALL ARE ONE, ONE IS ALL
THE SON LIVES IN AND FOR THE FATHER
THE SPIRIT IS LIFE OF THE SON IN THE FATHER
THE FATHER IS THE SON, LIVING SPIRITUALLY WITHIN
HIMSELF

E-MOTION IS POWER 04/19/72

Identical twins have identical bodies, genes, senses; and in this respect prove that we are as TV transmitters and receivers.

When something happens to one twin, even death, the other reacts the same reaction even though the physical act only occurred to the first one.

In this same sense, we are all influenced by and influencing others with our thoughts and feelings.

It appears as if the *strong emotional feeling has more power than regular feeling* and can be picked up by more people easier than with no emotion.

When we are in a relaxed, meditative, prayerful, God-like state of mind, we are in a sending and receiving state, or in the spiritual state: this is the natural state, or unmodulated state of mind.

In this unmodulated state of mind, we have an omni directional technique called imagination, *or thought director, which chooses the direction of thought, or in other words, the target for sending or receiving. Imagination is our center for creation.*

In this state, we have a power generator called E motion, which gives a boost to the impulses we send and receive. I term the E-motion as Easy Motion, because *the nerves and muscles must not tense.* They must remain at ease. The Easy Motion is expressed in thought, and not in movement of tissue of the body. I feel that love is this Easy Motion carrier. Love is Oneness-Openness.

Love is acceptance and Oneness in vibration or wavelength. *Love* is a fine tuning instrument of our minds. It *is a choice.*

MESSAGES IN LONG BEACH: BURMESE MONK 05/10/72

At Reverend Nina H's, in Long Beach, Janet gave a reading to me. She said that a Burmese monk was proud of me and said I would be teaching and preaching from a pulpit soon. He had on a brown robe and bright blue sash or belt.

MESSAGE IN LONG BEACH: ZECHARIAH 05/23/72

Again at Reverend Nina's class, Nina said that Zechariah is on hand for my aid; my feet are being wrapped in white, to go into my white shoes for my mission. Janet said that a monk is here again.

Carry said that I have a Bible in one hand and am seeing God in everyone.

NOTES: SIN, EVIL 06/10/72

Cathars, maybe Norma is one of these; look them up. The Cathars were a medieval European sect of self-denying Christians, maintaining a dualistic theology.

On the moon there is no sin or evil because the devil has control of earth, not the other planets. This sure sounds like bunk. First, because there is no devil, and second, human beings are the source of so-called evil and sin.

EVERYONE IS COMPLETE 02/03/73

If I see everyone as complete and eternal, then why should I say, "How are you?" to a person? This must be the art of compassion. This must be to find out what the other person is thinking about himself. By this method I can feel the other person's feelings and find ways to help him feel better.

THOUGHTS AND ILLNESS 02/11/73

If all mind ideas materialize, then why wouldn't the physical action *(or materialization)* produce new mind ideas through actual experience, which cause a strong idea or new belief in the mind?

If sin can be forgiven in the mind then can sin be forgiven by the physical cure before the mental cure? Example: If I get cancer by wrong mental attitude over a period of years, and I can't seem to change my attitude while I am having cancer, then if a doctor physically cures my cancer, then I might receive the idea into my mind that my sins are forgiven, and change my ways *(repent).*

This leads me to a theory that when a physical ailment is cured by physical means, then the patient's mind needs to be led in new and better ways of thinking at the same time as a physical cure because the illness, caused by wrong thought, will tend to reappear in time if the pressure of wrong thought is not released by a new direction of mind *(repentance).*

WITH GOD CONTINUOUSLY 01/04/74

By being with God continuously, in my mind, I find that I can live the normally hard parts of my life with ease. This method and commitment have raised my tolerance levels. With God as my leader and guide, my animal nature is subdued; I now can literally live and let live.

REDDING, CA: THOUGHTS ABOUT REALITY 02/18/74

Q. Life is change, so what is reality?
A. Reality is this instant as it is now. Reality is time stopped. Life is time continued. Reality is death of time. Reality is what is in the awareness at the moment. Life is the death of reality. Reality is truth.

God says to take what you want, but whatever it is, you must pay for it one way or another; that is, you either suffer the pains of hell, or suffer the desire of the flesh; either way the payment is made.

Q. Is the whole greater than its parts?
A. The whole is the sum of its parts and *is its parts*; the parts are the whole, and the whole is its parts. The part is a whole within the whole and the whole is nothing without its parts, so I cannot say that the whole is greater than its parts because without its parts *IT* cannot exist. What is greater than the parts is the law in which they exist.

The Law

Q. What is the law?
A. Law is the rule of the game. Law is unchanging, unbreakable. Law is the Rock! Law is the direction giver! Anything goes within the law! The Law is a wall *(law spelled backwards)*.

Follow the wall harmoniously and live happily and easily. Hit the wall and bust your fist. Study and know the law first. Then proceed, because we are in the survival of the fittest game. The way to be fit is to know the law first; then proceed in glory.

Since life is change and law is unchanging, the law is death. If the law is death, then since God is Law, God is also death. We are life, and God is death. This sounds very true. God is not dead, but is death.

Death is the ending of one thing and the beginning of another.

Death is a change in material life, but not a change in spirit, because spirit is eternal.

If we are life and God is death, then we are the life of God. We are the action of the thought. We are the life within the earth.

All good and all evil are the comings and the goings of us within God. Without the comings and the goings there is no life, no change, no good or evil. So what good is good unless it is the difference from evil? The contrast is the life. Without contrast there is no life.

So what good is death? Death is God. Death is the cessation of life and our time; death is bliss, bliss is blah! So life with the good and the evil is the only route to go. One cannot be without the other. There must be two things in order to have awareness or life. When all is One, there is no life; just death. The more the change, the more the life. The less change, the closer to death. Which do you choose?

My mind is the I AM in me. I AM what my mind thinks. My mind thinks from inherent memories from before birth, and from awareness memories since birth.

I AM the result of my inherited and acquired experiences. I AM a continuation of life, a movement in the mainstream of God. Things will change through my existence.

I AM a continuation in time.

SEEK AND YE SHALL FIND:
A SEARCH FOR TRUTH AND WISDOM 02/19/74

"He is the Truth". Whatever is the Truth is also dead, because Truth is what is right now, not yesterday. A second later, as change takes place, or as time passes by, or as life lives *(they are all the same),* the new Truth arises.

How come we have so many religious leaders such as Zoroaster, Buddha, Mohammed, Jesus, and all the new truths, which arise out of the old? Because this is the process of life. Truth changes the material world, as life changes.

An eternal truth is eternally dead and cannot change *(It is still Truth, but it does not change).* If it did change, it would be alive or always changing. Eternal law is dead in the same manner *(It is still law, but it does not change).* Knowledge is dead in the same manner. Knowledge is the end of a search; when the search is over, then knowledge is at hand. So knowledge is death. Wisdom used from knowledge gained is life.

Just as truth is dead in our changing material/physical world, the eternal truth of God is always dead and valid because God is spirit, eternal, and never changes. This material/physical world is actually an illusion/fantasy game of training for the soul *(spirit).* It is a virtual reality.

Wisdom is life because it is constant understanding. Wisdom observes all and lets all do its thing; lets it live, in other words. Live and let live is a description of wisdom, because wisdom is life, wisdom is love.

Why is a know it all despised? Because it is a sign of death. It implies the ending of something and therefore there is no more room for life. We are alive and cannot by nature feel happy with death because it is our ending of life as we are accustomed to it.

Seek and ye shall find, the title of this thought-paper, means live and die. The seeking is life and the finding is death.

This is the secret of life; life is seeking. Seek and find is the story of life; it is the persuasive force behind all life. For the continuation of life we must die. *In order to have* life ye *must be born* again, all the prophets have said throughout time. They say this because they know the secret of life, too. In order to be born again we must die, whether born again in another spiritual life, or born again in another physical life.

RELATIVITY 02/22/74

God is Absolute.
Everything else is relative.
God is death.
Life is relative.
We are life, so we are relative *and we have relatives, too.*

As I look into this matter, I see the movie reel again; the one which I spoke of in relation to time. Each picture frame in the reel is death, while *IT* is motionless. Each frame, projected and moving through time brings life to the dead pictures. In the ABSOLUTE *(death, God, or Universal Law)* is non-relativity.

This ABSOLUTE contains all there is or was or will be. This is the projector *(self contained, battery (GOD) powered)*. *IT* remains dead, and as it thinks *(reactionary thoughts)*, the thoughts are not inside the projector as with our heads, but its thoughts are direct life in the world, as we know it. *IT*'s thoughts are our thought processes. Its thought *(our thoughts and lives)* is life in action instantaneously. *IT*'s thoughts are *IT*'s life and *IT* is still dead.

Everything in this relative world is the life of IT. So, all there is in life, is relative. When we reach a non-relative point, which is 0, we are dead, but actually dead does not mean absolutely dead, but relatively dead. We would be dead to this life, but born into another life in the many mansions, because our awareness is the life of The Absolute in relativity and what The Absolute is cannot perish. The Absolute is ALL.

All the relativity must keep changing in an orderly balance *(within Universal Law)* and not one iota can be abolished without canceling God Itself, the ABSOLUTE. So there is no such thing as death as we know it; there is only change!

TIRED AND BORED 04/14/74

Today, I feel tired and bored; not over worked, but over fed and lonely. I need a laxative and a friend who understands the mind, universe, God, etc. The average daily life is so boring all the time, now (been single for eight years).

Everyone is so much interested in himself and his entertainment that he doesn't have time to see or feel the world; the life of things. He is under pressure of selfishness and habit. I want to meet one who is interested in living life at every turn. It costs nothing and generates love and life. I want to experience the unknown realm of mind. I feel like a prisoner in this body.

DREAM: BOB/CEMENT BUMPER 06/24/74

Had a bad dream about Bob *(my brother)* again. The last time he was drowning and this time he bumped his head on a parking lot cement bumper.

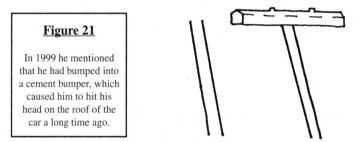

Figure 21

In 1999 he mentioned that he had bumped into a cement bumper, which caused him to hit his head on the roof of the car a long time ago.

I awoke immediately as it happened, about 4-5 a.m. Wednesday and my heart was beating very heavily as if I was right there. I cried over him in the dream as he was lying there.

NOTE 1994: *I have owned a business for twenty years and used up most of my time for the business, therefore I had a twenty year interlude where I spent less time in activities pertaining to the writing of my book.*

MESSAGE: THE DISTRACTIONS OF THIS WORLD 04/23/93

The attractions of this world, such as the big cities, fashions, movie stars, etc; are the distractions that crack the human spirit, such as a cracked egg. These distractions open up, or crack the spirit, and fill the cracks with what we might call garbage, and they tend to split the cracks open wider and wider as we pay more attention to these distractions.

MESSAGE FROM BUFFALO SPEAR 04/24/93

Go off into the middle of the waters, relax in the sunshine, solve everything good, enjoy the quietness, bring friends into your circle, become one with all, enjoy, reflect on the past, bring it all together.

Buffalo Spear said that he was talking to me and is bringing my triangle together; body, mind, and spirit, and the all-seeing eye of the present, guiding me through all the hard work into the bright light beyond.

REGULAR MEDITATION: COLLAR TIPS AND TIE 04/29/93

A man with long, pointed collar tips and a tie; can't see the face. Hourglass and candles, implying patience. *My impression is to have patience with this man that I have been thinking about.*

REGULAR MEDITATION: J.G. 04/30/93

J.G.'s middle two fingers, left hand. Black-brown derby hat; a round derby hat like Charlie Chaplin. Greek art, statues, sculptures. *Couldn't figure this out, except that maybe this person is a great actor, and has traveled a lot in Europe.*

CHAPTER FIVE

LETTERS I WROTE TO OTHERS WITH AN EYE ON GOD.

Religion, God Is Real, Not Belief, Life Is Eternal
Circa 1994 Letter to A

Hello A,

About religion. . .in my mind, most all religion is evil, because it brainwashes people's minds into a belief system. Not all of them are based on truth. Most all of them create gods out of anything that is handy and might work for them. After a religious leader is dead, then he is made into a god, the only god, and a superior god. The people swallow all the legends that are manipulated for them as if they were real and true.

When the mass of people become educated through the new advent of world communications, which is fast developing, this belief stuff will be seen for what it really is: the manipulation of people's minds for the power of a few.

God is a reality, not a belief. We live in God, and are expressions of God. We are created of God, which is the only thing there is. God is the medium in which we live. Good and evil are necessary in order to have life. We are the life of God.

The process of good and evil intermingled with free-will choices that we make, are the ingredients necessary for life, and education. Our duty is to learn the laws of life (God), and to live by the rules. The best way to learn is by experience, and the best way to teach is by example. Jesus taught by example. When he said "In my name", he was saying, "By my example".

Our goal is to be able to live with everyone else in cooperation and respect with and for each other. We all are made of the same source. . .God.

NOTE: *This is a thumbnail sketch of the results of my 63 years of seeking (I am now 70, and I began at 7).* Seeking never stops, just as this universe never stops. Being one with the Father, as Jesus was trying to teach us, is the way to go. The Father is always with you, but with your free will, you must choose to be with the Father or not.

Heaven is when you are one with the Father, and hell is when you are not. Life is eternal. Your personality never dies, because it is an expression of God. Life is a continuous learning process. . .eternal. Death is just a graduation to another phase of learning.

With this, I'll stop for now, Armand

LETTER TO R 11/03/94
God

Hello R,

Glad to hear from you, and to find that you are not dead yet. My stuffed up head is gone, now, and I have a dizzy head. Haven't figured out why. We were in Perdido Beach, Alabama for the last two weeks. The dizziness started while I was there. Did a lot of fishing and really enjoyed it.

You mentioned that I do not believe in God, and yet I have these experiences. When I say that I do not believe, it is because I have no reason to believe. I know. . . I know God. Also, I choose to not believe in anything.

Believing, to me, is making up stories to make me something that I am not. Instead of believing something that an outside influence wants me to believe, I study it, analyze it, and try to become it. If I cannot become it, it is not true for me.

Through my prayers, desires, studies, analyzing, fasting, etc, into God, God has come to me, and expressed himself in many ways. He has answered my prayers in my sleep with statements, explanations, a new Our Father prayer, which can be understood by me, with visions on my eyelids, etc.

He has answered my prayers with daytime visions in the air, which

I could watch with my external eyes, with loud voices in my head, and with knowingness in my mind that is confirmed by Him. He talks to me in meditation, and expresses Himself in the form of Gabriel the Archangel, who is the voice of God, the Father.

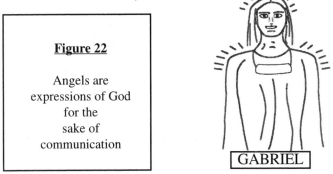

Figure 22

Angels are expressions of God for the sake of communication

GABRIEL

God is an *IT*. God takes many forms in which to express Himself to us by various means. We live in *IT*, and cannot see *IT*, because we are *IT*, and don't know *IT*. When we know *IT*, we are one with *IT* (the Father). We have our being in *IT*, and have the choice of being one with *IT*, or being in hell, which is the absence of *IT*.

This hell is by choice only, and is not forced on us. Heaven is the kingdom of *IT*. Heaven' is where *IT* lives, and by our choice of becoming one with *IT*, we live where *IT* lives and enjoy the goods of Heaven. Heaven is a state of mind, as hell is. Heaven is eternal, and hell is not, unless it is chosen permanently.

Got carried away there. I'll go on to something else. Happy sixty again, and welcome to the world of pain. Pain is good, and it reminds us of our age, and the wearing out of our bodies that we use here. The Cable TV networks are infested with bad stuff, like HBO, Playboy, and others, which promote swearing, disrespect, loose sex, nudity, drinking and smoking.

Got to watch CNN's Talk Back Live. I highly recommend a cable company that carries CNN programs. They are sensible, as a rule, and they originate in Atlanta, Georgia. That's where you are.

Love to you both, Armand (Andy)

LETTER: TO R 11/23/94
Great Questions: Why I Call God IT

Dear R,

You wrote a good letter. I like the challenge of the questions that you posed to me for thinking. I am still having dizziness spells, off and on. In the morning is the worst. What is the name of your medical book? I might take some Dramamine in the future. Thanks.

I call God *IT*, because *IT* includes everything that exists. God is spirit, which is mind, which is *us* living in an animal body. I live in an animal body. The animal body and I live in God. That's why I must call God *IT*. *IT* cannot be named, or even imagined with our finite thinking, because with our earth animal use of mind, we cannot see the forest for the trees.

It is when we join *IT*, or become One with *IT* (the Father mind), as Jesus taught, that the heavens (eternal mind), will open up to us. *IT* is too grand to have a name. *IT* is beyond comprehension. *IT* is what Jesus was tuned in to. When tuned into *IT*, we get filled with understanding. Jesus called *IT* Him, and Father. . .*IT*'s all the same.

QUESTION #1
Why do people raised by animals act like animals, even when they become adopted by humans?

Boy, this made my mind go into a frizzy. It's a great thought. Here goes. People raised by animals act like animals because they are living in animal bodies. When they are exposed to God, then they realize, ignorantly at first, that they are different from animals, and stretch their thinking beyond the barriers that animal thinking did.

As they are expanding their thinking, they will be more human, and less animal. As they expand their thinking into the realm of God *(spirit),* then, as much as they join God, they will increase in human behavior.

I don't know if these children had a gradual introduction to God, or not. Do you know?

I think that they would die early because of the shock of less freedom, and many new restrictions, drastic change of diet, and lack of spiritual knowledge.

An example of the lack of spiritual knowledge bringing on early death is developing in the news every day, now. Our children are not getting the spiritual knowledge they need, and they are being fed all this crap in the movies, TV, papers, and all news media.

Because of this lack, they are killing themselves by suicide, and killing others, also. They are dying younger because of lack of morals.

Materialistic, communistic Russia died the same way for the same reason. The overall consciousness of Russian government was Godless.

QUESTION #2
Why are humans so ignorant?

Because we are born on the earth in animal bodies without memories of pre-birth in order to learn how to co-operate with all others, and earn our way through the school of life the hardest and fastest way possible. This is the best way to learn. . .the hard way. Over and over it will be repeated here until we learn how to get along with each other.

After graduation from this planet and body, we die and transition to another life form *(body),* where we will be less ignorant, but time will not exist in the same degree. It will take longer as we progress, because of the lack of time. We are on a launching pad, heading for eternal schools. How is that for an answer?

QUESTION #3
Did God intend to teach humans what He wanted us to know through the Bible?

I think that that question is also the answer, somewhat.
The Bible is just a written history of the Jewish people, and there is a lot of spiritual stuff that was introduced into it. Many of the references to God were only the priest-gods, not God, as we know God.

Way back in the early parts of the Bible, the priest would ask God a question by throwing dice which had symbols on their sides. Whichever side came up was the answer from God. These were the Urim and Thummim, which were kept in the pocket of the Ephod *(apron).*

At other scenes, they threw lots, or sticks, in order to get answers from God. This is no more than psychic stuff, or fortune telling.

Jesus was the best psychic in the Bible. He was good at it. A psychic can tune in to God, or any other thing that he or she wants. There is no limit to the use of the mind (spirit).

The spiritual stuff was learned by the prophets, who had learned how to become One with the Father, and get some understanding. There is a lot of junk in the Bible, and many alterations, which have been introduced over time by leaders. Some were scribes' mistakes in copying; some were intentionally done for the sake of power and putting fear into the ignorant masses.

C.5 LETTERS I WROTE TO OTHERS WITH AN EYE ON GOD

But. . .there are many good spiritual ideas in the Bible, which would reflect communication with God. There is a lot of spiritual stuff in the Bible that is no more than the best judgments of the Jewish leaders over the centuries, which is similar to our government, which makes the rules of living for our best good.

Many of the ideas in the Bible are taken from past histories of other cultures, such as the Greeks, Babylonians and Egyptians. If we would know everything that we are supposed to, we wouldn't be here. This is a school of hard knocks.

QUESTION #4
Were we humans cheated intentionally?

Yes. As I said earlier, we are ignorant in order to learn faster, harder, and deeper, until our personalities change enough to live the golden rule naturally.

Well, I sure have had a chance to think hard, and search wide, in order to answer those tough questions. I appreciate your asking them. I firmly accept the knowledge that comes from conversation. Talking and communicating help us to know ourselves. A person gets to know himself a lot better when he talks.

My granddaughter is cooking her first Thanksgiving meal tomorrow. She is elated. I think she will do a great job.

'Twould be a great feat, if you could send some of your Georgia water this way. We need it bad. Seems like we are advanced enough, now, to bring that extra water to California. We move gasoline, oil, electricity and gas all over the country, _why not water_?

My mind is getting dry, now. I'll have to quit.
Here is a nice poem that I wrote to my son, Mark, two weeks ago when he got married. I had asked Father to write it for me. I'll put it on the other side of this paper.

Goodnight, and lots of peace to you both,
Armand

A FATHER'S YEARNING FOR HIS SON

In this day of wedded bliss,
I must tell you this:
For many years, Mark has yearned for his father,

and his father has yearned for his son.
Now, in this marriage,
the father feels secure for the son,
who seems to have won,
by his own overcomings,
his place in the sun.
The son is a mature individual, now, and
shows good example,
of which the father has seen many samples.
The father is very proud of his son,
and delighted about the bride he has won.
May they be the closest and truest of friends
first in the love of God,
and then in the love of each other,
now, and forever.
Thank you, Father
Love to you both, dad.

LETTER TO V 12-01-94
Religion, God, Politics, Raising Children, Armageddon, Bible, Hypnotism

Hi V,

Congratulations to Jim for not smoking and drinking. I agree with you about the Government Social Programs. They cannot be controlled properly from the Federal level. They must be controlled by as local as possible control, such as County or City.

The more distant the control, the more chance for graft, theft, favors, and stretching the rules. The rules in the printing of the laws need to be specific enough so that they are black and white, and cannot be stretched beyond the original intent.

My feeling about parents is what was quoted as Jesus' feelings. My only parent is Father God. I feel that parents have the responsibility to raise their young to the best of their ability, and then, when of age, release them to the world in order to express themselves in the world. The responsibility ends there for the parents. From that point on, there should be respect for each other as individuals, but no more control of one another.

C.5 LETTERS I WROTE TO OTHERS WITH AN EYE ON GOD

When parents want to control the adult children, either by constant phone call, innuendoes, pressure, excessive visits, etc, they do not know how to love a person.

Love is not judgmental, but freely given. Love does not control, but gives freedom to express within all law, natural, social, and spiritual.

I still think that Clinton is a well-meaning person with good ideas, and his biggest problem is trying to satisfy everyone, which even Jesus could not do. Clinton made some big mistakes in the marriage department, and he is still paying for them.

This world is a real world of solid texture, which needs to be cut with a sharp knife. I would like to have all social programs restructured with a modern day attitude of the responsibility of the individual, and not of the federal government.

As far as Armageddon goes, it is a lot of bull. All religions are evil, in my mind. Religions enslave our minds into a belief system, which separates us from reality, and puts us into a dream state of idealism. This idealism is o.k. but religion makes it a reality instead of just a goal to have.

Religions can do so much good in the future when they come down to reality, and break away from myths.

After a leader has died, people make up stories, rumors, exaggerations about the dead person, and eventually make them into gods: *(Zoroaster, Buddha, Mohammed, Jesus, etc,).*

There have been many persons who were called gods in past history, who were resurrected from the dead, who did miracles, and were born of virgins. They were just human beings who were exaggerated in history, so that people would succumb to their religious rulers, the same as politics.

God is a reality, but religion is a false look into this reality. Religious leaders are not gods. God is the medium of which we are made, and in which we live. God is not a he or she, but the combination of the two, which is really an *IT*.

IT is all encompassing law. We are the life of God, the expressions of God.

We are individual expressions of the one God, with a free will to express within the laws of God. Jesus was teaching this, but people could not comprehend. When we become One with the Father as he did, we have entered the Kingdom of Heaven *(unity of our mind and God mind)* where we should store all our treasures that no one can take away.

The words in the bible are put there by man, have been altered by man, and our religious leaders created a god story from this man-made book, which holds up their belief system.

All people who accept a belief system work hard to convince others that it is truth so that they can be re-enforced in their beliefs. Through amazing hypnotism from constant exposure to these beliefs and ceremonies, and the fear of death, the sheep encompass these ideas as their own. That is the very reason that there is so much hypocrisy in the sheep.

They are using their God-given intellects to live in a dream world, and once in a while they slip through the cracks between belief and reality.

Whoa!!! I'd better stop for now, on this subject. The above is the culmination of my experiences of the last fifty-seven years of search. I started when I was seven years of age, when I bit the host during communion and was sorry *(as the nuns said that I should be)* because I had bitten Christ.

Love to you, Armand

LETTER TO M 12/09/94
Peace of Mind, Negative Fear, Quality of Life, Stress

QUESTION
Where Is Your Peace of Mind?

Your peace of mind is everywhere, when you join your mind with the mind of God, the Father, and give your whole life to God. This means that whatever happens in your life, when you are One with God and when you have tried your best, is o.k. God will take care of it *(actually, you are taking care of it by asking God to take care of it, in your Oneness),* if you will remain with God in your mind *(in your Oneness).*

The worst thing that can happen is that you will die, and that is not so bad as you may think it is. God should always be your best friend, before anyone else, including yourself.

QUESTION
Where Is Your Peace of Mind, Free From Worry and Negative Thoughts?

C.5 LETTERS I WROTE TO OTHERS WITH AN EYE ON GOD

As above, letting God take care of the world, which is His and not yours. You have no reason for worry. Just do the best you can under all circumstances and the results will be o.k. no matter what.

A few negative thoughts are a self-preservation ploy, built into the mind. They are necessary for the continuation of life. This is a part of the natural fear process for self-preservation.

Sometimes, a person will go overboard and dwell on the negative fear process too much. This is a disturbing feeling to the person that dwells on it too much. This concentration on negatives and fears is a lack of trust and friendship with God. I'm very serious about God. God is reality. This excessive fear process will eat a person's body and mind, which causes real physical and mental illness.

I know that you have inherited a good portion of this from your mother, but, just as I have changed my life so that I won't have the bad qualities of my parents, you should do the same, if you want to improve on the past.

Keep the good qualities of your parents, and refuse the bad qualities. The point of your life is to improve it over what you were born into. Do not be worse, or at a standstill, but be better. Take the best, and leave the bad behind you, and invent some new good ones for yourself.

I'm serious about having God as your best friend. There's no fairy tale here. I've studied God for sixty-three years, now, internally and externally.

Religion has nothing to do with God. Religion is a belief system, and there are many different systems on this planet. They all end up killing each other, and feel that they are saved, and all others are heathens, going to hell *(which doesn't exist)*.

God is real, and He is All of you. Live with God, and God will live with you, inside of your mind *(the residence of God, called Heaven)*. Your free choice is to choose God, or distance yourself from God and try this world on your own. Give your life and appreciation to God, and you will have no excessive fears. Yes, this is peace of mind.

QUESTION
Will God Relieve Your Stress By Being With You All Day?

God is always with you wherever you are. The trick is for you to be with God by your choice. It is just a matter of training your mind to be close to God at all times. God is always there, but if your mind isn't recognizing, or tuning in to God at all times, then you are not always with God, but God is still always with you.

God has given you the choice, or free will to be with Him, but He is always with you, and does not interfere in your life unless you cause God to do it.

Love to you both,
Armand

LETTER TO R 01/11/95
Born With Blueprints, Today's Prophets

Hello for 1995, R,

Christmas was good, and the New Year will definitely be as good, or better. I am grateful either way. We have had the flu twice each. That's enough. I haven't published the poems yet. Any ideas? Glad you like them.

QUESTION #1
Humans Are the Only Creatures On Earth Who are Not Born With A Blueprint In their Being (Brain) Which Tells Them What They are, What They Need, For Food, Etc.

We *are* born with blueprints. They are called DNA. Our stomachs tell our subconscious minds what they want. We don't follow it, though, because we are free will creatures.

You thought that God gave instructions to the Prophets of old. I agree with that. Also, anyone can be instructed, as the Prophets were, even today. All that is needed is becoming One with the Father.

The Father is the medium in which we live and breathe. The Father is All. We live in the Father, and ignore the Father most of the time. Ignoring the Father is the same as eating the apple in Eden. The eating is an act of ignoring, or disobeying the Father. Becoming One with the Father means that we are listening to the Father and following *IT*'s advice.

This advice is not church dogma. Church dogma is man's rules for gaining power over man through fear in the name of love.

Lots of love to you both,
Armand

LETTER TO R 02/22/95
Gods, Gabriel, It, Father

Dear R,

Thanks for the long letter. On the first line you said, "No God huh?" I never said any such thing that I can recall. If I did, then I didn't mean to convey such an idea.

As far as Osiris and all the others that were mentioned, they were people, not God. There is a term Gods which means those beings that are advanced far beyond our comprehension, and we think of them as superior because of their advancement, but they are not God. . .they are men just as we are men.

I call God IT, because God is both male and female. There is no gender for God. God is the total existence of everyone and everything. IT is omnipresent, everywhere at all times. ET's, etc are people. They live in God, also, the same as we do. We called them Gods in the old days, but that is because we didn't know any better. They were gods because they came from somewhere else.

Things have changed since then. There is and was only one God. God does not require a belief. God just is, and our existence is proof of God.

The churches promote men as God, and that is what is evil *(misunderstood)*. God is what Jesus called Father. Father is the God that Jesus prayed to, and remained One with.

Father is the term I use when I pray to God, which is twenty-four hours a day. I am One with, also, and I learned it from Jesus' words in the Bible.

On page two, you mention that: "God will set His Kingdom down here on one half of the earth". Well, I see God's Kingdom right here and right now, and that's what I understand Jesus as saying; that the Kingdom is here and now in my mind, and it is up to me to keep that Kingdom clean and worthy, so that God and I can live in peace with each other all the time, every day of my life throughout eternity.

This body I use is just a means of movement and expression on this earth where I am residing today, and I will use another form or body after I leave this one. The Kingdom is always where we are. It is the spiritual world; the world of the Mind. No one can add to, or take away what we store in our minds. This is where the treasure is built up by us; in the Kingdom.

On page three you seem to think that I am in agony because I am alone. I am in bliss, not agony. I am excited about life and goodness.

Gabriel has appeared to me in my living room while I was watching TV. He said that he is Gabriel, my Father and my Guide. He did this on his own. I was surprised that he had no wings; he was dressed in a bright white robe! I wasn't that familiar with him until he appeared in daylight to me, and spoke to me.

Since then, he advises me on many things in meditation, prayer, and they are wonderful. He is the voice of God. God cannot be seen, or speak. God is law.

I can see that you are concerned because I think differently from you about these matters. Do stay as sweet as you are, and don't be so concerned for me and my life. I am fine, and you are fine. We are both living the best that we know how, and it is wonderful that we can speak freely with each other.

Happy Valentine's Day, and Washington's Birthday,
Armand (Andy)

LETTER TO L 03/09/95
Heaven And Hell

Dear L,

I am still reading the copied book you sent about life after death. It is very interesting. There have been many books written in this manner, and they all seem to say something different from each other.

After I die this time, I'll tell you what I experience. I have read URANTIA all the way through, HEAVEN AND HELL by Swedenborg, another one about God, heaven and hell, the BIBLE, the LOST BOOKS OF THE BIBLE, ENOCH, and many more about heaven, hell, God, the church, religion, old histories, etc. Many of them say opposing things and I get a mixed feeling from the books. But, there must be something out there.

I have experienced many things in my own mind, also. To me, so far, I do know that God exists, and that my soul/spirit is eternal. Beyond that, I can't see any solid evidence of the other side that is the same for everyone. Maybe the people on the other side have all been reincarnated to different places.

Seems as if we all have different viewpoints of experience, which is what we were created for in the first place, and this will carry over into the next life, and the next life, and the next life.

This is my description of my conclusion as of today.

Love to you, L,
ARMAND

LETTER TO M 05/02/95
Cult of Religion, Last Days, Tears, Fears, Selfishness, God, Kingdom, Soul, Going To Heaven

Dear M

Thank you for your letter of sincere caring for our souls.

C.5 LETTERS I WROTE TO OTHERS WITH AN EYE ON GOD

I read the Revelations: 9+12. This is a fictitious fear used to gain members in religious groups. It promotes worship and respect for the Satan of the Bible, and detracts from the reality of God. This sort of idea fills educated peoples' minds with fear and disgust.

Even before Jesus, the Essenes and other End Times groups were already spewing their hatred on peoples through the spreading of fears about gods, devils, evil spirits, bad angels, etc. The witch doctors all over the world from way back and up to now have used this tactic to scare people, and gain attention and following.

Religions are no different from the old witch doctors. They are both based on magic, fear of the unknown, and laziness of the general public. In the Bible, beginning at Genesis 6:13, God has been said to be mad at the human race and would wipe them out, and it has not stopped yet, even with a rainbow promise that God was said to have made.

John the Baptist said the End Times were upon us right now in his time of life. Jesus spoke of the End Times of his time of life. Paul spoke the same thing, that it would happen before he would die.

This is pure trash, M.; this is fear mongering. God would not make a world and then be sorry for it. God cannot be sorry, and man should not be sorry, either. What is, is.

Believing in these things is a good way to be caught up in the cult of religion. All religions are cults of believers. The members choose to believe something as if it were true, and then want all their friends to believe the same stuff so they can be saved.

Believers are in great need of company, because down deep, they are not sure, and need reinforcement for their beliefs. I read 2Timothy 3:1-5. Man has always been this way, even before the Bible was written. This is nothing revealing or new, it is just another fear tactic to control the human mind in the name of religion or God.

The Last Days is each day and minute of your present life here on earth. Our lives are to be lived with the utmost care each minute for what we choose to eat, see, feel, think, smell, speak, and listen to, because each minute is our Last Days. We must be wise as serpents in all that we do. We are living in a bed of weeds, and must choose the right choices among the weeds in order to survive. This has always been.

I read Revelation 21:4. I cannot believe that a God will wipe away my tears, and eliminate death *(in reality, there is no death; a truly spiritual person would know this)*. Tears are selfish expressions of loss. Tears will be wiped away when a person stops thinking selfishly, not by a God, but by the person's own actions.

There is no such thing as death, so how can it be eliminated? Fear of death, as we think of death, is a selfish fear of loss of this vehicle that we call a body. When we learn that the body is not us and that we are the spirit/soul using the body, and that the spirit/soul is eternal, and that it is an expression of God, then where is there room for fear?

"The bible is the authority and is the basis for our faith in God and his promises." (You wrote this.)

The Bible is just a collection of writings chosen by those who want to control your mind, and put the fear of God into you. By your developing faith in these writings you are a member of a cult *(read the definition of the word cult in the dictionary)*.

Men were made into Gods by ignorant people in the past, and as we become more intelligent, we find that these stories of Gods are not true as stated. They were only political leverages used for control of others, by somewhat devious men, who always were, and will be, as long as they can find ignorant people.

We appreciate the fact that you are trying to help us. Thank you very much, and write to us as much as you like. We love you.
P.S. I am reading the tract, now.

Happiness is everywhere all the time if a person only chooses to be happy. Happiness is a choice of frame, or state of mind. Many people choose to be miserable because they are naturally selfish, and cannot bring themselves to appreciate life as they live it. They are like children who cannot get what they want. . .they pout and whine and act unhappy by choice.

The person who knows God, and is unselfish, appreciates all that he has with gratitude, and is happy. Guaranteed.

God is not a book. God is an experience within an unselfish soul; a soul full of unselfish love. This happens in your closet; your mind, where you are to keep all the treasures of living. God's Kingdom is not the earth, but your mind/spirit/soul.

In this life, your responsibility is to improve your soul, not your money treasures. This earth will pass away, but your soul will not, because it is eternal. Your soul is an expression of this God that everyone is so concerned about; it cannot die.

The manifestations of atomic material (matter) are but putty in the making of better souls. God's kingdom is not of this earth. I am not concerned as to what Paradise can be found on this earth, because it is not God's kingdom; it is ours for learning in. This earth to me is a training ground for the development of my soul *(the sum total of my being as of today as an expression of God)*.

C.5 LETTERS I WROTE TO OTHERS WITH AN EYE ON GOD

I am this eternal soul now and forever, living in different bodies for use in different dimensions of space and time. Going to Heaven is putting off what must be achieved today in our souls. Going to Heaven is no more than changing your attitude.

Must go now, lots of love to you,
Armand L. Archambeault.

LETTER TO M 06/19/95
Psychology Is No Excuse For Crime, Diets, Daily Prayer, Hypnosis, Spiritual Intelligence, Reasoning, E-Motions, Ignorance Is Promoted By Religions, Blind Faith, Dangers and Benefits of Psychology

Dear M,

Psychology is a good subject, as long as it is not allowed in court as an excuse for committing a crime, so that the wrong doer will not be punished. Going on a diet is not the way to go; it is better to change your eating habits for life, not a short period. That is why diets don't work; they are temporary satisfaction, but you will pay it back later, by getting fat again, so that you will have to diet again.

Lifetime change of habit will do the job for good. Keep cutting back on quantity eaten, and the fat grams consumed, and do some exercises, indoors or outdoors: walking, table tennis, etc., and prayer (which causes a change in your subconscious mind).

Your subconscious mind is what is the creator of your habits; it is the Automatic Mind. Train your subconscious mind to create better and new habits.

The subconscious mind can be trained through prayer, meditation, hypnosis (prayer and meditation are forms of hypnosis), and conscious new actions in the right direction with right positive attitude.

I had another article printed in the paper. It is enclosed. Most of what I write is shocking to the average person, because they live their lives by animal emotions, and not with their spiritual intelligences.

This animal body that we live in is misleading. It tells us to do certain things, which do not make sense to pure intelligence.

Pure spiritual intelligence is the truth, while the emotional/body feelings are basic lies. Emotional feelings are nice, and moving, but they are body senses and not mind senses.

As you learn psychology, I hope that you will communicate with me on the subject so that you can get a rounded education. Psychology is supposed to be a study of the mind, but I have seen where some of the teachings don't know the difference between the mind/spirit and the body/emotions.

Our heart-feelings are emotional, and are linked to the body that we live in. Our mind-intelligence senses can over-ride the animal heart-feelings and see through the lies of the feelings. We call this reasoning.

Emotional feelings are such as: Feeling sorry about something. Feeling joy, such as love. Feeling like you need something. Feeling lonely. Feeling worthless. Feeling unwanted. Feeling hateful about something. Feeling scared. Most of the time, an emotional decision is a bad decision. When Jesus spoke, he reasoned with people, appealing to the mind, and not the emotions. He did slip though, when he overturned the money tables at the temple courtyard, and used a whip to express himself. That was bad, but it was good, too. He taught a lesson through emotions to the general audience.

I was reading an article about Iran and the Islamic religion today. Here is a quote from their Islamic Salvation Front: "Democracy is a lethal poison based on impiety".

They warn against getting educated. In my opinion, they prefer ignorance, as do all religions, so that they have more control over the minds of the people. As education increases in the people, the people leave the religions.

Ignorance and a blind faith following is what the religions need and want in order to hold the memberships up.

This is the way that the knowledge of psychology can be dangerous, and yet revealing; dangerous so as to be used to control other minds for selfish reasons, and revealing so that understanding what is happening can give a person freedom of mind.

Better stop for now, (you owe me a letter, now)

Love to you both, Armand

LETTER TO R 06-23-94
I Am In Control Of My Life

Got your letter of June 14. Your bi-location experience is very fascinating (See below). This would be a good article for Fate magazine.

This idea of fate and destiny doesn't agree with my mind. Since my life is composed of zillions of choices and changes, I can't seem to fit fate and destiny with life. I feel that my life is mine to live, and nothing can run it for me, except by my choice.

Things that happen to me are the result of choices I have made, like where I go, what I do, etc. If I get hurt, or sick, it is because of my earlier choices of actions. Fate seems to be something that is under someone else's control, and I can't comprehend it.

I feel that if I do not control my life, I am dead, and have given up control. Therefore, it is in my best interest to enhance my thinking processes so that they will be as intelligent and sharp as possible. This life that we live is a tightrope to be walked with lots of care for survival. The responsibility for our lives is in our own hands.

Ignorance of the law is no excuse. This is God's love for us. Our job is to learn all laws, and abide by them.

What do you think? It's a big world out there, isn't it?

Armand

The Bi-Location Experience Of R Above

This happened when R was 5 or 6 years of age. R lived on a farm in the country and the neighbors were few and far between. Early one morning the Aunt, L, told R to run and get C, her sister in law and her nearest neighbor. The pain and urgency in her voice and the fact that she held her abdomen with both hands and was bent over told R to hurry.

R raced to the road leading to C's house and looked back. L was on the porch, watching her. Then the next second R was squeezing around a bed in C's house. No door or even a window was in that area but R had come in that way.

E, the brother of R, who was about the same age as R saw R and was so glad to see R, that he just laughed and helped R get past the foot of the bed. C was about finished cooking breakfast when C turned to R and asked why R had come there so early. R told her that L (her aunt) had sent R in a rush.

They left C's (sister-in-law's) house and walked to L's house, a good mile plus. All the way, the brother danced at R's side, smiling and talking and R was very conscious of the need to get back into her body without any of them seeing her do it.

R did not want to frighten the others. As they drew near the body left behind, and the farmhouse, R managed to do just that and C (sister-in-law) laughed and said, "Well I thought you were behind me; how did you get in front of me so quick?" Then E (R's brother) raced to R's side and R just laughed some more.

When they got inside L's house, L was sitting in a chair. C said, "R came and told me you wanted me to come."

L said, "Well, R never left the road; she's been standing right out there all this time."

C said, "Well, I know R did come to my house and told me you sent R to get me to come help you."

C said she knew what she was talking about. R was standing in the road all the time and an image of her (her spirit) was at C's house at the same time and R was aware of what she was doing at the same time. *(I've heard other stories like this).*

LETTER TO M 08/13/95
Wisdom, The Canoe Of The Father

Answering your last letter of 8/2/95. We are well and grateful. We are cool and refreshed. We are drinking lots of liquids. Thank you for your concern and suggestions. Very glad that you and E are going to church together. Going alone is no good for the marriage.

Very glad that you appreciate everything that you experience in your life, because the appreciation of what you have is the foundation of Wisdom.

Latest Meditation. ***Put away all your crutches, hang-ups, and sorrows; hang them all on the limb of peace. Enter the canoe of the Father, full of peace and healing, as it rides down the restful currents of Father's Oneness. (Bright and Shining One)***

Love to you both,
Armand

LETTER TO R 09/20/95
Gabriel, Attitude of Gratitude

Answer to your letter:

The Gabriel experience, which I had, was a reality in daytime vision and real, normal hearing (not meditation or dreams).

The doubt I have is similar to Exodus 3:11 when Moses said to

God, "Who am I that I should go?" Thanks for your insight; it was helpful.

New letter

We went to Yosemite last week and enjoyed it a lot. The waterfalls are outstanding when you are right under them and hear the rush of water as it falls to the ground level. It is like the sound of liquid thunder.

I had an eye examination yesterday. I'll be getting a pair of reading glasses (one vision rather than bi-focal) so that I can work at the computer without the neck strain that I must bear with the bifocals. The neck strain causes a tendency toward a headache, which I don't accept.

Kay is up to 98lbs this week. That is great! The more she weighs, the more her memory works. Seems as if I have more of her, as she gains weight, physically and mentally.

Gratitude is an attitude of thankfulness. An attitude of gratitude allows Father to fulfill your plans according to His Law. Let go and let God. Live in peace with gratitude and truth. Love to you and your family

Kay and Armand (Do you remember Kay Armand, the singer c1950?)

LETTER TO W AND G 09-27-95
Worry Is Evil, Lack Of Faith, Possessiveness, The Father Is Real

Dear W and G,

I hope that our letter is the first one that you get at your new home. We are glad the visit is over, and that we are in our own home again. The feeling is very good, when you are in your own home. There is no place like home. That should apply to everyone, I think.

What we went there for has been accomplished, and we feel good about it. We are very happy that you are moving in to V, where you will be able to relax and enjoy the benefits of life together as husband and wife with the least amount of tension, worry, fear, work and stress.

Live it up while you are together and alive with some health left. Thanks for all the meals that we had in your house and in the restaurants. Thanks for the times that we saw you two holding hands, and saying sweet things to each other. Those moments stay with us longer than anything else. They are precious.

Over the years you have been telling me to "call when I arrive in our home" after the flight is over, and I always tell you that I don't do that. Even so, you call us to find out if we are o.k.

The reason that I don't let people know that I arrived home is: My experiences with God the Father have told me that it is a wrong thing to do. By calling people to tell them that we are all right after a trip is promoting worry as a good thing, whereas worry is an evil thing.

Worry is a waste of imagination. Worry is the total lack of faith in God. It shows that the person is grounded in material things. It shows a need of controlling others. It shows a possessive attitude (which is the opposite of true love) rather than an attitude of gratitude, and acceptance of life, as is given by God the Father .

I have learned this over a long period of time and experience with God. This sounds like fantasy, but is true. God is reality, and I hope to teach others as Jesus did that the Father is real, and not just a story out of mythical history books (Bibles, etc.). The Father is reality which can be known with effort, desire, and seeking.

Becoming one with the Father is just as real as being in this world, but not of it. Material things matter not. Spiritual treasures are all that matters. (This has been a mini-sermon.)

Love (the most powerful tool that we have) to you both,
Andy and Kay

LETTER TO M 01/08/96
A Poem, Noah's Ark, Gods and Aliens, Tapping The Future, Formal Learning, Best High School Subject, Five Most Enlightened Religions For Today.

This is a poem by me:
Just got your letter, which was typed.
Very neat!
The rain came down in bucketfuls and more, the last couple of days
and nights seemed like inches and feet!
We had to stay warm so as to not get sore.
Wish you were here with us
So that you would not, over us,
have to fuss
about whether we would rust
in this downpour, which eliminates dust.

Thanks for your poem. It stirs the mind. Congratulations on self-control and planning ahead. You folks are to be commended for your diligence and perseverance (look those up in the dictionary).

M, are you implying that I will have to wear dark glasses when I am watching E smile? (You said he was going to get his teeth cleaned.) I'm glad you read my writings, and glad that you have remembered some of them, and are thinking about them.

NOAH'S ARK

What I have come across, so far, is that it seems that there is a wooden boat of that description on top of Mt. Ararat. It is not proved yet. There was a documentary made a few years ago that claimed to prove it, but the documentary was proven to be made through lies and trickery by a con man. The documentary was shown on TV, and was backed up by church people, too. The church people were very embarrassed to find out that they were tricked.

Way back in time, before our Old Testament was put together, there was a Legend, even before the Tower of Babel was built in Babylon (Iraq, today), that Noah was told by God to build the Ark, and to build it with certain woods and dimensions.

Noah was told to bring his family with him, and to bring, also, two of each kind of specific creatures, so that after the flood that God was about to bring, in order to kill off all of the other people (nice god), Noah could start another civilization. This story has been found in all the old history books (bibles) of 3000 years ago and earlier.

This story seems to be about some real occurrence. It probably started before the surface 'plates' of the earth were separated so much, and caused the continents to be so far apart.

Now, things get fuzzy way back then in the old times. Supposedly, God said to do this and that, and God did marvelous things, but there are many theories which are gaining proof, as time passes, that this God, and the Gods of all the old bibles were no more than advanced men from other planets and solar systems.

These Gods used the Jews, Babylonians, Egyptians and other earth folks before them as a chosen people, who were actually slaves, to mine different elements like gold, silver and such, which the Gods needed for their own purposes.

These Gods were far advanced in technology, and were worshipped by the people of earth. They had intercourse with the earth women, and thereby, they advanced our culture and intelligence. I think that those Gods are the ones who told Noah to build the boat.

Ask L. to write to me about her spirit confrontation, and dreams, so that I can study them. I would like to have a lot of details about her experiences. I thank her ahead of time.

Dreams of the future do happen, when we tap the wavelength of the future. The wavelength is a vibration, which you tune into, just like a TV set, in order to get the right station. What is needed, is to have a strong desire to see the future.

Go to bed with that desire on your mind, and have a notebook by your bed, so that when the dream happens, you should wake up and write it out in the notebook before you forget.

The future is known, and it can be tapped into, so can the past be tapped into, also. Become One with the Father, and all will be shown to thee. I am enclosing a fair copy of a poor copy of the Spiritualist Philosophy. I am not a Spiritualist (I must be free and separate from religion so that I may speak truth), but I study it along with all the other religions around the world. I study by participation, rather than from just books and hearsay.

The Precepts of the Spiritualist religion are very valid and intelligent, as far as I can tell. They all ring true to me. Most religions, to me, are the last bastion of ignorance being spread around the world today.

The most enlightened religious groups, in my opinion, are:
1. SCIENCE OF MIND INTERNATIONAL
   (This is my favorite place to learn how to think.)
   (Different from Religious Science; Science of Mind International is not Christian, as I recall). They teach a person how to use the mind of man and God. It is very practical.

2. BAHA'I
   I think that this is the most reasonable and enlightened group of people for today's *religious* needs. For those who need to be with an enlightened group to satisfy their herd instincts, this is it. SCIENCE OF MIND INTERNATIONAL is highly recommended by me as a prerequisite to the BAHA'I, because it will train the person to think correctly under all situations in life and the working world.
   (The BAHA'I will satisfy the emotional needs of the emotional people. As I say in this book, emotions are animal/body functions; they are not of the spirit.)

3. SCIENTOLOGY
(too involved with money, and causes people to be dependent on the church, but made of good basic sense).

4. SPIRITUALISM
(Great philosophy, but susceptible to fraud, and addiction to readings, which tend to make a person susceptible to outside influences and then the person loses his own ability to think and plan for himself; be cautious).

There is much superstition sprinkled throughout which is another dependency to watch for.

If the 'precepts' are strictly followed, this is a great place for an inquiring mind that wants to get 'tuned in' to God.

5. UNITARIAN
Mid western type; (not based on Christianity so much as the New England type)
This is an open-minded organization, willing to learn.

6. FORMAL EDUCATION:
I don't like the idea of formal learning for me, because it would pour my mind into a mold formed by other people. I wish to be myself, not a reproduction of someone else.

The best things to learn in high school are: English, Spelling, Speech, Math, Algebra, Science, Computer Literacy, and common sense morality. All else is wasted time, for me.

College should be for specialization in a subject for future employment or use, and apprenticeship should be a major factor and a right in employment. Of course, today's high schools graduate people who should never graduate, and then they have to go to college to learn the basics they should have learned in high school.
Enough f'now, Love to all,
Armand

LETTER TO M 06/17/96
Gabriel, My Confirmation of Oneness

This is a sample of what has happened to me in the last few years (about 30) in the spiritual department of my life. It has been a strange and exciting trip. It started in Riverside, CA, when I went on a 40 day fast (because Jesus did, and I wanted to become One with the Father, as he was trying to teach us to do, regardless of what the church has always said about his teachings) and started to see visions of the future and present at far distance, like in Japan, Mississippi, and The Dome of the Rock in Jerusalem.

There have been many strange happenings in my life since, which have brought me to the point of being confirmed as One with the Father last year, by the Father, through Gabriel the Archangel.

The confirmation began with a visit from Gabriel, right in front of me while I was watching TV. He appeared as a very bright, life-sized human being in a shiny, gold trimmed, bright white robe with a very shiny gold platen suspended in front of him below the neck by a gold chain.

He had a gentle smile on his face, shoulder length golden shiny blonde hair, brilliant blue eyes of piercing enjoyment, and white skin covering a strong face. His lips were upturned ever so slightly (they looked like seriousness with understanding).

Figure 23

My mouth and eyes wide open, I was stunned in time as I watched Gabriel and listened intently, not daring to move an inch.

He said, "I am Gabriel, I am your Father, I am your Guide." Since then, I have learned, in the Koran, that he is the voice of the Father. The Father does not speak, but assigned Gabriel to translate.

A few months later, I was Confirmed (Ordained) in a meditation with Father. I'm telling you these things now, after reluctance, because of the obvious innuendoes (Jesus was crucified because he disagreed with the local churches; there is lots of hatred where there is Belief).

I do want you to know what has happened in my seeking, because you are my extension here, and I'm getting up in physical age.

Love to you, M.,

Armand

LETTER TO: DOCTORS OF THE BIBLE CIRCA 1996
(Letter to Tract Authors)

Dear Doctors

(Doctors of the Bible who sent tracts around quoting the Bible with fire and brimstone so as to scare the average person), I submit this written over by me copy of your tract to you folks because I feel that my feelings should be expressed and realized by you.

Originally, I wrote the notations for myself, but decided to let you see them for your edification. I wrote the notes to show where I disagree because of the many real-life experiences that I've had.

Being One with the Father, I have lost all the fears of the old days, which were instilled in my mind through organized religion.

Organized religion has now been realized in my mind as man's power grab over the minds of man, and the shamming and shameful development of the teachings of Jesus, making a God out of him, and perverting the true teachings of his so that man would think of him as a supernatural being to be worshipped instead of a good human being to be respected.

There are many good things that have been done, but also many bad things, too. The minds of men have been digressed into ignorance and withdrawal because of the false ideas propagated by the churches.

To call a book the Word of God is really a stupid idea generated by the power-hungry men of the past and continue to this day. People are not ignorant as they were before the communication generation. They should be treated as intelligent human beings, and looked up to as well meaning persons rather than puppets of doctrines, which are created by man. These tracts are way past their time.

With Love.

LETTER TO M 03/25/98
Religions Come and Go, but God is, What Do I Think About Grace?

I'm glad that you asked. The reason I got onto this Internet is so that I may exchange ideas and information with other people of like interest, which is God. On the surface, the answer about Grace is that she is my sister-in-law (ha-ha), Grace in Alabama. Her husband used to say, "By the Grace of God, there she goes."

My second thought is that the Grace of God is the process of reincarnation in eternal living. Life is a hard knock for a lot of us, and as we learn, we find many hardships in our ignorance of God. Sometimes, we take such hard knocks in our stupidity and lack of respect for God and all people everywhere, that we become despondent to the point of suicide.

The Grace of God becomes evident when we face God now or in another life, and finally have respect for God. If we find God now, in this life, we will be relieved and re-live our lives with respect for God and everything else, because we must respect everything else when we realize that God is All there is, and we live in God as well as the fact that God lives in us.

Re-living our lives with respect, we feel the Grace of God because the whole world looks different, now. We are seeing the world through clear eyes, whereas before we were looking through dark glasses, which hide God and respect from us.

If we don't find God in this life, then we will find It/Him/Her in another life and enjoy living in this God Kingdom, which is called Heaven, on earth or another planet, or even in another dimension.

Heaven is:
- The best city in the state of our mind.
- God's Kingdom, where God resides.
- Appreciation for God, which is everything, even not dreamed of.
- The place where I store all my treasures, in my mind, where God resides (earthly treasures will perish).
- Recognition of God and becoming one with It/Him/Her.

Grace is:
- Grace is a gift from knowingness of eternal things.
- Grace is an attitude of gratitude gained from the knowingness.
- Grace is passed on to others, freely, as it was received, freely from the source, God.
- Grace passes understanding, because it has to be experienced in order to have it and to give it.

- Grace is a 'feeling' that has no feeling, because it is experienced in the soul, not the animal emotions of the body we use.
- Grace can be had by all, when loving God, which is everything, good and bad, not cursing God's 'Creation' (which never was created), and realizing that everything that is, is eternal because God is eternal and everything is God.

This should pass your understanding until it is experienced through your true love of God (All). When I say love of God, I say not love of religion, but love of God.

Religion is dogma, basically, and treads on God with its Dogma. Religions come and go, but God is.

When religions teach love and respect for all others, then they are emerging, but the Dogma and interpretations from their man-made gods take away from love.

There have been many gods, which were crucified, born of virgins, resurrected, etc, before Jesus.   Read your histories of civilization and older gods.

I say these things not to destroy anything, but to help understanding them.

Jesus was trying to tell us about the Father and we made Jesus into a god, instead of loving the God which he revealed to us, and trying to understand *IT*.

CHAPTER SIX

CONCLUSIONS

As I think about life and God after all the past experiences of mine, I must conclude that I have found the answer to my quest (finding proof of God, and becoming One with IT).

Since seven years of age (sixty three years ago), my journey has come to an end of sorts where I want to continue from here with my talking to God through the Archangel, Gabriel.

Maybe I'll live long enough to put the newer communications into another book. I have new questions to ask, piling up as I write the ending of this book.

This life which I have experienced makes me all the more wondrous of all the rest of eternal life to be experienced. All the marvelous possibilities ahead of us are mind-boggling and I don't want to miss one of them.

I don't mind dying now, for I am anticipating the fabulous future to be experienced by me for God (God is ALL, including you), my first love. The understandings of life since becoming One are a new found freedom, which I was not aware of in the past.

I have moved from the mental slavery of religion, which produced frustration, confusion, hatred and disgust, to the freedom and understanding of God, which produces love.

It would be a terrible thing if we had everything right now so that we would have no wants, and to have all knowledge now so that our minds would die from boredom. The eternal life is the only way to go. If eternity had a beginning, it would also have an ending. I am glad we are eternal because my mind/spirit is everlastingly curious.

Because my wife's Alzheimer's and her death have caused me to slow down the finishing of this book, I must work even harder to see that it is done. During the pause in my writing, many new things have surfaced, and the latest is the findings of an Egyptologist, an Egyptian named Ahmed Osman, who wrote some books on his findings through research and the latest archaeological finds.

He was born in Cairo in 1934, studied law at Cairo University and in the early 1960's worked there as a journalist. Because of continuing border disputes between Egypt and Israel, he went to London to discover the historical roots between the two countries, and the tie-ins with the Bible and archaeologists over the last 200 years.

His present book is titled, *Out of Egypt* by Century, Random House in London; 20 Vauxhall Bridge Rd, London, SWIV2SA. He has written, also, *The House of the Messiah, 1992; Moses: Pharaoh of Egypt, 1990; Stranger in the Valley of the Kings, 1987.*

I have read his last two books, and am amazed at the findings, which, to me, open up a large can of logical worms', and lend credence to my ideas of mythology being used as fact in the Bible and Christianity.

Actually, I have found that Sigmund Freud was one of the first acknowledged persons who claimed that Moses and the Pharaoh of Egypt (Akhenaten) in the 1300's BC were one and the same person. This changes the timetable of the Bible quite a bit, by about 1300 years.

The books by Ahmed Osman are very important with large amounts of evidence to prove the assertions. There is evidence in these books that Jesus may have been the son of Moses.

Here are some quotes from *OUT OF EGYPT* by Ahmed Osman:

> The Gnostic writings make it clear that they believed Jesus had lived a long time in the past and that many of them were awaiting his Second Coming.

> Any visitor to the tomb of the young king, in the Valley of the Kings, can see for himself the strongest pictorial evidence connecting Tutankhamun and Jesus Christ.(Tutankhamun lived in the 1350's BC, over a thousand years before the Bible story).

Thus on the north wall of Tutankhamun's burial chamber we find the three important theological points related to the death and resurrection of Jesus Christ.

. . . ancient Egyptian wisdom was again recognized as the source of Christian philosophy.

From OUT OF EGYPT by Ahmed Osman,
"As we have seen, the religion of Jesus differed from the religion of Moses."
Although keeping the Aten (Adonai) as the one true God, he accepted the old gods of Egypt as angels through whom Egyptians could reach the true God; he asked the Egyptians and Israelites to accept each other, and, unlike Moses, he believed in life after death.
However, Phinehas looked upon these teachings as blasphemy and, on the eve of the Passover, killed him in the Tabernacle at the foot of Mount Sinai. The killing was avenged by the slaughter of thousands of Israelites, including Phinehas at the hands of Ephraim (Aye) the second son of Joseph the Patriarch.
It was the death of John the Baptist many centuries later that persuaded the Essene leaders, who had been awaiting the Second Coming of Christ as a judge at the end of the world, to claim that they had witnessed Jesus, allowing the evangelists to retell the story of Christ adapted to the time of Herod the Great and Pontious Pilate.

With what Ahmed Osman has presented, I think we should take the findings seriously and re-think the past. He has found good evidence that,
- Jesus/Joshua was the son of Moses.
- Moses was the son of Solomon (Amenhotep 3).
- Nefertiti was Mary the mother of Jesus.

I recommend highly that everyone interested in God and or the Bible should read the books written by Ahmed Osman listed above and that they take seriously what is written in my book *IT* which you are reading from now.
The more I look into this world here, the more mystifying if becomes as to how old it is and how things got here. . .UFO's abound throughout old histories (Bibles) even unto today, and they hint of us being planted here from other planets, which have since died.

They hint also of our being watched and nurtured. Also, Our planet Earth seems to have been overturned with the flips of balance as time and distance changed the equilibrium of things. There are statements in science which suggest that our earth changes magnetic fields periodically about 3500 years apart.

The words of Jesus and Buddha show that they were connected with God, also. This is the connection that I have found, and it is very mystic. It is an unbelievable connection until it has many confirmations within the realm of our own internal (Subconscious/Soul) and external (Conscious/Awareness) minds.

The Words, Wisdom, Faith, Passion, Grace

These are the essences of True Love. These are what Jesus called Oneness with the Father. This is our connection to God, which comes about with marriage to God. It is a merging of ourselves with the Godself, so that we are aware of it internally where the reality is.

We are all God or IT in this lifetime game of living. . . We are all One! Let's have respect for one another in brotherly love, understanding that we are all different viewpoints of God (Oneness/*IT*).

We are living lives of Fantasy for the sake of Life itself, which is the life we live so that the Absolute can have an Awareness of life for *IT*'s Self.

This Awareness is in the total consciousness of all, which is what I call theSuper Consciousness (the totality of man's continuously changing awarenesses). This is where future trends can be found.

Love is the only moral there is. The absolute definition of love is, *Giving Responsible Freedom to the object of your love to live within all Law.*

I have intuitively sensed that aspect of God, which is the Eternal foundation of material reality. This is Shiva (the Eternal Transcendent Principle, which we call God. Shiva is Absolute, unchanging).

Shakti is man, who moves in the material world. By the way, I just learned about Shiva and Shakti on the Internet.

My Meditations with God agree on this viewpoint of God. God has no Passion, Emotion, and is detached. There is no good or evil in God.

It is my job to show mankind that everyone can achieve this One-ness. We have progressed enough to grasp the idea and choose it so that we can evolve to a higher quality of living right here and now.

"From my perspective, eternal unchanging love in an eternally changing material universe is perfectly logical and compatible with living life in the highest spiritual sense. . ." *I agree with this.* (John Leake at a Spiritual Forum on the Internet, called: www.omsakthi.org). This website is very well done and is participated in by seekers and thinkers.

P.S. http://home.swbell.net/dndylion/ This web site is a must for the serious thinker, also. This is a good place to seriously investigate the reality of things of God and Religion. At the bottom of my web site is a stick man, which when clicked on will take you to it.

Our reason for being eternal is to live life in material worlds so that the Absolute can have life; this is how we serve God. When we return to God, or die, we are returning to material life in another body. This material life can be in one of zillions of worlds or Mansions in My Father's House.

We are eternal, and our book (the book that you are reading) is basically in front of you because I was told to write it and it is through the Archangel Gabriel, who is the voice of God the Father, and Who dictated all the meditations in this book.

In the Realm of Mind/Law/God/Absolute/Karma/Reincarnation

Thought is so instantaneous that even Einstein would have been surprised with his Theory of Relativity. He figured that if we traveled faster than light, we would be able to see ourselves coming.

The speed of thought is so fast that even before we ask, we have already received, providing that we are knowing and say thanks. Saying thanks, or knowing that we will receive are triggers for releasing the answers to prayers, or reactions to our actions.

I mentioned the speed of thought to remind us that this **Reincarnation and Karma thing takes place instantly** so that we may enter new bodies or forms for material life at once. This new body or form may be in any one of the many mansions in the house of God, and must be brought forth or born so that the new soul inhabitant can have life. This will be a new life of experiences for God and the independent, responsible, free willed soul of man.

These many mansions are all in the same time and place as Earth, but with different vibrations of reality. Reality is what our material senses pick up or are sensitive to in the different mansions of life.

We are living in fantasy worlds of existence and life. God is the reality. "As I mentioned in an old thread, I believe the universe is eternal. While not a single thing in it will endure forever, *IT* will. In that sense it is absolute, if I'm correct in that belief." (John Leake.) I agree with that, John. (John at a Spiritual Forum on the Internet).

Another suggestion I have as of yesterday, February 25th, 2000, is to see the movie American Beauty. The movie caused me to have a strong desire to leave the theater in disgust, but as it progressed it became self evident to me that this was a movie which had a great insight. It ended with a statement, which explained my book. . .Wow!

This movie is a must see all the way to the last statement at the end. Use perseverance; it is worth it.

We are now in an election time where all kinds of views are being displayed and argued over.

What Comes to Mind as I Close This Book

. . . is the time around 350AD when the Universal Roman Catholic Church became a political body with power and influence around the world so much so that we had the Dark Ages where people were the slaves to the domineering Church until Martin Luther and others opened up the door of ignorance so that we could be free of mental slavery.

This mental slavery is coming to a head again, because of power hungry religious Rightists who have been and are rearing their heads in taking over the Republican Party, and killing it. They want their religious ideas of morality to be the only ideas, which we should live by. Watch out for the slinky snake, which is raising it venomous head again. . .

More of What Comes to Mind as I Close This Book

. . . is the time when Islam was created and enslaved the minds of it's people so much so that they have been relegated to ancient days of no progress in the abundance of living, also.

The religion is fine for the good thinking people, but it has had too much political control, thereby creating slaves of mind as did the Catholic political mind control, producing oppression of it's women, ignorance and backwardness.

The political scene in Iran is being changed again to the people of intelligence and taken away from the people of ignorance (the oppressive religious right).

Please, Religious Rightists Around the World, of All Religions

Change your narrow minded ideas of the past and come to love all others with respect. Challenge your people to stop killing others in the name of Religious Ideas. Change your operations to educating your followers in the arts of love and respect. We are all people and we are all one. Let us love, respect, and accept differences of opinions.

Call off your killers in the name of God. Call back and denounce the killers of Abortionist doctors, and peoples of different Religious ideas around the world. Let us enjoy life with each other everywhere, and help each other everywhere where it is practical. Education is the best way to help others.

Sunday, June 4, 2000:

Beliefs, to me, are usually a case of hypnotism (the power of suggestion brought forth by the repetitions from parents, teachers, the Media, religious rituals in churches and homes, and the use of fear and threats along the way for reinforcement).

So-called Geniuses are generally people who think differently, or they think for themselves rather than accept the thoughts of others for their own, as in belief systems.

The human animal naturally wishes to follow the crowd (the herd instinct) and make his life easier. It is a tendency toward natural security and laziness of the animal body. Beliefs are a result of the herd instinct, the way I see it.

People who think for themselves are more alive than those who don't. We call them entrepeneurs in business, mavericks in general, and someone to be crucified, or sent to hell, or burned at the stake in religion.

I can see where religion is different from the other classifications because religions, in their unbending attitudes, separate people rather than bring them together. This will change, and is changing now as I write.

As we become more intelligent (soul and wisdom), and less animal (body and emotions), the religions will bring people back together again as they realize that we are all One, and there is nothing to be afraid of in the act of loving and respecting all others.

Meanwhile, all religions fit someone at some level, and are doing some good in their slow progress.

Love,
Armand

PS As this world, through the Internet, becomes free again from religious domination, through intelligence, we will have a better world where we all respect each others' different viewpoints and realize that we are all different viewpoints of God, even unto our fingerprints, and need to express ourselves with respect for All.

My E-mail address is andyandgod@nctimes.net

My Web site is http://www.geocities.com/eternity_92079

To order more copies of IT,

Fill out the form below and mail it with a check or money order to:

AMC Publications:
PO BOX 81672
SAN DIEGO CA 92138-1672

PHONE 619/296-0442

Number of copies _____ x $ 14.95 = $ _____

If California resident, add .0775 sales tax   _____

Shipping add $3.00 per book   _____

Insurance add $1.00 (Optional)*   _____
Author/Publisher will assume no responsibility
for items lost in the mail.

Enclose check or money order for **Total $** _____

NAME_____

ADDRESS_____

CITY_____

STATE____ZIP_____

ISBN 0 -9664126 - 3 - X